Springer Proceedings in Business and Economics

D1740394

More information about this series at http://www.springer.com/series/11960

Francisco J. Martínez-López •
Juan Carlos Gázquez-Abad • Alexander Chernev
Editors

Advances in National Brand and Private Label Marketing

Fifth International Conference, 2018

 Springer

Editors
Francisco J. Martínez-López
Department of Business Administration
University of Granada
Granada, Spain

Juan Carlos Gázquez-Abad
Department of Economics and Business
University of Almería
Almería, Spain

Alexander Chernev
Kellog School of Management
Northwestern University
Evanston, Illinois, USA

ISSN 2198-7246   ISSN 2198-7254   (electronic)
Springer Proceedings in Business and Economics
ISBN 978-3-319-92083-2   ISBN 978-3-319-92084-9   (eBook)
https://doi.org/10.1007/978-3-319-92084-9

Library of Congress Control Number: 2018944267

Printed on acid-free paper

This Springer imprint is published by the registered company Springer International Publishing AG part of Springer Nature.
The registered company address is: Gewerbestrasse 11, 6330 Cham, Switzerland

Preface

The Internet has dramatically changed the ways in which consumers engage with brands, the role brands play in people's lives, and the value brands can create for companies and their customers. As an increasing number of consumers are virtually always online with their smart phones, tablets, and computers, companies are presented with unique opportunities to gain a better understanding of how these customers think and design more effective and cost-efficient strategies to build and manage strong brands. To stay relevant, companies must evolve with times and ensure that their brands are in tune with the digital lifestyle of their customers.

Along with brand building opportunities come challenges. The availability of product-related information is eroding the role of brands as a signal of product quality. Rather than relying on the brand image to infer product performance, consumers can easily gain the relevant information from blog posts, customer reviews, and online ratings. Product performance, rather than the company's advertising, is becoming the key factor in defining brand image. The increased importance of product performance not only de-emphasizes the impact of the company's brands and decreases customers' willingness to pay a premium for branded products, but it also levels the playfield between national brands and established mega-brands on the one hand and private labels and newly launched niche brands on the other. In addition to the threat of becoming less relevant, traditional brands are also facing the challenge stemming from the exponential growth of the social media that has dramatically reduced the company's ability to control the image of its brands. Today's customers effectively co-own the company's brands by creating unique brand content, developing brand narratives, and shaping brand meaning.

Another profound change in the ways companies position their brands involves a shift from focusing on functional benefits of the company's offerings to emphasizing the role of brands as a means of self-expression. Lifestyle branding has become an increasingly common approach among managers, especially in categories in which functional differences are hard to discern. A growing number of companies—from consumer packaged goods companies, to car manufacturers, and technology companies—are adopting lifestyle positioning as a way to break free of the cutthroat competition within a category by connecting with consumers on a more personal level. This trend toward lifestyle branding is facilitated by Facebook, YouTube, Twitter, and other social media platforms that help companies identify the touch points where brands engage and influence their target customers. At the same time, social media platforms provide unprecedented opportunities for consumers to assert their individuality by interacting with one another without relying on lifestyle brands. The ubiquity of such nonbrand means of self-expression raises the hurdle that lifestyle brands must overcome to stay relevant to their customers.

Despite the changes, one aspect of building brands in the digital age has remained constant: consumers want offerings with a clear and relevant brand promise. The key function of brands as a means of creating customer value above and beyond the value delivered by the company's products and services has not changed. What has changed is the context in which brands create customer value, the means by which they create value, and the specific tools that companies can use to design and manage their brands. Understanding the impact of digital transformation is essential to the company's ability to build strong brands that create market value.

Looking at those aspects underlying this new marketing context offers exciting opportunities for researchers. It is with this goal in mind that this Fifth International Conference on Research on National Brand & Private Label Marketing (NB&PL 2018) has been launched and organized. After the success of the four previous editions, this fifth edition is still believed to be a unique international forum to present and discuss original, rigorous, and significant contributions specifically on national brand and private label issues.

Each paper submitted to NB&PL 2018 has gone through a stringent peer review process by members of the Program Committee, comprising 46 internationally renowned researchers from 14 countries.

A total of 19 papers have been accepted, and they address diverse areas of application such as consumer decision-making, premium private labels, digital transformation, ethical aspects, cultural dimensions, sales promotions, brand equity, private label pricing, and dual branding, among others. A wide variety of theoretical and methodological approaches have been used in these areas.

We believe that this fifth edition has continued with the same goals as the four previous editions: promote, stimulate, and publish high-quality contributions on national brands and private labels, which could help retailers and manufacturers deal with diversity of issues. Nevertheless, we hope to keep organizing this conference which is aimed to become an international reference for advancing this promising research field.

Finally, we wish to acknowledge the support of the sponsors *Open University of Catalonia, Information Resources Inc. (IRI), Manufacturers-and-Retailers Spanish Multisectoral Association (AECOC),* and *EAE Business School.* We would also like to thank all the contributing authors, members of the Program Committee, and the

rest of the Organizing Committee for their highly valuable work in enabling the
success of this fifth edition of NB&PL. Thanks for your generous contribution—IC-
NB&PL 2018 would not have been possible without you all.

Granada, Spain   Francisco J. Martínez-López
Almería, Spain   Juan Carlos Gázquez-Abad
Evanston, Illinois, USA   Alexander Chernev

Organization

Conference Chairs

Francisco J. Martínez-López – University of Granada (Spain)
Juan Carlos Gázquez-Abad – University of Almería (Spain)
Alexander Chernev – Northwestern University (USA)

Program Committee

Kusum L. Ailawadi, Tuck School of Business at Dartmouth (USA)
Nawel Amrouche, Long Island University (USA)
Chris Baumann, Macquarie University (Australia)
José J. Beristain, University of the Basque Country (Spain)
Enrique Bigné, University of Valencia (Spain)
James Brown, West Virginia University (USA)
Cristina Calvo-Porral, University of La Coruña (Spain)
Ioannis E. Chaniotakis, University of the Aegean (Greece)
Liwen (Brandon) Chen, City University of Hong Kong (China)
Chan Choi, Rutgers Business School (USA)
Gérard Cliquet, Université de Rennes 1 (France)
Giuseppe Colangelo, Catholic University of Milan (Italy)
Ronald W. Cotterill, University of Connecticut (USA)
Barbara Deleersnyder, Tilburg University (The Netherlands)
John Dawes, University of South Australia (Australia)
Els Gijsbrechts, Tilburg University (Netherlands)
J. Tomas Gomez-Arias, Saint Mary's College of California (USA)
Oscar González-Benito, University of Salamanca (Spain)
Csilla Horváth, Radboud University (The Netherlands)
Marco Ieva, University of Parma (Italy)

Eugene Jones, The Ohio State University (USA)
Robert Paul Jones, The University of Texas at Tyler (USA)
Lien Lamey, Katholieke Universiteit Leuven (Belgium)
Elisa Martinelli, University of Modena and Reggio Emilia (Italy)
Mercedes Martos-Partal, University of Salamanca (Spain)
Sebastián Molinillo Jiménez, University of Malaga (Spain)
Dirk Morschett, University of Fribourg (Switzerland)
Martin Natter, Goethe University Frankfurt am Main (Germany)
Magdalena Nenycz-Thiel, University of South Australia (Australia)
Nicoletta Occhiocupo, Oxford Brookes University (UK)
Michael Pepe, Siena College (USA)
William P. Putsis, University of North Carolina at Chapel Hill (USA)
Natalia Rubio-Benito, Autonomous University of Madrid (Spain)
Hanna Schramm-Klein, University of Siegen (Germany)
Fiona Scott Morton, Yale University (USA)
Raj Sethuraman, Southern Methodist University (USA)
Randall Shannon, Mahidol University (Thailand)
Ian Clark Sinapuelas, San Francisco State University (USA)
Yaron Timmor, Arison School of Business (Israel)
Rodolfo Vázquez-Casielles, University of Oviedo (Spain)
Gianfranco Walsh, Friedrich Schiller University of Jena (Germany)
María Jesús Yagüe-Guillén, Autonomous University of Madrid (Spain)
Jie Zhang, University of Maryland (USA)
Cristina Ziliani, University of Parma (Italy)
Pilar Zorrilla, University of the Basque Country (Spain)

Program Organizing Committee

Irene Esteban-Millat, Open University of Catalonia (Spain)
María Pujol Jover, Open University of Catalonia (Spain)
José Luis Ruiz-Real, University of Almería (Spain)
Alejandro Alegret, EAE Business School (Spain)
Cintia Pla García, Open University of Catalonia (Spain)

Contents

Part IV Modelling and Theoretical Research

Part I
Consumer Behaviour

Status Consumption: Both an Antecedent and a Moderator of Private Label Brand Proneness

Hanna Gendel-Guterman and Shalom Levy

Abstract Status consumption has received little attention from scholars of private label research, and the results of the few existing studies were inconclusive about its influence on private label brand proneness. The aim of this research is to explore how status consumption is involved in the decision process to buy private label brands. An integrated model was constructed and empirically tested in a survey of 603 consumers. The findings show that although the impact of status consumption on private label proneness is not significant, but rather positive and small, it has a negative influence on quality perception and a positive influence on familiarity. The findings also revealed the interesting moderator function of status consumption on the relation between quality perception and buying proneness.

Keywords PLB proneness · Status consumption · PLB quality · PLB value for money · Familiarity

1 Introduction

The popularity of private labels continues to grow throughout Europe. The latest Nielsen data shows that market share for retailer brands has climbed to all-time highs, reaching 40% in 6 out of 19 European countries; yet, it varies considerably among countries (PLMA 2016). The factors that influence private label brand (PLB) attitudes and shopping behaviors have been extensively researched over the last several decades. Research has found that demographic factors do not explain PLB proneness; however, Ailawadi et al. (2001, p. 73) have found that they influence consumers' attitudes toward PLB indirectly, through their moderating effects via psychographics.

H. Gendel-Guterman (✉) · S. Levy
Department of Economics and Business Administration, Ariel University, Ariel, Israel
e-mail: hanag@ariel.ac.il; shalom@ariel.ac.il

© Springer International Publishing AG, part of Springer Nature 2018
F. J. Martínez-López et al. (eds.), *Advances in National Brand and Private Label Marketing*, Springer Proceedings in Business and Economics,
https://doi.org/10.1007/978-3-319-92084-9_1

3

One of the main researched psychographic traits, which has been found to have an important effect on purchasing behavior, is *status consumption tendency* (SCT), sometimes referred to in the literature as *social value consumption* or *self-concept consumption*. However, research on PLB proneness in relation to SCT, especially in grocery products, is rare (Kakkos et al. 2015). Moreover, the findings of these studies remain inconclusive (Kara et al. 2009).

General marketing research has revealed that SCT has a negative effect on perceived low-quality products. The aim of this research is to determine whether SCT has a negative impact on PLB proneness through the main factors that were found to effect proneness—quality, value for money (VFM), and familiarity. Furthermore, the current study attempts to answer the question of whether SCT is an antecedent to these factors or a moderator between them and PLB proneness.

2   Theoretical and Empirical Backgrounds

Regarding PLB buying proneness, meaning, the intention of consumers to adopt and purchase PLB, longitudinal research studies have established that there are three main influencing factors—PLB Quality, VFM, and familiarity (Richardson et al. 1996).

Private Label Brands (PLB), sometimes referred to as store brand are products manufactured on behalf of retailers, sold through their own outlets, and under the retailer's own name or trademark. Traditionally, PLB are sold to consumers at lower prices compared to national brand products (Koschate-Fischer et al. 2014).

Product proneness is "the possibility that consumers will plan or be willing to purchase a certain product or service in the future" (Wu et al. 2011, p. 32). Product proneness is considered as the exactly precedent stage before indulging in the actual buying behavior (de Magistris and Gracia 2008)

Product *perceived quality* can be defined as "the consumer's judgment about a product's overall excellence or superiority" (Zeithaml 1988, p. 3; Cronin et al. 2000). Perceived quality drives consumers to choose one brand over other competing brands. PLB are usually considered to be of lower quality compared to national brands (NB) (González Mieres et al. 2006), a perception which decreases PLB proneness.

A product or service's perceived *VFM* refers to how consumers evaluate a product relative to its price (Wu et al. 2011). VFM equation is an important factor in the PLB buying process; PLBs are sold at lower prices than NB, therefore this will cause consumers to evaluate fairly the quality of the PLB brand, followed by a positive influence on both its VFM and its proneness.

Familiarity with a brand—or *brand awareness*—reflects one's ability to recall and recognize a brand within a given category and has a positive influence on the PLB VFM and its proneness (Richardson et al. 1996). According to the existing literature, it can be assumed that:

H1a PLB quality perception will be positively correlated with PLB buying proneness.

H1b PLB familiarity will be positively correlated with PLB buying proneness.

H1c PLB VFM perception will be positively correlated with PLB buying proneness.

H1d PLB familiarity will be positively correlated with PLB VFM.

Status consumption is defined as the motivational process by which individuals strive to improve their social standing through the conspicuous consumption of consumer products that symbolize status—in their own eyes and in the eyes of others (Eastman et al. 1999). It is based more on affective then cognitive attitudes. O'cass and McEwen (2004) argued that "status consumption is more a matter of consumers' desires to gain prestige from the acquisition of status-laden products and brands; however, conspicuous consumption focuses on the visual display or overt usage of products in the presence of others". This distinction implies that the acquisition itself could be a measure of social success, without display or overt usage of products in the presence of others (O'cass and McEwen 2004).

There is a great deal of research about status consumption in the general marketing literature, but only a few of these studies examined SCT in relation to the issue of PLB in comparison to NB (Kakkos et al. 2015; Richie et al. 2018). Therefore, this paper included research that referred to this process as *social value consumption* (Kakkos et al. 2015) or as *self-concept consumption* (Richie et al. 2018).

The findings of these studies remain inconclusive (Kara et al. 2009). In some studies, SCT is found to have a negative effect on PLB proneness (Shannon 2016; Richie et al. 2018), while others found that SCT has either an insignificant or a positive effect on PLB proneness in certain situations (Richie et al. 2018). Several explanations were provided for these contradictory results; some researchers argue that supermarkets' PLB are consumed at home; therefore, the consumption is inconspicuous and is irrelevant to SCT consumers (DelVecchio 2001; Weiß 2015, p. 86). Others explain that SCT is trait that is similar to the "shopping maven" trait. Consumers who think they are expert shoppers tend to be familiar with market products and prices, and take pride in searching and finding the best deals (Weiß 2015, p. 86). Thus, consumers with high SCT will be more familiar with PLB and regard more favorably its VFM.

Although the results are inconclusive, based on the majority of recent literature, it is assumed that:

H2 SCT will have a negative effect on PLB buying proneness.

H3a SCT will have a negative effect on PLB quality perception.

H3b SCT will have a positive effect on PLB VFM.

H3c SCT will have a positive effect on PLB familiarity.

Due to the irrelevancy of PLB quality to consumers with high SCT buying decision, the following hypothesis is suggested:

H4 SCT will be a moderator between PLB perceived quality and PLB buying proneness.

3 Methodology

Sample: Participants were randomly recruited from eleven grocery stores of a major well-known retailer, spread out over extended geographic areas in Israel. Overall, 603 shoppers agreed to participate and completed the questionnaire. Most of the participants were female (66%); for the most part, ages ranged between 26 and 65 (92%); the majority of participants possess a full high school education or above (88%); and have an average or above-average income (66%). All subjects said they usually participate in family shopping trips (100%). The sample's external validity was confirmed by comparing it to the socio-demographic traits of the total cumulative population of the chain's shoppers.

Measurement: The items were partly taken from multiple studies and partly phrased based on the literature. Following Richardson et al. (1996), the dependent variable—private label buying proneness—was examined using six items—one general question and five questions relating to different product categories (basic food, cleaning materials, beverages, cookies and preserves). As for the independent variables, four items for store brand quality (e.g. "There is a great difference in overall quality between nationally advertised and store brands grocery items"), one item for VFM ("Private label brands offer great value for money"), and one for familiarity with store brand ("I am well familiar with private labels brands of this store") were taken from Richardson et al. (1996). Three items of status consumption (e.g. "Status is important to me") were based on Eastman et al. (1999) and O'cass and McEwen (2004). Respondents were asked to indicate their level of agreement with the different statements, regarding their attitudes about grocery shopping behavior. A five-point Likert scale was used, ranging from 1 = strongly disagree, to 5 = strongly agree. Demographic variables were also collected.

4 Results

Validity and reliability: Exploratory Factor Analysis (EFA) with Varimax rotation was used, explaining 57.2% of the cumulative variance factors. All items demonstrated internal consistency. Confirmatory Factor Analysis (CFA) was used for validity. The results confirm the constructs ($\chi 2$ value (55) = 126.03, p < 0.05 ($\chi 2$/ df < 3); CFI = 0.975; NFI = 0.957; (RMSEA) = 0.043. The CFA shows that the scale items loaded satisfactorily on the relevant latent variables. Convergent validity

Fig. 1 Path analysis model
(parameters are standardized
parameter estimates and
only significant paths are
displayed. Dotted lines
represent moderation. R^2
appears in the right-hand
corner. *p < 0.05;
** p < 0.01)

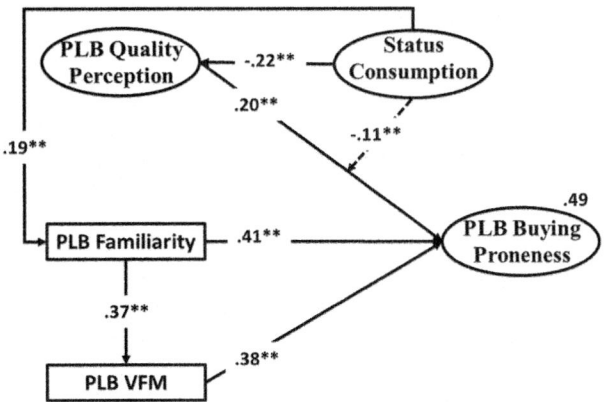

Table 1 Hypotheses testing—total and direct significant relationships

Relationship	Standardized effect		Regression weights (direct)		
	Total	Direct	Estimate	C.R.	p
PLB quality → PLB buying	0.196	0.196	0.335	4.553	<0.01
PLB VFM → PLB buying	0.383	0.383	0.260	8.870	<0.01
PLB familiarity → PLB buying	0.551	0.410	0.268	9.292	<0.01
PLB familiarity → PLB VFM	0.368	0.368	0.355	9.371	<0.01
SCT → PLB buying	0.183	0.089	0.121	1.804	N.S.
SCT*PLB quality → PLB Buying	−0.108	−0.108	−0.083	−3.112	<0.01
SCT*PLB VFM → PLB buying					N.S.
SCT*PLB familiarity → PLB buying					N.S.
SCT → PLB quality	−0.218	−0.218	−0.173	−3.377	<0.01
SCT → PLB VFM	0.152	0.081	0.162	1.547	N.S.
SCT → PLB familiarity	0.192	0.192	0.397	3.343	<0.01

SCT status consumption tendency

and internal consistency were examined using the following measurements: The standardized loading estimates for all items are significant and above 0.5; therefore, the constructs show acceptable convergent validity. The Cronbach's alpha coefficients range was 0.56–0.83.

Model testing: A path analysis was conducted to check the research hypotheses using Structural Equation Modeling (SEM), based on the maximum likelihood approach. The path analysis results show that the overall fit statistics (goodness of fit measures) exhibit an acceptable level of fit ($\chi2$ value (89) = 192.63, $\chi2$/Df < 3, p < 0.05; CFI = 0.962; NFI = 0.932; RMSEA = 0.044), indicating that the path model is valid. The path model, regression standardized coefficients, and their significance are illustrated in Fig. 1. Table 1 shows the variables' total and direct relationships and the statistical measures.

Figure 1 indicates that, as expected, direct relationships exist between PLB quality perception and PLB buying proneness (β = 0.20); between PLB familiarity

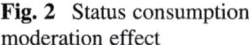

Fig. 2 Status consumption
moderation effect

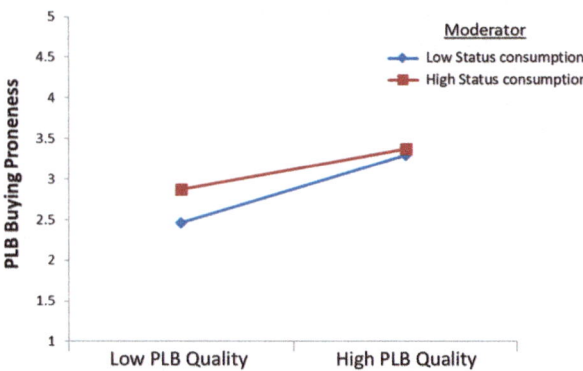

and PLB buying proneness ($\beta = 0.41$); and between PLB VFM and PLB buying proneness ($\beta = 0.38$). Additionally, PLB familiarity has a direct positive relationship with PLB VFM ($\beta = 0.37$). Hence, hypotheses H1a, H1b, H1c and H1d were supported.

The model further shows that status consumption has a direct negative relationship with PLB quality perception ($\beta = -0.22$) and a positive relationship with PLB familiarity ($\beta = 0.19$). However, no significant relationship was found to exist between status consumption and PLB VFM ($\beta = 0.08$ ns). Thus, H3a and H3c were supported, while and H3b was not supported.

In contrast to our expectation, no significant direct relationship was found to exist between status consumption and PLB buying proneness ($\beta = 0.09$ ns). The relationship was found to be positive and rather indirect ($c\text{-}c' = 0.09$), mainly through PLB familiarity. This path indicates full mediation of PLB VFM and PLB familiarity on PLB buying proneness (bootstrap with 95% CI: 0.04–0.24; $p < 0.05$). Hence, H2 was not supported.

Additionally, status consumption negatively moderates the positive relationship between PLB quality and PLB buying proneness ($\beta = -0.11$). This indicates that status consumption dampens the positive relationship between PLB quality and PLB buying proneness which means that PLB quality perception has a significantly stronger positive effect on PLB proneness when status consumption is lower (see Fig. 2). Status consumption has no moderating effect on the relationships between PLB VFM and PLB buying or between PLB familiarity and PLB buying. Therefore, H4 was supported.

5 Discussion and Implications

This research has found that the influence of SCT on PLB proneness is positive and small. These results are in accordance with some of previous research (Weiß 2015). Nevertheless, it is contrary to our assumption that it would be negative due to the still-existing perception that PLB quality is inferior compared to that of NB

(Shannon 2016; Richie et al. 2018). The current research provides a theoretical contribution to the literature, as it proved that SCT plays a major role, with different effects, both positive and negative on the consumer's decision process regarding PLB proneness. First, it was found that SCT is an antecedent to the main factors effecting PLB proneness. As assumed, consumers with high STC have negative attitudes about PLB quality, regarding them as inferior, compared to NB. High SCT consumers are familiar with PLB, perhaps because they are also "shopping mavens", who like to have as much information as possible when shopping. Another interesting result is the finding that high SCT consumers hold positive attitudes about PLB VFM. This positive reaction is subjected to the realization that most PLB are not consumed in public; thus, the status issue is irrelevant to them. Additionally, the attitude that PLB has good VFM could arise from its contribution to self-image, through their decision to be smart shoppers with "intellectual independence" (Granzin 1981; O'cass and McEwen 2004).

Second, SCT was found to be a moderator between the poor image of PLB quality and PLB proneness. PLB quality perception has a significantly stronger positive effect on PLB proneness when status consumption is lower. One explanation for this is that consumers with lower SCT don't include the affective aspect of social status in their decision, and instead depend only on the cognitive aspect of perceived quality. On the other hand, for those with high SCT, the perceived quality is less important in the equation of status and quality.

The implication of the findings for retailers is that SCT can have two different angles: one, status brands as *social value* and two as supporting *self-image*. Retailers could use a strategy to promote PLB as the right alternative for shopping mavens and as a self-image enhancing tool.

6   Limitations and Further Research

The current research has some limitations. First, the product categories included in the current research belong to a grocery products' private label, which are products that are more basic and consumed in private rather than public situations. It is possible, that different food categories (like wine or delicatessen products) or non-food categories may reveal different results. Another limitation is that SCT is only one of consumer's psychographic traits. Including other traits in the process, such as extrinsic cues, could enhance our understanding about the influence of SCT on PLB proneness. Therefore, further research should examine other product categories and other psychographic traits.

References

Ailawadi, K. L., Neslin, S. A., & Gedenk, K. (2001). Pursuing the value-conscious consumer: Store brands versus national brand promotions. *Journal of Marketing, 65*(1), 71–89.

Cronin, J. J., Brady, M. K., & Hult, G. T. M. (2000). Assessing the effects of quality, value, and customer satisfaction on consumer behavioral intentions in service environments. *Journal of Retailing, 76*(2), 193–218.

De Magistris, T., & Gracia, A. (2008). The decision to buy organic food products in Southern Italy. *British Food Journal, 110*(9), 929–947.

DelVecchio, D. (2001). Consumer perceptions of private label quality: The role of product category characteristics and consumer use of heuristics. *Journal of Retailing and Consumer Services, 8* (5), 239–249.

Eastman, J. K., Goldsmith, R. E., & Flynn, L. R. (1999). Status consumption in consumer behavior: Scale development and validation. *Journal of Marketing Theory and Practice, 7*(3), 41–52.

González Mieres, C., MaríaDíaz Martín, A., & Trespalacios Gutiérrez, J. A. (2006). Influence of perceived risk on store brand proneness. *International Journal of Retail & Distribution Management, 34*(10), 761–772.

Granzin, K. L. (1981). An investigation of the market for generic products. *Journal of Retailing, 57* (4), 39–55.

Kakkos, N., Trivellas, P., & Sdrolias, L. (2015). Identifying drivers of purchase intention for private label brands. Preliminary evidence from Greek consumers. *Procedia-Social and Behavioral Sciences, 175*, 522–528.

Kara, A., Rojas-Méndez, J. I., Kucukemiroglu, O., & Harcar, T. (2009). Consumer preferences of store brands: Role of prior experiences and value consciousness. *Journal of Targeting, Measurement and Analysis for Marketing, 17*(2), 127–137.

Koschate-Fischer, N., Cramer, J., & Hoyer, W. D. (2014). Moderating effects of the relationship between private label share and store loyalty. *Journal of Marketing, 78*(2), 69–82.

O'cass, A., & McEwen, H. (2004). Exploring consumer status and conspicuous consumption. *Journal of Consumer Behaviour, 4*(1), 25–39.

PLMA. (2016). *PLMA's 2016 private label yearbook: A statistical guide to today's store brands.* http://plma.com/share/press/resources/PLMA2016YB_COMB_RPT.pdf

Richardson, P. S., Jain, A. K., & Dick, A. (1996). Household store brand proneness: A framework. *Journal of Retailing, 72*(2), 159–185.

Richie, L. L., Sprott, D. E., Spangenberg, E. R., Czellar, S., & Voss, K. E. (2018). Consumer preference for national vs. private brands: The influence of brand engagement and self-concept threat. *Journal of Retailing and Consumer Services, 41*, 90–100.

Shannon, R. (2016). Contrasting Thai and Chinese Shopper Behavior and Satisfaction with PL Brands. In *Advances in National Brand and Private Label Marketing* (pp. 121–128). Springer.

Weiß, S. (2015). *Determinants of private label attitude: Predicting consumers' brand preferences using psychographics.* Wiesbaden: Springer.

Wu, P. C., Yeh, G. Y. Y., & Hsiao, C. R. (2011). The effect of store image and service quality on brand image and purchase intention for private label brands. *Australasian Marketing Journal, 19*(1), 30–39.

Zeithaml, V. A. (1988). Consumer perceptions of price, quality, and value: A means-end model and synthesis of evidence. *The Journal of Marketing, 52*(3), 2–22.

Differences in the Effect of Ethical Labels on National Brand and Private Label Brand Products on Store and Brand Perception: A Preliminary Work

Vanessa Steppuhn

Abstract Over the last years, consumers' engagement towards socially aware consumption increased and there is not only a growing demand for ethical products (i.e. organic and fair-trade products) and corporate social responsibility initiatives, but also consumers tend to punish companies promoting unethical goods. Although several studies have investigated the effect of ethical labels on national brand (NB) products, research in the context of private label (PL) products is rare. This study contributes to existing research by investigating the effect of ethical labels on products in the context of NB and PL products, examining the effect sizes of product brand trust on store and brand perception. The study provides evidence that the effects are stronger for private label brand (PLB) products, indicating that ethical labels are of high relevance for private label brands.

Keywords PLB products · NB products · Ethical labels · Product brand trust · Store perception · Brand perception

1 Introduction

Owing to their ongoing global increase in market share (Nielsen 2011), PLBs have attracted growing attention during the past several years. Previous studies provide a basic understanding of the competition between PLBs and NBs (e.g., Cotterill et al. 2000), and which factors play an important role for customers during the decision-making process for PL product purchase (e.g., Hoch and Banerji 1993; Nies and Natter 2012; Richardson et al. 1994). To address these needs and to compete successfully against NBs, retailers create multi-tiered PLBs with different levels of price and quality: generic, standard, and premium PLBs (Geyskens et al. 2010; Kumar and Steenkamp 2007). This differentiation strategy and the wide range of

V. Steppuhn (✉)
Institute of Marketing, University of Muenster, Münster, Germany
e-mail: v.steppuhn@uni-muenster.de

© Springer International Publishing AG, part of Springer Nature 2018   11
F. J. Martínez-López et al. (eds.), *Advances in National Brand and Private Label Marketing*, Springer Proceedings in Business and Economics,
https://doi.org/10.1007/978-3-319-92084-9_2

PLBs enable retailers to attract and satisfy different target groups. First studies were conducted addressing the idea of using ethical label PLs to use this opportunity (e.g., Bodur et al. 2016).

2 Background

Due to its high relevance and potential positive impact on consumers and retailers, there was an increasing number of empirical research and publications on ethical label products over the last years. Various studies showed that consumers' engagement towards socially aware consumption increases (Auger and Devinney 2007; Karjalainen and Moxham 2013). There is not only a growing demand for ethical products (i.e. organic and fair-trade products) and corporate social responsibility initiatives (Bhattacharya and Sen 2004), but also consumers tend to punish companies promoting unethical goods (Trudel and Cotte 2009). Most of the previous research focused on customer values (e.g., altruistic and egoistic values) and motives for purchasing ethical products (e.g., Cowe and Williams 2001; Yamoah et al. 2016).

In contrast to the NB context (e.g., Du et al. 2007; Henderson and Arora 2010), research on how ethical labels on PL products affect consumers and retailers is rare. Nevertheless, there are valid reasons to investigate the effect of ethical labels on private label products on customer perception. Not only are PLBs important for the retailer's competition against NBs (Bodur et al. 2016), but also they are often associated with the brand itself, since they are only available at the store of one retailer (Richardson et al. 1994; Sethuraman 2003). Moreover, ethical label PLB products might offer the possibility to attract a new customer group, which has not bought PLBs or shopped at the retailer before (Corstjens and Lal 2000) due to missing trust towards the products offered. Previous research revealed that the perception of facing high risk when purchasing PL products is one of the most important factors inhibiting PL product purchase (Nies and Natter 2012).

Building on the principal-agent theory, investigating the effect of ethical labels on PL products is of high relevance, since they might offer a way for the retailer to reduce the customers' perceived risk provoked by information asymmetry. Ethical labels have an influence on sensory acceptance of products (De Andrade Silva et al. 2017) and might symbolize good quality, as they are judged by objective standards. This can reduce the feeling of uncertainty (Batra and Sinha 2000) and bring NB and PLB products closer together (Batra and Sinha 2000; Richardson et al. 1996). Moreover, there have been just very few studies dealing with the impact of ethical attributes in a PLB context (e.g., Bodur et al. 2016).

To the author's knowledge, there is just one study by Bauer et al. (2013) which investigates differences in the effect of organic labels on global, local and private brands. None of the existing studies has investigated the differences of the effects of different ethical labels. This study will close this research gap and contribute to scientific research by comparing the effects of three different ethical label combinations on PLB and NB products on customers' product brand trust. Moreover, this study provides evidence that this trust is a stronger predictor of the perception of brand and store perception for PLB than for NB products.

3 Conceptual Framework and Hypotheses

In order to account for the different possibilities of ethical labeling, three different types of ethical label products have been chosen for the model: (1) organic labeled NB and PL products, (2) fair-trade labeled NB and PL products, and (3) organic and fair-trade labeled (combined in one label) NB and PL products.

3.1 Product Brand Trust

Previous research has shown that labels are able to reduce customers' uncertainty about the product quality, because they follow objective standards (Harbaugh et al. 2011). Ethical labels fulfill objective ethical standards and products fulfilling those standards are highly linked to the brand trust (Singh et al. 2012). Following this research, it is assumed that:

H1 Fair-trade labels on products have a positive effect on customers' product brand trust.

H2 Organic labels on products have a positive effect on customers' product brand trust.

H3 Fair-trade and organic labels on products have a positive effect on customers' product brand trust.

3.2 Brand and Store Perception

As previous research revealed, spillover effects from product perceptions to the customers' store and brand perception are likely to occur, because the offered products are linked to the retailer and store in customers' mind (e.g., Ellison et al. 2016; Nies and Natter 2012). Hence, the following is proposed:

H4 Product brand trust has a positive effect on customers' brand perception.

H5 Product brand trust has a positive effect on customers' store perception.

However, the perception of NB products is not as strongly linked to brand and store perception as it is for PLB products (Rao et al. 2004). This is because customers perceive a stronger connection between PLB products with the brand and store, since

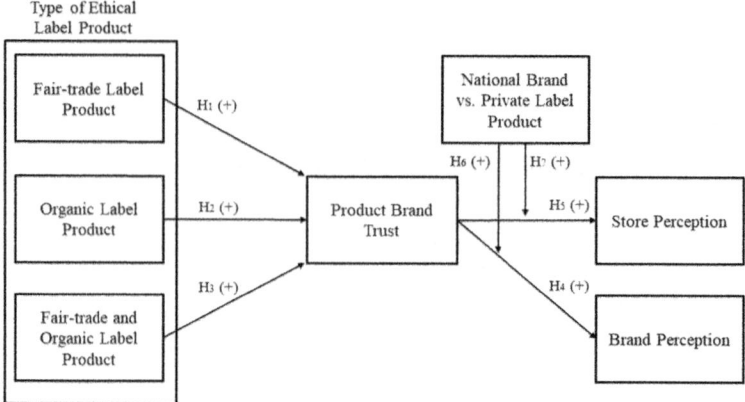

Fig. 1 Conceptual model

these products are only available at one retailer (Richardson et al. 1994; Sethuraman 2003). Following this research findings, it is hypothesized that:

H6 The effect of product brand trust on customers' brand perception is stronger for private label brand products than for national brand products.

H7 The effect of product brand trust on customers' store perception is stronger for private label brand products than for national brand products (Fig. 1).

4 Methodology

In order to test the proposed relationships, three pretests were conducted. Firstly, fictitious brand labels tested, used, and provided by Noormann (2017) were again checked for the presence of associations with other brand labels. 22 random participants took part in the online survey that tested for recall and recognition for the fictitious brand labels with existing ones. The pretest revealed that there were still no considerable associations with existing labels. A second pretest with 34 random participants was conducted online to check whether participants were able to classify the labels into the correct PL categories. Attributes like quality and price perception as well as label congruency between PLB products and ethical labels (i.e. fair-trade, organic and one label including both) were measured. Results of this pretest have shown that ethical labels are not suitable for the generic PL and questionable on the standard PL.

Working from the results of the pretests, two online experiment studies were designed. The first study examines the effect of ethical label PL products on brand trust as well as on brand and store perception. A random sample of 504 participants, balanced for gender, age, education, and occupation was acquired. One PL product portfolio with ethical label was shown to each participant and after that, relevant dependent variables were measured on established scales. The second study examines the same relationships as in study 1 with the same experiment structure for the NB context. 676 random participants took part in this online survey, again balanced for relevant demographics.

5 Expected Results and Discussion

The pretest confirmed the expectation that ethical labels are not advantageous for retailers on all stages of their PLB portfolio. First empirical results of the main studies indicate a significant difference for ethical label products compared to products without a label for both product types. Moreover, a difference in the effects of the three different labels on product brand trust seems to be supported by the data. Third, significant differences in brand and store perception was found for the two different product types. It is expected that the results of a deeper empirical analysis will show that there is an overall positive effect of ethical labels on PLB as well as on NB products on customers' product brand trust. Furthermore, it is proposed that there is a spillover effect of product brand trust on store and brand perception, which is stronger for PLB products than for NB products. This would underline the potential and relevance of ethical label PL products for retailers.

6 Conclusion and Implications for Theory and Practice

The study will show that ethical labeling of PL products can increase brand and store perception more effectively than offering ethical label NB products. This demonstrates that the consideration of providing PL products with ethical labels is of high relevance for retailers. Ethical labels offer the opportunity to not just differentiate from other retailers and their PLBs, but also to have a better baseline in the competition with NBs. Moreover, the study will show that ethical labels can increase customers' product brand trust. Further research should investigate the underlying psychological processes more deeply.

References

Auger, P., & Devinney, T. M. (2007). Do what consumers say matter? The misalignment of preferences with unconstrained ethical intentions. *Journal of Business Ethics, 76*(4), 361–383.

Batra, R., & Sinha, I. (2000). Consumer-level factors moderating the success of private label brands. *Journal of Retailing, 76*(2), 175–191.

Bauer, H. H., Heinrich, D., & Schäfer, D. B. (2013). The effects of organic labels on global, local, and private brands: More hype than substance? *Journal of Business Research, 66*(8), 1035–1043.

Bhattacharya, C. B., & Sen, S. (2004). Doing better at doing good: When, why, and how consumers respond to social initiatives. *California Management Review, 47*(1), 9–24.

Bodur, H. O., Tofighi, M., & Grohmann, B. (2016). When should private label brands endorse ethical attributes? *Journal of Retailing, 92*(2), 204–217.

Corstjens, M., & Lal, R. (2000). Building store loyalty through store brands. *Journal of Marketing Research, 37*(3), 281–291.

Cotterill, R. W., Putsis, W. P., & Dhar, R. (2000). Assessing the competitive interaction between private labels and national brands. *Journal of Business, 73*(1), 109–137.

Cowe, R., & Williams, S. (2001). *Who are the ethical consumers?* CO-Operative Bank/Mori Survey.

De Andrade Silva, A. R., Sodré Bioto, A., Efraim, P., & de Castilho Queiroz, G. (2017). Impact of sustainability labeling in the perception of sensory quality and purchase intention of chocolate consumers. *Journal of Cleaner Production, 141*, 11–21.

Du, S., Bhattacharya, C. B., & Sen, S. (2007). Reaping relational rewards from corporate social responsibility: The role of competitive positioning. *International Journal of Research in Marketing, 24*(3), 224–241.

Ellison, B., Duff, B. R. L., Wang, Z., & White, T. B. (2016). Putting the organic label in context: Examining the interactions between the organic label, product type, and retail outlet. *Food Quality and Preference, 49*, 140–150.

Geyskens, I., Gielens, K., & Gijsbrechts, E. (2010). Proliferating private-label portfolios: How introducing economy and premium private labels influences brand choice. *Journal of Marketing Research, 47*(5), 791–807.

Harbaugh, R., Maxwell, J. W., & Roussillon, B. (2011). Label confusion: The Groucho effect of uncertain standards. *Management Science, 57*(9), 1512–1527.

Henderson, T., & Arora, N. (2010). Promoting brands across categories with a social cause: Implementing effective embedded premium programs. *Journal of Marketing, 74*(6), 41–60.

Hoch, S. J., & Banerji, S. (1993). When do private labels succeed? *MIT Sloan Management Review, 34*(4), 57.

Karjalainen, K., & Moxham, C. (2013). Focus on fairtrade: Propositions for integrating fairtrade and supply chain management research. *Journal of Business Ethics, 116*(2), 267–282.

Kumar, N., & Steenkamp, J.-B. (2007). Brand versus Brand. *International Commerce Review, 7*(1), 46–53.

Nielsen. (2011). *Global private label report the rise of the value-conscious shopper.* Accessed March 3, 2018 from http://www.nielsen.com/us/en/insights/news/2011/global-private-label-report-the-rise-of-the-value-conscious-shopper.html

Nies, S., & Natter, M. (2012). Does private label quality influence consumers' decision on where to shop? *Psychology & Marketing, 29*(4), 279–292.

Noormann, P. (2017). *Mehrstufige Eigenmarken.* Wiesbaden: Springer.

Rao, V. R., Agarwal, M. K., & Dahlhoff, D. (2004). How is manifest branding strategy related to the intangible value of a corporation? *Journal of Marketing, 68*(4), 126–141.

Richardson, P. S., Dick, A. S., & Jain, A. K. (1994). Extrinsic and intrinsic cue effects on perceptions of store brand quality. *Journal of Marketing, 58*(4), 28–36.

Richardson, P. S., Jain, A. K., & Dick, A. (1996). Household store brand proneness: A Frame-work. *Journal of Retailing, 72*(2), 159–185.

Sethuraman, R. (2003). Measuring National Brands' equity over store brands. *Review of Marketing Science, 1*(1), 1–26.

Singh, J. J., Iglesias, O., & Batiste-Foguet, J. M. (2012). Does having an ethical brand matter? The influence of consumer perceived ethicality on trust, affect and loyalty. *Journal of Business Ethics, 111*, 541–549.

Trudel, R., & Cotte, J. (2009). Does it pay to be good? *MIT Sloan Management Review, 50*(2), 61.

Yamoah, F. A., Duffy, R., Petrovici, D., & Fearne, A. (2016). Toward a framework for understanding fairtrade purchase intention in the mainstream environment of supermarkets. *Journal of Business Ethics, 136*, 181–197.

Consumer Attitudes During Periods of Economic Downturn: Embodying Responsible Behaviors

Maria Sarmento, Mercedes Galan-Ladero, and Susana Marques

Abstract This study addresses consumer attitudes towards PLs and NB promotions during recessions. The research adopts a mixed method approach, combining interviews and a survey applied to consumers in a context of economic crisis. The results show that economic contractions change consumer behavior, highlighting the consumers' rational dimension. They also establish bases for structural learning. Consumers assumed that the crisis helped them to become more economically and socially responsible, assuming an intention to maintain rational and responsible behaviors in a post-recession stage.

Keywords Private labels · National brands · Consumer behavior

1 Introduction

Since the beginning of the twenty-first century sales growth for Private labels (PLs) has outperformed the growth of National brands (NBs) (Bao et al. 2011; Batra and Sinha 2000; Steenkamp and Geyskens 2014). Part of this growth might be attributed to the economic crisis that began in the 2000s and continues to affect the Eurozone (e.g. Diallo and Kaswengi 2016; Kaswengi and Diallo 2015). The competition between NBs and PLs has been a key research area (Cheng et al. 2007). Nonetheless,

M. Sarmento (✉)
Nova School of Business and Economics, Lisbon, Portugal

Open University Business School, Milton Keynes, UK
e-mail: maria.sarmento@novasbe.pt

M. Galan-Ladero
University of Extremadura, Badajoz, Spain
e-mail: mgalan@unex.es

S. Marques
University of Aveiro, Aveiro, Portugal
e-mail: susana.vasconcelos@ua.pt

© Springer International Publishing AG, part of Springer Nature 2018   17
F. J. Martínez-López et al. (eds.), *Advances in National Brand and Private Label Marketing*, Springer Proceedings in Business and Economics,
https://doi.org/10.1007/978-3-319-92084-9_3

consumer attitudes towards PLs and NB promotions in periods of economic down-turn is a question that remains unanswered. Our main objective is to understand if, during recessions, attitudes change in a structural way, or if the consumer is forced to consume the cheapest brands just because of the loss of purchasing power.

2   Background and Hypotheses

Companies generally brand their products with a National Brand (NB) or a Private label (PL) (Dawes and Nenycz-Thiel 2013). NB (also called as manufacturer brands) are brands developed and sold under the brand name of manufacturers, while PLs (also called as store brands, private brands, or distributor brands) are brands devel-oped and distributed under retailers or wholesalers' own labels (Dawes and Nenycz-Thiel 2013; Bao et al. 2011; Burton et al. 1998).

Price Consciousness is defined as the "degree to which the consumer focuses exclusively on paying low prices" (Lichtenstein et al. 1993, p. 235). Price is a key marketing variable (Diallo and Kaswengi 2016) and consumers enjoy paying prices that are lower than the reference price (Chandon et al. 2000). The loss of income, grant consumers incentives to experiment with lower-priced brands (Diallo and Kaswengi 2016), favoring more purchases of PLs and NB promotions (Burton et al. 1998; Chandon et al. 2000. Consumers seeking to save money can also search for a NB being marketed on deal (Chandon et al. 2000). The monetary savings gained from buying a NB promotion versus a PL may often be very similar (Garretson et al. 2002). Thus, it is hypothesized that, during recessions:

H1 Price consciousness has a positive effect on attitude towards PLs

H2 Price consciousness has a positive effect on NB promotion attitude

Perceived price unfairness is defined as "the consumer's subjective evaluation that he/she has been charged more (i.e., asked to pay an unfair premium than that called for by the costs incurred by the seller)" (Sinha and Batra 1999, p. 241). In periods of economic crisis, consumers question the fairness of companies' price strategies. On the basis of this judgement consumers punish (e.g. do not buy the brand) when they consider the price imposed by the seller to be unfair or inadequate (Sinha and Batra 1999) which is the case of NBs that are perceived as being too expensive for what they deliver (Nenycz-Thiel and Romaniuk 2009). In this situa-tion, consumers may opt to buy PLs instead of NBs as they are marked at a lower price and therefore judged as being fairer. Thus, it is hypothesized that, during recessions:

H3 Perceived price unfairness of NBs has a positive effect on attitude towards PLs

Risk Aversion is defined as "the extent to which people feel threatened by ambiguous situations, and have created beliefs and institutions that try to avoid these" (Hofstede and Bond 1984, p. 419). Consumers with high risk aversion feel threatened by uncertain and novel situations (Bao et al. 2003). As the perceived risk of a purchase increases, consumers are more likely to rely on a higher price as a signal of quality (e.g. Bao et al. 2003; DelVecchio 2001). The greater variability in quality across the PL products increases the risk that a given PL will not perform in a satisfactory manner, suggesting that consumers who are more risk averse are less receptive to PLs (Batra and Sinha 2000; Burton et al. 1998). Thus, it is hypothesized that, during recessions:

H4 Risk aversion has a negative effect on attitude towards PLs

Smart shoppers are "thoughtful consumers who take pride in their decision-making ability" (Burton et al. 1998, p. 296). Smart shoppers believe that there are advantageous purchase opportunities available in the marketplace, act less impulsively in their decision-making, and take pride in capitalizing on these opportunities (Burton et al. 1998). Buying a promoted product can be a means of becoming recognized a smart shopper (Chandon et al. 2000; Garretson et al. 2002). Additionally, consumers who have a positive attitude toward PLs view themselves as smart shoppers who are more purposeful in their behaviour and are willing to procure PL versions of a product rather than purchasing on impulse (Burton et al. 1998; Garretson et al. 2002). Thus, it is hypothesized that, during recessions:

H5 Smart shoppers' self-perception has a positive effect on attitude towards PLs

H6 Smart shoppers' self-perception has a positive effect on NB promotion attitude

3   Method

The research method entails a combination of qualitative (phase 1) and quantitative (phase 2) approaches.

Phase 1 An empirical qualitative study was conducted to gain in-depth insights into the topic, aiming at a better comprehension of consumer attitudes towards PLs in periods of economic downturn. The study was conducted in 2014, during Portuguese recession. The qualitative phase comprised eleven semi-structured interviews with Portuguese consumers. This stage was fundamental to better comprehend the subject as it allowed the comparison between consumer attitudes in the stages before and during the recession. It also allowed to capture consumers' future intentions.

Phase 2 The quantitative stage comprised the development of a survey aiming at testing the conceptual model. All measures were bored from previous research. To measure PL attitude, we used the scale proposed by Burton et al. (1998) and to measure NB promotion attitude, we used Garretson et al. (2002) scale. The scales of price consciousness and perceived price unfairness of NBs were adopted from Sinha and Batra (1999). Smart shoppers' self-perception was measured based on Garretson et al. (2002), and Risk aversion scale used the items proposed by Bao et al. (2003). The questionnaire was administrated on-line and a snowball sampling was adopted, starting with a pool of consumers that nominated, through their social networks other consumers that could potentially contribute to the study. At the end, we obtained 280 valid responses that constitute the base of the study.

4 Findings

The results of the structural equation model involving the hypothesized relationships yielded an adequate fit for the data: $\chi2 = 300$, df $= 176$, P < 0.001, CFI $= 0.95$, RMSEA $= 0.05$ (Hair et al. 2009). Regarding the effects of price related variables, findings support H1 and H2, suggesting that price consciousness is a very important predictor of consumer's attitude towards PLs and NB promotions. There is a significant large coefficient representing the effect of price consciousness on attitude towards PLs ($\beta = 0.527$, t $= 5.99$), and a significant large coefficient of the effect of price consciousness on attitude towards NB promotions ($\beta = 0.507$, t $= 6.97$). Findings also confirm H3, showing a positive significant effect of perceived price unfairness of NBs on attitude towards PLs ($\beta = 0.167$, t $= 2.37$). The results from the survey are also in line with the interviewees' comments. In general, interviewees mentioned that, particularly during the hard times of recession, the price of the products became determinant in their choices and the main concern was to save some money. In this search for economic rationality, interviewees also mentioned the adoption of other behaviors like going shopping more often and avoiding stocking a large quantity of products. Consumers also referred an additional concern of not wasting.

Regarding the effects of personality related variables, findings from the survey reject H4, showing that the effect of risk aversion on attitude towards PLs was non-significant ($\beta = 0.02$, t $= 0.28$). The findings from the interviews are in line with the survey's findings, corroborating the idea that buying PLs is not risky. In periods of economic recession, the determinant buying criteria is price if the minimum levels of quality are assured. Globally interviewees trust PLs, although in some categories of products they have more confidence than in others. Findings support H5 and H6, revealing that the variable smart shopper self-perception is a positive predictor of attitudes towards PLs ($\beta = 0.191$, t $= 2.81$) and NB promotions ($\beta = 0.415$, t $= 6.59$). These findings are aligned with previous research that addressed the conceptual antecedents of attitudes toward PLs and NB promotions (Garretson et al. 2002; Manzur et al. 2011). Results also show that the effect of smart shopper self-perception is higher on attitude towards NB promotions than the effect on attitude towards PLs ($\beta = 0.415$ vs $\beta = 0.191$).

5 Conclusion

Economic recessions constitute 'periods of change', engendering moments of human reflection that influence consumer behavior. In this context, consumers adjust their actions to lessen economic resources. Our study confirms that, under these circumstances, consumers become more price sensitive and the human dimension of the 'rational man' gains dominance. In general, as a result of the increased price consciousness, consumers are more willing to spare some money, opting for cheaper solutions, such as PLs and NB promotions. Our research shows that consumer's perception of price unfairness of NBs has an impact on consumer's attitude towards PLs. In addition, risk aversion is not a trait that prevents consumers from buying PLs. In periods of economic downturn, risk dimension in neglected in favor of behaviors (for example in the price dimension) that allow rational decisions and utility maximization. In this pursuit for economic rationality, consumers assume new behaviors that allow them to accommodate the reduced income, which also translates in increased social responsibility. Besides looking for utility maximization and switching to cheaper options, consumers revealed new habits, such as (1) more organization and planned behavior; (2) going shopping more frequently; (3) reducing stocking behavior; and (4) avoiding wasting.

Consumers also referred to the learning opportunity that recessions usually engender, instigating structural changes in people's lives, that is, behaviors adopted during these periods are assimilated and become part of consumers' everyday life. Consumers claim that nothing will be the same, once they learned the lesson and intend to continue to be more rational and responsible consumers in a post-recession stage.

References

Bao, Y., Zheng-Zhou, K., & Su, C. (2003). Face consciousness and risk aversion: do they affect consumer decision-making? *Psychology and Marketing, 20*(8), 733–755.

Bao, Y., Bao, Y., & Sheng, S. (2011). Motivating purchase of private brands: Effects of store image, product signatureness, and quality variation. *Journal of Business Research, 64*, 220–226.

Batra, R., & Sinha, I. (2000). Consumer-level factors moderating the success of private label brands. *Journal of Retailing, 76*(2), 175–191.

Burton, S., Lichtenstein, D., Netemeyer, R., & Garretson, J. (1998). A scale for measuring attitude toward private label products and an examination of its psychological and behavioral correlates. *Journal of the Academy of Marketing Science, 26*(4), 293–306.

Chandon, P., Wansink, B., & Laurent, G. (2000). A benefit congruency framework of sales promotion effectiveness. *Journal of Marketing, 64*(October), 65–81.

Cheng, J., Chen, L., Lin, J., & Wang, E. (2007). Do consumers perceive differences among national brands, international private labels and local private labels? The case of Taiwan. *Journal of Product and Brand Management, 16*(6), 368–376.

Dawes, J., & Nenycz-Thiel, M. (2013). Analyzing the intensity of private label competition across retailers. *Journal of Business Research, 66*, 60–66.

DelVecchio, D. (2001). Consumer perceptions of private label quality: The role of product category characteristics and consumer use of heuristics. *Journal of Retailing and Consumer Services, 8,* 239–249.

Diallo, M., & Kaswengi, J. (2016). What drives store brand purchases during crisis periods? Evidence from panel data in four product categories. *International Journal of Retail and Distribution Management, 44*(3), 301–319.

Garretson, J., Fisher, D., & Burton, S. (2002). Antecedents of private label attitude and national brand promotion attitude: Similarities and differences. *Journal of Retailing, 78,* 91–99.

Hair, J., Black, W., Babin, B., & Anderson, R. (2009). *Multivariate data analysis* (7th ed.). Upper Saddle River, NJ: Prentice Hall.

Hofstede, G., & Bond, M. (1984). Hofstede's culture dimensions: An independent validation usingll Rokeach's value survey. *Journal of Cross-Cultural Psychology, 15,* 417–433.

Kaswengi, J., & Diallo, M. (2015). Consumer choice of store brands across store formats: A panel data analysis under crisis periods. *Journal of Retailing and Consumer Services, 23,* 70–76.

Lichtenstein, D., Ridgway, N., & Netemeyer, R. (1993). Price perceptions and consumer shopping behavior: A field study. *Journal of Marketing Research, 30*(2), 234–245.

Manzur, E., Olavarrieta, S., Hidalgo, P., Farias, P., & Uribe, R. (2011). Store brand and national brand promotion attitudes antecedentes. *Journal of Business Research, 64*(3), 286–291.

Nenycz-Thiel, M., & Romaniuk, J. (2009). Perceptual categorization of private labels and national brands. *Journal of Product and Brand Management, 18*(4), 251–261.

Sinha, I., & Batra, R. (1999). The effect of consumer price consciousness on private label purchase. *International Journal of Research in Marketing, 16,* 237–251.

Steenkamp, J., & Geyskens, I. (2014). Manufacturer and retailer strategies to impact store brand share: Global integration, local adaptation, and worldwide learning. *Marketing Science, 33*(1), 6–26.

Usage of Private Label Brands Among Street Vendors in Thailand

Jiaranai Chaiyakarn Zheng and Randall Shannon

Abstract Despite aggressive attempts to develop and market private label brands by retailers in Thailand, acceptance remains low. If used as an ingredient, private labels could be a lower cost alternative to national brands and the end user would likely never know the difference. This study explores usage of private label brands among street vendors in Bangkok, Thailand.

Keywords Private label · Asia · Consumer behavior · Street vendors · Bangkok · Thailand

1 Introduction

After a wave of foreign food retailer expansion swept through Thailand, the number of private label brands offered increased exponentially, to the point that Thailand was in the top five fastest growing markets for PL. However, figures from Nielsen (2014) have shown that this growth was mainly a sharp increase from less than 1%, growing to roughly 1.5%, which has been stable over the past 15 years. It seems the growth was more from the push by retailers rather than actual consumer acceptance. A variety of papers have been published exploring various aspects of attitudes and behaviors in regards to PL acceptance among Thai consumers, (e.g. Mandhachitara et al. 2007), but not among providers of foods or beverages, such as the hotel, restaurant or catering businesses (HoReCa). As there are huge numbers of street vendors in Bangkok, this study set forth to explore whether they use private label brands, and the reasons as to why or why not.

J. C. Zheng (✉)
Faculty of Management Science, Ubon Ratchathani University, Ubon Ratchathani, Thailand

R. Shannon
College of Management, Mahidol University (CMMU), Bangkok, Thailand
e-mail: Randall.sha@mahidol.ac.th

© Springer International Publishing AG, part of Springer Nature 2018   23
F. J. Martínez-López et al. (eds.), *Advances in National Brand and Private Label Marketing*, Springer Proceedings in Business and Economics,
https://doi.org/10.1007/978-3-319-92084-9_4

Thailand has remained one of the fastest growing food retail markets in the world, with total retail sales of US$ 88.2 billion in 2016 (USDA Gain Report 2017), with $83.5 billion coming from store retailing. Street vendors are small entrepreneurs operating their businesses along sidewalks or the roadside, and can be mobile or static (Narathorn 2014). These vendors are a part of daily life for many people in Thailand, especially in big cities, like Bangkok, which has a population of roughly ten million people. The Department of City Planning estimates there are roughly 22,000 street vendors in Bangkok, with a market value of roughly $2.5 million (Department of City Planning 2012), although the HoReCa market in Thailand has been estimated to have a value of $32,040,000,000 (Thansettakij 2015). The vast majority of street vendors are selling food or beverages (Walsh 2010). Street vendors are included in the HoReCa sector, and need to frequently purchase goods to use as ingredients for their products. Since these ingredients are typically not seen by the end consumers, there is a high potential for street vendors to be drawn to use PL brands and enjoy cost savings. PL brands have long faced problems with extrinsic cue reliance (Richardson et al. 1994), and many Asians have been found to have high uncertainty avoidance and avoid risk (Batra and Sinha 2000; Shannon and Mandhachitara 2008), which reduces the chance that they would move away from national brands and try private labels. Emerging markets, in general, seem slow to adopt PL brands (Cuneo et al. 2015).

This study aims to investigate awareness and usage of private label brands among street vendors in an emerging market to facilitate a better understanding of why they use them or why they do not.

2 Research Methodology

Based on a report by the Department of City Planning, three districts within Bangkok were selected as the focus of the research due to having the highest concentrations of street vendors (BMA 2012). The authors opted to use depth interviews because of the exploratory nature of the study, and also because many street vendors have low education and income, thus may not be willing or able to participate in a survey. In line with recommendations by Ghauri and Gronhaug (2010), the interviews were often conducted using the dialect with which the street vendors spoke, primarily from the northeast. Ten depth interviews were conducted among vendors of food and beverages from each of the three selected districts, for a total of 30 interviews, which were recorded for later analysis.

3 Research Findings

From the 30 respondents, 23 sold food and 7 sold beverages, and among them, only 7 claimed to use private label brands, 1 selling beverages and 6 selling food.

All respondents were aware of the concept of private label brands, but the majority reported shopping in fresh markets for their supplies, and private label is typically not available in such venues.

Most of the street vendors buy their materials on a daily basis, paying cash, with more than half buying on credit in the morning, then paying the money back at the end of the day (with no interest charged). They work from small budgets and do not want to stock raw materials. With low income and no fixed salary, they are usually not qualified to apply for credit cards. Informal credit and also being able to call the retailer and have their order prepared both highlight how traditional trade is still able to survive in the midst of widespread modern trade food retail expansion. However, convenience sometimes wins over price, as some vendors said they preferred buying heavy items close by, and if they run out of inventory during the day, they may run to a nearby convenience store and buy more.

Among those who reported using PL brands, they cited attractive promotions and use of low risk products, which did not risk affecting the quality of their products, such as tissue paper and toothpicks. When especially attractive promotions were available, they said they would buy PL (cooking oil buy one get one free, for example). Several of the vendors reported repackaging PL products so that they appeared to be national brands. This was partially to hide the actual brand, but sometimes was in response to consumer questioning their use of PL. In general, PL brands were perceived to be of lower quality and thus not only risky, but also not particularly a value for money, since more of the product might be required for similar results (dish washing liquid). The price difference was also reportedly very low, thus not particularly attractive versus the perceived risk. Close imitations of packaging were found distasteful, with more appreciation given to the functional side of packaging, such as being waterproof or not leaking or easily breaking. While several street vendors claimed to use PL, they tended to be low involvement products. In general, vendors were afraid of taking risks that might affect the taste of their products, thus tend to stick with national brands.

4   Conclusions

This study has found that street vendors very often buy their ingredients on a daily basis, many buying on credit in the morning and paying back the cash in the evening. This has implications in terms of PL brands generally not being offered in traditional trade formats. Can retailers find a way to get their PL brands into traditional trade outlets? If retailers would consider providing credit or perhaps just offering to deliver to street vendors or mom and pop shops, they might be able to increase sales of PL through the enhanced value for money provided. Educating street vendors about PL as being used as an ingredient brand might also help increase sales, as long as they feel assured that the quality of their food or beverages will not be negatively affected. Low involvement products are still deemed safer choices among respondents, but if they have positive experiences, it would be expected their trust in PL would grow, as would acceptance and usage. With widespread adoption of smartphones, future research could explore the extent to which consumers shop online. Lower prices and convenience of delivery might be a way to attract street vendors to shop online, which then also offers PL brand options and more savings.

References

Batra, R., & Sinha, I. (2000). Consumer-level factors moderating the success of private label brands. *Journal of Retailing, 76*(Summer), 175–191.

Cuneo, A., Milberg, S. J., Benavente, J. M., & Palacios-Fenech, J. (2015). The growth of private label brands: A worldwide phenomenon? *Journal of International Marketing, 23*(1), 72–90 https://doi.org/10.1509/jim.14.0036.

Department of City Planning, Bangkok Metropolitan Administration. (2012). *Street vendors in Bangkok report.* Accessed January 12, 2018 from http://cpd.bangkok.go.th:90/web2/strategy/DATA54_55/15UNM.pdf

Ghauri, P. N., & Gronhaug, K. (2010). *Research methods in business studies* (4th ed.). London: FT Pearson.

http://www.thansettakij.com/content/107693 Accessed January 15, 2018, Thai news article with figures about the HoReCa market in Thailand.

Mandhachitara, R., Shannon, R., & Hadjicharalambous, C. (2007). Why private label grocery brands have not succeeded in Asia. *Journal of Global Marketing, 20*(2/3), 71–87.

Narathorn, N. (2014). *Fighting poverty from the street: A survey of street food vendors in Bangkok.* Bangkok: International Labor Office (ILO).

Nielson. (2014, November). *The state of private label around the world, where it's growing, where it's not, and what the future holds.* Accessed January 5, 2018 from http://www.nielsen.com/content/dam/nielsenglobal/kr/docs/global-report/2014/Nielsen%20Global%20Private%20Label%20Report%20November%202014.pdf

Richardson, P. S., Dick, A. S., & Jain, A. K. (1994). Extrinsic and intrinsic cue effects on perceptions of store brand quality. *Journal of Marketing, 58*, 28–36.

Shannon, R., & Mandhachitara, R. (2008). Causal path modeling of grocery shopping in hypermarkets. *Journal of Product and Brand Management, 17*(5), 327–340. https://doi.org/10.1108/10610420810896086.

USDA Gain report: Thailand Retail Foods. (2017). Accessed February 20, 2018 from https://gain.fas.usda.gov/Recent%20GAIN%20Publications/Retail%20Foods_Bangkok_Thailand_12-28-2017.pdf

Walsh, J. (2010). The street vendors of Bangkok: Alternatives to indoor retailers at a time of economic crisis. *American Journal of Economics and Business Administration, 2*(2), 186–188.

Private Label Consumers and National Brand New Products: An Empirical Investigation

Ian Clark Sinapuelas

Abstract Previous research finds that national brands take market shares from private labels when they introduce new products. Which consumers they attract with the new product introduction however remains unknown. Using data from the carbonated beverage category and a cure model approach, this research empirically investigates which consumer segments are regained. Our results suggest that new national brands mostly regain brand users, though they are more likely to attract light private label users. Our results have implications for national brand managers designing launch and targeting strategies and for private label managers designing defensive strategies.

Keywords New products · Purchase adoption · Private label share · Split population

1 Introduction

Private labels draw consumers away from national brands (Gielens 2012). To maintain competitiveness, national brands innovate and introduce new products (Kumar and Steenkamp 2007). From an aggregate perspective, Gielens (2012) find that when certain national brands introduce certain types of products, they can affect the private label market shares. At the consumer level perspective, Abril et al. (2015) find that consumers are less likely to switch to private labels when national brands introduce new products.

While the issue of prevention of switching has been addressed by Abril et al. (2015), their study is limited to prevention and is unable to trace the recovery of customers lost to private labels. While Gielens' (2012) aggregate results may hint that some recovery happens, as this explains the decrease in private label market

I. C. Sinapuelas (✉)
San Francisco State University, San Francisco, CA, USA
e-mail: sinapuel@sfsu.edu

© Springer International Publishing AG, part of Springer Nature 2018   27
F. J. Martínez-López et al. (eds.), *Advances in National Brand and Private Label Marketing*, Springer Proceedings in Business and Economics,
https://doi.org/10.1007/978-3-319-92084-9_5

shares upon a national brand's introduction, their research however does not identify which private label consumer purchases the new product. It is likely that the decrease in private label shares may arise from previous national brand users switching to private labels and eventually switching back to the national brand's new product. It is equally likely that the decrease in private label shares may arise from national brand non-users. While both scenarios may be beneficial to the national brand, the two scenarios require different launch and targeting strategies.

To address this issue, this research proposes a cure model to empirically determine who among existing private label users purchase a national brand's new product. In particular, this research proposes a typology of private label users based on their private label shares and brand experience. Using this classification system, this empirical research measures the likelihood of purchase for each consumer type. Our results suggest that new products introduced by national brands attract consumers who have brand experience though their likelihood varies according to their private label purchases. Thus, national brands introducing new products may be able to recover consumers "lost" to private label brands.

2 Background and Hypotheses

There is a general consensus among researchers that private label consumers are more budget constrained, price conscious, value conscious, and more deal prone (see Muruganantham and Priyadharshini 2017 for a review). Decades of research on the private label consumer consistently find that the primary reason for their continued patronage of private label brands is the value that these consumers find in private labels (Sethuraman and Gielens 2014). However, when given a chance, as when the price is right, consumers still prefer national brands over private labels (Kara et al. 2009). This suggests that the basket of goods purchased by these consumers over a period of time, e.g. in a year, contains both private label and national brands. In fact, Ailawadi and Harlam (2004) suggest a wide range of consumer private label shares, i.e., the share of a customer's purchases that are private labels. They find that light users tend to have more items in their baskets than heavy users. They propose that heavy private label users may have more financial constraints, buy and consume less, and have smaller families. Given a light users' more frequent purchase of national brands, we suggest that the private label's value proposition is less appealing to light users compared to heavy users. As new products change a consumer's perception of value (Rindova and Petkova 2007), we propose that when presented with new national brand products, light users are more likely to purchase. Thus, the decrease in private label share that follows a national brand new product introduction can come from the low share private label customers.

Alternatively, it is possible that the decrease in private label share following a national brand introduction can be explained by the national brand regaining its consumers "lost" to private labels. Previous research (Sinapuelas et al. 2015) find that experience with the parent brand is a consistent predictor of new product

		Parent Brand Experience	
		Yes	No
Private Label	High	Q1: Strong Possibilities	Q2: Low Conversion
Share	Low	Q3: Low Hanging Fruit	Q4: Competitors Turf

Fig. 1 A typology of private label consumers

adoption. With experience, the consumer is able to transfer his quality perceptions of the parent brand to the new product. Such transfer reduces the uncertainty and facilitates new product trial. Moreover, because brand experience influences brand loyalty (Brakus et al. 2009), we suspect that brand experience also impacts the consumer's value perception. Thus, consumers with brand experience may find greater value in the new product than those without.

Given competing explanations, we propose in Fig. 1 a typology of customers using two variables: private label share (high/low) and brand experience (Yes/No).

We predict different product adoption patterns across the four segments:

Q1. From the perspective of the national brand introducing a new product, high private label share consumers with brand experience offer strong possibilities. Although they heavily purchase private label brands, they can draw on their experience to evaluate a new product. Yet their behavior of relying heavily on private labels indicate that they may not be attracted to the value offered by a new product. We label this segment as "strong possibilities."

Q2. From the perspective of the national brand introducing a new product, high private label share consumers without brand experience are the most difficult to convert to the new product. Like the "strong possibilities" segment, they are less likely to be find value in the new product. More importantly, they have no experience on which to draw in evaluating the new product. We label this segment as "low conversion."

Q3. Low private label share consumers who have brand experience are most likely to try the new product. Unlike high private label share customers, they may find the value of the private label less appealing. Additionally, their experience allows them to easily find value in the new product. From the national brand's perspective, these consumers are a "low hanging fruit," thus we label them as such.

Q4. Low private label share consumers with no experience of the parent brand may not be inclined to try the new product at all. Their low shares suggest that they rarely find value in private labels, and their lack of experience with the national brand suggest that they patronize the national brand's rivals. National brands introducing new products may find appealing to these individuals very difficult as they already show weak preference for the said brand. From the national brand's perspective, these consumers belong to the "competitor's turf."

The previous discussion suggests that the "low hanging fruit" segment is most likely and the "low conversion" segment are the least likely to purchase a new product. Whether the other two segments are more or less likely to adopt than these segment remains an empirical issue. We address this question in our empirical analysis.

3 Data and Methodology

The data used in this study is a subset of the consumer panel data from the 2008 IRI Marketing Dataset (Bronnenberg et al. 2008). The IRI data set provides information for panelists in two BehaviorScan markets, and consumer panel data provide demographic and purchase data from 2001 to 2005. The product category under investigation is carbonated beverages. The carbonated beverage category has the shortest purchase cycle among products with low perishability which make it conducive to new product trial. In addition, the carbonated beverage category generates the highest revenue and has the highest household penetration rate, which make it of great interest to retail managers. We restrict our sample to panelists who have purchased a private label 2 years prior to the introduction of the new product. In order to obtain complete purchase histories, we limit our sample of 11 new products introduced between 2003 and 2005. Although a new product's window of acceptance is only 6 to 12 months (Gielens and Steenkamp 2007), we track a panelist's purchases until the product is withdrawn from the market or until the end of our observation period.

3.1 Model and Variable Definitions

Since the research objective is to compare the purchase likelihoods of each customer type in Fig. 1, we utilize survival modeling, where the variable of interest, product adoption, is considered a "failure". This approach is similar to (Abril et al. 2015) in the sense that "failure" is indicated by product adoption. While most survival models assume that everyone in the sample eventually fails, full market penetration is unrealistic in this context as consumers do not purchase every new product introduced in the market. Thus, there is a need to utilize split population or cure models (Peng and Taylor 2014) which are a special class of survival models. Applied to our context, cure models assume that a certain fraction of the population, π, will never adopt a product. The phenomenon we are interested in, the proportion of consumers who will adopt a product, is denoted by $1-\pi$. If we let T be the time until product adoption, the survival function equals $P(T > t) = \pi S_u(t) + (1-\pi)S_c(t)$, where $S_u(t)$ is the survival function for uncured individuals, and $S_c(t)$ is the survival function for cured individuals which equals to 1 (Peng and Taylor 2014).

We model π as follows: $\pi = \beta_0 + \beta_1 Q_1 + \beta_2 Q_2 + \beta_3 Q_3 + \delta Inc$, where Q_1, Q_2, Q_3 are dummy variables equal to 1 if the consumer belongs to Fig. 1's first, second, or third quadrant, respectively, zero otherwise. Inc_i is a dummy variable equal to 1 if the individual has a household income less than $45,000, zero otherwise. Though not a variable of interest, we include income because previous research consistently find that private label users tend to have lower income (Sethuraman and Gielens 2014). Additionally, low income individuals are less inclined to try new products (Bartels and Reinders 2011).

One type of split population estimation technique (Lambert 2007) incorporates baseline hazards in estimating the parameter π. Baseline hazards allow the possibility of "failure" due to factors other than the ones under consideration. Baseline hazards are calculated using the full sample (private label users and non-users) in the data. We estimate the model for each of the 11 new products in the sample using Lambert's (2007) strsnmix STATA procedure.

We measure private label share as the household's private label (unit) purchases in the category as a percentage of its total (units) purchases from the category. Following Ailawadi and Harlam (2004), we define a market share cut-off of 35%. Thus, individuals are classified as high share if more than 35% of their unit purchases in the 2 years immediately preceding the new product launch are private labels. We classify consumers as having parent brand experience if they have purchased the product at least once in the 2 years prior to launch.

3.2 Descriptive Statistics

Table 1 shows the descriptive statistics. Table 1 shows that 67% of our sample belong to the "low hanging fruit" segment and they tend to have the highest adoption rates. The smallest segment are "low conversion" individuals, and they tend to have the lowest adoption rates. While "strong possibilities" individuals tend to be fewer, they have the second highest adoption rate compared to "competitor's turf" individuals which comprise the second largest segment.

Table 1 Descriptive statistics

Segment name	Private label market share	Parent brand experience	Average proportion of consumers (%)[a]	Average adoption rate (%)	Range of adoption rates (%)
Strong possibilities	High	Yes	5.17	12.94	3.54–30.19
Low conversion	High	No	4.68	2.52	0–5.21
Low hanging fruit	Low	Yes	67.24	18.01	7.10–35.74
Competitor's turf	Low	No	22.92	4.67	0.46–12.18

[a]The average is taken across the 11 new products under consideration

4   Results

Table 2 shows estimation results for the 11 new products from the carbonated beverage category. The intercept term is the estimated cure fraction of the high income individual belonging to the "competitor's turf" segment, our base case. The estimated coefficients in columns 4, 6, and 8 show the differences in cure fractions for individuals in other segments relative to "competitor's turf". In particular, Table 2 shows the estimated cure fractions for "low hanging fruit" consumers are consistently less. This is because the estimated coefficients are negative and statistically significant for all 11 products in the sample. The average of these estimated coefficients equals −0.153 which suggests that though they have the same private label share individuals with brand experience are less likely to be "cured", or equivalently, more likely to try the new product.

"Low conversion" consumers, who like "competitor's turf" have no parent brand experience, but have higher private label shares, tend to have higher cure fractions than the base case. Five out of nine products have positive and significant estimated coefficients which suggest higher cure fractions or lower likelihoods of trial. Though they have no brand experience like "competitor's turf" individuals, their higher private label shares suggest that these consumers may find better value in private labels than national brands.

Table 2 Estimation results

| | Estimated coefficients | | | | |
| | Intercept | Q1 | Q2 | Q3 | |
New product	Competitor's turf	Strong possibilities	Low conversion	Low hanging fruit	Income
7up plus	0.911***	−0.076*	0.059***	−0.085***	−0.005
Coke C2	0.986***	−0.022		−0.080***	0.005
Diet Coke with Lime	0.888***	−0.127***	−0.014	−0.231***	0.083***
Mountain Dew Pitch Black	0.993***	−0.049*		−0.098***	−0.010
Mountain Dew Live Wire	0.931***	−0.114***	0.031***	−0.217***	0.004
Pepsi Vanilla	0.975***	−0.139***	−0.020	−0.162***	−0.003
Diet Pepsi Vanilla	0.943***	−0.124***	0.016	−0.162***	0.032**
Pepsi Holiday Spice	0.989***	−0.023	−0.011	−0.075***	0.000
Sierra Mist Free	0.774***	−0.228***	0.072***	−0.300***	0.120***
Sprite Remix	0.957***	−0.060**	0.031**	−0.102***	−0.001
Sprite Tropical Remix	0.870***	−0.085***	0.064***	−0.169***	0.046***
Mean	0.929	−0.095	0.025	−0.153	0.025

*p < 0.10, **p < 0.05, ***p < 0.01

"Strong possibilities" consumers tend to have lower cure fractions than "competitor's turf" individuals, which suggest that they are more likely to try the new product. Nine of the eleven estimated coefficients are negative and statistically significant. Their higher likelihoods persist despite their high level of private label shares.

Given the estimated coefficients, we find a certain ordering in terms of the private label consumer's tendency to try new national brands. Those most prone to try a new product are "low hanging fruit", followed by "strong possibilities", "competitor's turf", and finally "low conversion". This ordering suggests that brand experience is a significant factor in predicting new product trial. Private label experience on the other hand appear to be secondary since its effects are greater among those with brand experience compared to those without.

We conduct a robustness check to determine if the results are sensitive to the private label market share cutoff and the operationalization of the brand experience variable. For private label market share, we use the sample average private label market share as the cutoff instead of 35%. For brand experience, we use three purchase occasions (trial, first repeat, and second repeat) instead of a single purchase. We assume individuals who purchase the parent brand beyond second repeat have amassed positive experiences. The results are similar, we find that the most prone to try a new national brand product is the "low hanging fruit" individual, and the least prone to try is the "low conversion" individual. "Strong possibilities" and "competitor's turf" individuals have the same tendency to try the new national brand product.

5 Discussion

The objective of this research is to demonstrate empirically which private label consumer is prone to switch to new products introduced by national brands. National brands introduce new products as a non-price related strategy to counter the emergence of private label products. Extant research find that indeed new national brand products tend to draw from private label shares, but fail to identify these customers. Since private label customers tend to patronize national brands when given a financial incentive, they get to occasionally experience them. From the national brand's perspective, it is interesting to determine if their new products recover their consumers who occasionally purchase private labels, or the heavy private label user.

By classifying private label users according to their private label purchases and experience with the national brand, and using cure analysis techniques, we are able to determine which of the four types of customers are more prone to try national brand new products. Though limited in its breadth, our study of 11 new products from the carbonated beverages category suggest that previous users of the parent brand are more susceptible to try the new product, though those that have low private label shares are more likely to do so than those with high private label shares. Low private label share users may not find value in private labels as much as high users and may be more susceptible to new products. This effect however appears to be weak among consumers with no parent brand experience.

National brand managers should take comfort in the fact that their consumers who purchase private labels can be "recovered." However, they must continue to introduce new products for this to happen. Whether they want to recover these consumers will depend on the costs of new product introduction and the value of these customers. If desired, they can design programs to target the low private label share segment first and the high private label share after. Oppositely, private label managers should heed this as a warning that while these consumers may purchase private labels, they can easily switch back to national brands. They can design preemptive or defensive strategies to reduce the chances that their private label customers try the new national brand product.

5.1 Limitations and Further Research

This study does not account for the price gap between the new product and existing private label brands which previous literature finds as a significant factor in the decision to switch to private labels. The new national brand product may offer a low enough price that private label consumers find value in them. This issue however is outside the scope of the current research, and can be investigated in future work. Regardless, the price gap between private label and the new product should be the same for all individuals, thus we do not expect significant variation within the sample investigated. It is expected to vary between new products. With additional products from more product categories, these effects can be tested.

Another limitation is the absence of product specific factors. For example, some products are more innovative, which may attract more, or less, attention from the private label consumer. Gielens (2012) and Geyskens et al. (2010) find different types of new products have different impact in private label market shares which imply variation in cure fractions due to product specific factors. In fact, our limited sample shows that even for the same parent brand (Pepsi), Pepsi Holiday Spice's cure fraction is higher than Pepsi Vanilla's cure fraction. One potential explanation is that Pepsi Holiday Spice is rated innovative while Pepsi Vanilla is not. Further research can explore this issue with more products and categories.

References

Abril, C., Sanchez, J., & García-Madariaga, J. (2015). The effect of product innovation, promotion, and price on consumer switching to private labels. *Journal of Marketing Channels, 22*(3), 192–201.

Ailawadi, K. L., & Harlam, B. (2004). An empirical analysis of the determinants of retail margins: The role of store-brand share. *Journal of Marketing, 68*(1), 147–165.

Bartels, J., & Reinders, M. J. (2011). Consumer innovativeness and its correlates: A propositional inventory for future research. *Journal of Business Research, 64*(6), 601–609.

Brakus, J. J., Schmitt, B. H., & Zarantonello, L. (2009). Brand experience: What is it? How is it measured? Does it affect loyalty? *Journal of marketing, 73*(3), 52–68.

Bronnenberg, B. J., Kruger, M. W., & Mela, C. F. (2008). Database paper: The IRI marketing data set. *Marketing Science, 27*(4), 745–748.

Geyskens, I., Gielens, K., & Gijsbrechts, E. (2010). Proliferating private label portfolios: How introducing economy and premium private labels influence brand choice. *Journal of Marketing Research, 47*(5), 791–807.

Gielens, K. (2012). New products: The antidote to private label growth? *Journal of Marketing Research, 49*(3), 408–423.

Gielens, K., & Steenkamp, J. B. E. (2007). Drivers of consumer acceptance of new packaged goods: An investigation across products and countries. *International Journal of Research in Marketing, 24*(2), 97–111.

Kara, A., Rojas-Méndez, J. I., Kucukemiroglu, O., & Harcar, T. (2009). Consumer preferences of store brands: Role of prior experiences and value consciousness. *Journal of Targeting, Measurement and Analysis for Marketing, 17*(2), 127–137.

Kumar, N., & Steenkamp, J.-B. E. M. (2007). *Private label strategy: How to meet the store brand challenge*. Boston: Harvard Business School Press.

Lambert, P. C. (2007). Modeling of the cure fraction in survival studies. *Stata Journal, 7*(3), 351.

Muruganantham, G., & Priyadharshini, K. (2017). Antecedents and consequences of private brand purchase: A systematic review and a conceptual framework. *International Journal of Retail &Distribution Management, 45*(6), 660–682.

Peng, Y., & Taylor, J. M. (2014). Cure models. *Handbook of Survival Analysis*, 113–134.

Rindova, V. P., & Petkova, A. P. (2007). When is a new thing a good thing? Technological change, product form design, and perceptions of value for product innovations. *Organization Science, 18*(2), 217–232.

Sethuraman, R., & Gielens, K. (2014). Determinants of store brand share. *Journal of Retailing, 90* (2), 141–153.

Sinapuelas, I. C. S., Wang, H. M. D., & Bohlmann, J. D. (2015). The interplay of innovation, brand, and marketing mix variables in line extensions. *Journal of the Academy of Marketing Science, 43*(5), 558–573.

Does PDO/PGI Labels Contribute to Consumers' Intention to Buy Premium Private Labels Products? An Empirical Survey

Elisa Martinelli and Francesca De Canio

Abstract The paper focuses on a specific Premium Private Label (PPL), featured by a double branding: the retailer premium brand and the Protected Designation of Origin (PDO)/Protected Geographic Indication (PGI) label. Specifically, the study investigates if the use of an EU quality label might contribute in enhancing the intention to buy the PPL (PPLINTB), through the mediating role of PPL perceived quality (PPLQ) and attitude towards PPL products (PPLATT). The paper contributes to the literature on store brands and quality labels giving empirical evidence to the positive impact of EU quality labels on the PPL. The role of PDO/PGI labels is evaluated through three constructs: the brand guarantee they offer (PDO/PGILG), their role as products supporting the local economy (ES), their perception as authentic local products (AUT).

A survey was performed on a sample of retail customers. Our hypotheses were confirmed applying SEM, apart from the impact of AUT. PPLQ resulted as the main antecedent of PPLATT, followed by the PDO/PGI label guarantee (PDO/PGILG). PPLQ, ES and PPLATT mediate the indirect effects of the PDO/PGI labels on the PPLINT.

Keywords Premium Private Labels (PPLs) · PDO/PGI quality labels · Attitude towards the PPL · Intention to buy · Grocery retailing

1 Introduction

The private label's (PL) role has greatly evolved over time: PLs have increased their perceived quality (Steenkamp et al. 2010); they have expanded to non-food categories (e.g. clothes, appliances, etc.) and services (travel booking, financial services, etc.) (Martinelli et al. 2015); they can now be divided into three main tiers: economy,

E. Martinelli (✉) · F. De Canio
Department of Economics Marco Biagi, University of Modena and Reggio Emilia, Modena, Italy
e-mail: elisa.martinelli@unimore.it

© Springer International Publishing AG, part of Springer Nature 2018   37
F. J. Martínez-López et al. (eds.), *Advances in National Brand and Private Label Marketing*, Springer Proceedings in Business and Economics,
https://doi.org/10.1007/978-3-319-92084-9_6

standard and premium PLs (Lamey et al. 2012; Geyskens et al. 2010). In sum, PLs have substantially modified their nature over time, passing from a price convenience option aimed at supporting retailer profitability to a real brand option, aimed at satisfying shoppers' needs and wants, in innovative ways. The Premium Private Label (PPL) tier gained particular attention as it is considered as the fastest-growing (IRI 2016) and most profitable tier (Ter Braak et al. 2014). PPLs are defined as "consumer products, produced by or on behalf of retailers with high quality and priced close to national brands, that contribute to differentiating the retailer from its competitors" (Huang and Huddleston 2009, p. 978). Examples are Tesco's "Finest" in UK, Loblaw's "President's Choice" in Canada, and Conad's "Sapori & Dintorni" in Italy. As many PPLs consist in local products labelled with a Protected Designation of Origin (PDO) or a Protected Geographic Indication (PGI) brand too as vehicle to increase the perceived value of the PPL, this study investigates if the use of an EU quality label might contribute to enhancing consumers' intention to buy the PPL (PPLINTB), through the mediating role of the perceived quality level of the PPL (PPLQ) and of attitude towards PPL products (PPLATT). The paper contributes to the literature on store brands and quality labels giving empirical evidence to the positive impact of EU quality labels on the PPL consumers' perceptions, attitudes and INTB. Specifically, previous research did not test the indirect effects of EU quality labels on product attitude and intention to buy through the role of perceived product quality. As far as the authors are concerned, this could be a novel result. Moreover, managerial implications might be interesting too. In fact, according to IGD (2017), PPL will be the most important of the top trends to shape the global retail market in 2018; the second one will be offering local products. Consequently, investigating if the match of both brands, the retailer brand and the PDO/PGI label, stimulates its perceived product quality, a positive consumer attitude and intention to buy the PPL, would extend the scientific and managerial knowledge.

The paper is structured as follows: first, the conceptual model and the hypotheses proposed by our study are presented. The methodology used follows, pointing out the validity of the measurements applied. Then, results are depicted, ending with some managerial implications for retailers and EU quality labels producers.

2   Conceptual Model and Hypotheses

We propose a model in which the dimensions of the EU quality label are impacting the perceived quality of the PPL (PPLQ), considering it as a mediating variable with respect to the other widely accepted mediating relationships that the literature unanimously recognizes regarding the attitude towards PPL products and then the intention to buy the PPL. We want also to examine whether the PDO/PGI label yields an effect on PPLINTB through the mediating role of PPLATT.

Our hypotheses are as follows.

PPL tiers are at the top end of the market and deliver quality comparable to premium-quality NBs, with similar (and sometimes even higher) perceived quality

(Huang and Huddleston 2009). As PPLQ was found as being an antecedent of PPLATT (Chaniotakis et al. 2010), we postulate the following hypothesis:

H1 PPL perceived quality (PPLQ) has a significant positive impact on PLLATT.

The EU introduced PDO/PGI labels to legally protect the origin of local and traditional products and foods of the members countries, supporting its quality policy regarding agriculture. The result is an enhanced perceived product value, rending PDO/PGI products more easily accepted by consumers (Fotopoulos and Krystallis 2003). Thus, the PDO/PGI label guarantee might increase PPLATT.

H2 PDO/PGILG has a significant and positive impact on PPLATT.

In our study, the role of PDO/PGI labels is evaluated through three constructs (Van Ittersum et al. 2000): the brand guarantee that they offer (PDO/PGILG), their role as products supporting the local economy (ES), their perception as authentic local products (AUT). As a matter of fact, the prevailing literature ascertained that consumers associate the EU quality labels with quality (Grunert and Aachmann 2016). Moreover, the EU created the EU quality labels to support local farmers and led them to get higher margins from their quality production (Van Ittersum et al. 2000). With respect to regional products, guaranteeing the region of origin of the product by means of the PDO/PGI regulation will increase the consumers' confidence that s/he purchased the "real thing" and not some cheap imitation (Van Ittersum et al. 2000). These factors might contribute to a better quality perception towards the PPL that employs also the PDO/PGI label. In sum, we might postulate the following HPs:

H3 PDO/PGILG has a significant and positive impact on PPLQ.

H4 ES has a significant and positive impact on PPLQ.

H5 AUT has a significant and positive impact on PPLQ.

There is a common and general consensus in considering that attitude toward a product relates positively to its purchase behavior (Ajzen and Fishbein 1980). This has been found true also when PLs are considered (Garretson et al. 2002).

H6 PPLATT positively impacts on PPLINTB.

3   Methodology

To empirically test the postulated hypotheses, we conducted a survey administering a structured questionnaire to a convenience sample of shoppers of an Italian-based retailer chosen because of its great involvement in offering PPLs labelled with an EU quality labels too.

258 completed questionnaire were collected, during a period of 10 days in November 2017. As not all respondents claimed to be consistent users of the PPL, 210 knowledgeable respondents were selected from the initial sample. Within the sample, women were overrepresented (172; 81.9%) in line with the Italian shopping habits. In terms of

Table 1 Constructs and measures factor loadings

Original scale	Constructs	Items		F.L.	T-value
Adapted from Grewal et al. (1998)	*Intention to buy PPL (PPLINTB)*	I will continue to buy the PPL "X" products	PPLINT1	0.98	n.d.
		I will buy again the PPL "X" next time I go grocery shopping	PPLINT2	0.87	28.65
		I am willing to buy again the PPL "X products"	PPLINT3	0.99	51.52
Adapted from Aaker and Keller (1990)	*Attitude towards PPL (PPLATT)*	The buying of PPL "X" product is. . ..			
		Negative/positive	PPLATT1	0.90	n.d.
		Useless/useful	PPLATT2	0.90	10.97
		Bad/good	PPLATT3	0.83	9.82
DelVecchio (2001)	*PPL Quality (PPLQ)*	I think PPL "X" products have a superior quality	PPLQ1	0.93	n.d.
		I think that PPL "X" products are excellent	PPLQ2	0.87	16.71
Van Ittersum et al. (2000)	*PDO/PGI label Guarantee (PDO/PGILG)*	Buying a PPL product with a PDO/PGI label is more trustworthy	PDO1	0.77	n.d.
		I prefer to buy a PPL product with a PDO/PGI brand	PDO2	0.96	9.43
		I feel more guaranteed when the PPL has a PDO/PGI label too	PDO3	0.99	9.61
	Economic Support (ES)	The PDO/PGI protection. . .			
		Leads to more employment in the region of origin	ES1	0.79	n.d.
		Leads to higher farmer incomes	ES2	0.95	9.98
		Guarantees the product is produced in a traditional way	ES3	0.84	8.76
	Product Authenticity (AUT)	The PDO/PGI protection protects the authenticity of the product	AUT1	0.58	n.d.
		The PDO/PGI protection preserves the exclusivity of the product	AUT2	0.85	4.25

participants' age: 7.6% interviewees were younger than 25 years of age, while 17.1% of them were older than 65. Others age clusters are as follows: 13.8% (25–35 years); 34.3% (36–50 years); 27.1% (51–65 years). The family composition is heterogeneous: 8.6% were singles. 18.1% live in a family of five or more members; 19.0% live in a family of three components. 26.7% live in couple and 27.6% in family composed by four components.

The items used in the model (Table 1), previously pre-tested and validated on a limited sample of grocery shoppers, were evaluated using a 7-point Likert scale,

(1 = strongly disagree and 7 = strongly agree), apart from PPLATT in which we used a semantic differential scale (1–7 points).

3.1 Measure Validity

To assess the validity of the hypotheses a two-step approach to analyze the data was used, as recommended by Anderson and Gerbing (1988): first a confirmatory factor analysis (CFA—to test the unidimensionality and convergent validity of the constructs) and then a structural equation model with Maximum Likelihood method (SEM) were performed. The software Lisrel 8.80 was employed.

The psychometric analysis of the scales investigated assesses their convergence and discriminant validity. Table 1 reports the results of the factor analysis confirming that all items are significantly (t-values > 4) and substantially (factor loading > 0.576) loaded onto the expected latent constructs. Thus, the convergent validity of the measures was confirmed (Hu and Bentler 1999). Accordingly, all the 16 items exhibited a high item-total correlation, indicating their capability to measure the investigated constructs.

Average Variance Extracted (AVE) and Composite Reliability (CR) assess the convergent validity (Table 2) showing good levels of AVE and CR as very close to their conventional cut-off AVE > 0.5 (Fornell and Larcker 1981) and CR > 0.7 (Steenkamp and van Trijp 1991). Following the criterion for discriminant validity proposed by Fornell and Larcker (1981), we tested that the square root of AVE by the underlying construct is larger than the correlation of this construct and the others. In this way, we tested that each construct shared more variance with its own measures than it shared with other constructs. As shown in Table 2 this condition was verified for all the six investigated constructs, showing a good internal validity of the measurement model.

Indicators of the model fit show a good overall fit. Although the significant Satorra and Bentler chi-square $\chi^2_{(SB)(95)} = 164.836$, p < 0.01 indicates that the

Table 2 Convergent and discriminant validity and correlation matrix

Constructs		AVE	CR						
Intention to buy PPL	PPLINT	0.859	0.966	**0.927**					
Attitude towards PPL	PPLATT	0.770	0.909	0.674	**0.878**				
PPL Quality	PPLQ	0.816	0.899	0.509	0.755	**0.903**			
PDO/PGILG	PDO/PGILG	0.831	0.936	0.240	0.356	0.338	**0.912**		
Product Authenticity	AUT	0.535	0.689	0.077	0.114	0.130	0.180	**0.732**	
Economic Support	ES	0.751	0.900	0.146	0.217	0.256	0.290	0.524	**0.866**

hypothesized model does not mirror the pattern of covariance contained within the raw data, both $\chi 2/df$ indicator (1.735) and the not-significant Close-Fit RMSEA (p-value = 0.153) confirm the goodness of the model fit. The model has no substantial problems with residuals as shown by the Standardized Root Mean Square Residual (SRMR = 0.0773) and the incremental fit measurements are greater than 0.95 (NFI = 0.961; CFI = 0.983).

3.2 Results

The proposed structural model (Fig. 1) presents a substantial predictive ability for Attitude Towards PPL products ($R^2_{(PPLATT)} = 0.582$) and an interesting predictive ability for the Intention to Buy PPL products ($R^2_{(PPLINT)} = 0.454$). Moreover, an acceptable predictive ability is found for the PPL Quality ($R^2_{(PPLQ)} = 0.142$).

PPL perceived quality is the main driver of PPLATT. In fact, the more consumers perceive PPL products as of high quality, the more they develop a positive attitude towards them, confirming our first hypothesis (H1: $\beta = 0.717$, $p < 0.01$). The PDO/PGI label that accompanies the PPL brand (PDO/PGILG) acts positively on increasing both PPLQ and consumers' PPLATT, supporting our hypotheses (H3: $\beta = 0.288$, $p < 0.01$; H2: $\beta = 0.114$, $p < 0.05$). Furthermore, the interest of consumers towards a production system economically fair for producers and linked to local methods of production (ES) positively influences PPLQ: so, our fourth hypothesis is accepted (H4: $\beta = 0.181$, $p < 0.05$). Conversely, we reject the fifth hypothesis analyzing how the opportunity to buy a genuine and unique product (AUT) impacts on the PPLQ. Results showed that AUT has no significant effect on PPLQ (H5: $\beta = -0.016$, not significant). Last but not least, in accordance with the consumer behaviour literature, the greater the attitude towards the PPL, the greater the intention to buy PPL products: in fact, H6 ($\beta = 0.674$, $p < 0.01$) is confirmed.

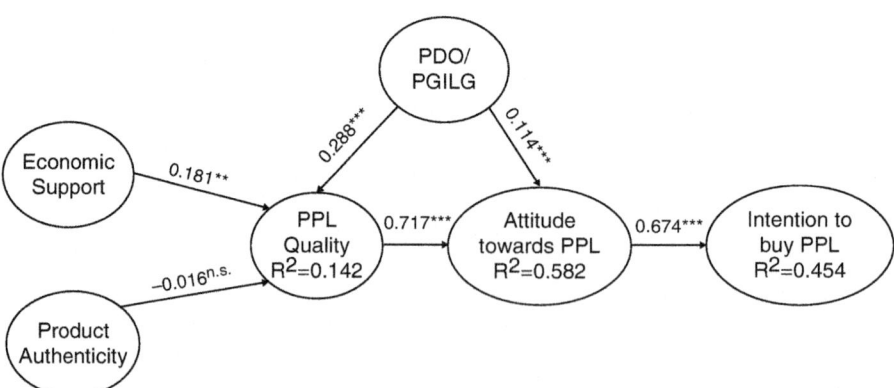

Fig. 1 Research model. **All factor loadings are significant at the $p < 0.05$ level. ***All factor loadings are significant at the $p < 0.01$ level

Mediation Analysis

The Sobel-test was performed to verify indirect effects proposed in the theoretical model as it is considered the most parsimonious mediation test. Specifically, we tested the indirect effects of PDO/PGILG, ES and PA on the PPLATT by the mediating effect of PPLQ. Results show that both PDO/PGILG ($\beta = 0.179$, $p < 0.000$) and ES ($\beta = 0.100$, $p < 0.063$) express an indirect effect on the PPLATT, while due to its not significant effect on the mediating construct, authenticity has no indirect effect ($\beta = -0.022$, $p < 1.114$) on the PPLATT. Moreover, PPLQ ($\beta = 0.831$, $p < 0.000$) and PDO/PGILG ($\beta = 0.109$, $p < 0.064$) show also an indirect effect on the PPLINT channeled by the PPLATT.

4 Conclusions

Our findings contribute to the literature on PLs proving that not only the high perceived quality of PPLs stimulates a positive attitude and intention to buy this offering, but also that the PDO/PGI labels influence shoppers. To this regards, we have to notice that it is the EU quality guarantee that strongly reinforces the PPL improving the perceived quality of products and consumers' attitude towards EU quality label products. Moreover, PPL shoppers buy these products in order to support farmers and typical local production, as the products origin and their production rules are considered a high guarantee about their overall quality. Conversely, the perceived authenticity of the local food products does not exert any effect on the PPLINTB. Our results might help retailers in correctly position their PPLs on the market. The importance given to the PPL quality demonstrates that this PL is firstly evaluated for its intrinsic characteristic. Consequently, retailers should stress their quality control efforts to enhance PPLs quality and communicate them in most effective manners. Moreover, as shoppers consider PDO/PGI labels as an antecedent of PPLQ and they feel more guaranteed when these labels accompanies the PPL, retailers might base their PPL communication strategies on enhancing the role of the PDO/PGI label, at the moment almost unused. Even PDO/PGI producers and consortiums can benefit from our findings: they might increase their negotiating power towards retailers and pursue the use of co-marketing tools to jointly activate with grocery retailers. Consequently, the PDO/PGI protection label may lead to higher farmer incomes, more employment in the area of origin and signal traditional agricultural methods used to produce these products, confirming Van Ittersum et al. (2000) assumptions.

This study presents some limitations. First, the survey relates to a generic concept of PPL, although the impact of the PL might also depend on the product category. Then, we do not check the effect of any moderator (*i.e.* PL familiarity, customer involvement), even if the PL literature proved their effect. Lastly, the survey was performed in a sole country, while a comparison with other EU retail contexts should strengthen current results.

References

Aaker, D. A., & Keller, K. L. (1990). Consumer evaluations of brand extensions. *Journal of Marketing, 54*(1), 27–41.

Ajzen, I., & Fishbein, M. (1980). *Understanding attitudes and predicting social behavior*. Englewood Cliffs, NJ: Prentice-Hall.

Anderson, J. C., & Gerbing, D. W. (1988). Structural equation modeling in practice: A review and recommended two-step approach. *Psychological Bulletin, 103*(3), 411–423.

Chaniotakis, I. E., Lymperopoulos, C., & Soureli, M. (2010). Consumers' intentions of buying own-label premium food products. *Journal of Product and Brand Management, 19*(5), 327–334.

DelVecchio, D. (2001). Consumer perceptions of private label quality: The role of product category characteristics and consumer use of heuristics. *Journal of Retailing and Consumer Services, 8*, 239–249.

Fornell, C., & Larcker, D. F. (1981). Evaluating structural equation models with unobservable variables and measurement error. *Journal of Marketing Research, 18*(1), 39–50.

Fotopoulos, C., & Krystallis, A. (2003). Quality labels as a marketing advantage. The case of the "PDO Zagora" apples in the Greek market. *European Journal of Marketing, 37*(10), 1350–1374.

Garretson, J. A., Fisher, D., & Burton, S. (2002). Antecedents of private label attitude and national brand promotion attitude: Similarities and differences. *Journal of Retailing, 78*(2), 91–99.

Geyskens, I., Gielens, K., & Gijsbrechts, E. (2010). Proliferating private-label portfolios: How introducing economy and premium private labels influences brand choice. *Journal of Marketing Research, 47*(5), 791–807.

Grewal, D., Krishnan, R., Baker, J., & Borin, N. (1998). The effect of store name, brand name and price discounts on consumers' evaluations and purchase intentions. *Journal of Retailing, 74*(3), 331–352.

Grunert, K. G., & Aachmann, K. (2016). Consumer reactions to the use of EU quality labels on food products: A review of the literature. *Food Control, 59*, 178–187.

Hu, L.-T., & Bentler, P. M. (1999). Cutoff criteria for fit indexes in covariance structure analysis: Conventional criteria versus new alternatives. *Structural Equation Modeling: A Multidisciplinary Journal, 6*(1), 1–55.

Huang, Y., & Huddleston, P. (2009). Retailer premium own-brands: creating customer loyalty through own-brand products advantage. *International Journal of Retail and Distribution Management, 37*(11), 975–992.

IGD. (2017). *Global retail trend predictions for 2018*. Accessed January 15, 2018 from https://www.igd.com/about-us/media/press-releases/press-release/t/igd-unveils-global-retail-trend-predictions-for-2018/i/18009

IRI. (2016, June). *Private label in western economies*, Special Report.

Lamey, L., Deleersnyder, B., Steenkamp, J.-B. E. M., & Dekimpe, M. J. (2012). The effect of business-cycle fluctuations on private-label share: What has marketing conduct got to do with it? *Journal of Marketing, 76*(January), 1–19.

Martinelli, E., Belli, A., & Marchi, G. (2015). The role of customer loyalty as a brand extension purchase predictor. *International Review of Retail, Distribution and Consumer Research, 25*, 105–119.

Steenkamp, J.-B., & van Trijp, H. (1991). The use of lisrel in validating marketing constructs. *International Journal of Research in Marketing, 8*(4), 283–299.

Steenkamp, J. B. E. M., Van Heerde, H., & Geyskens, I. (2010). What makes consumers willing to pay a price premium for national brands over private labels? *Journal of Marketing Research, 47*(6), 1011–1024.

Ter Braak, A., Geyskens, I., & Dekimpe, M. G. (2014). Why premium private label presence varies by category. *Journal of Retailing, 90*(2), 125–140.

Van Ittersum, K., Candel, M. J. J. M., & Torelli, F. (2000). *The market for PDO/PGI protected regional products: Consumer attitudes and behaviour*. The socio-economics of origin labelled products in agri-food supply chains: Spatial, Institutional and Co-ordination Aspects, 209–221.

Trajectories to Making Botswana a Destination of Choice: An Evaluation of the Current Awareness and Perception Levels

Tshepo Maswabi, Ntonghanwah Forcheh, and Resego Taolo

Abstract This paper presents findings of a study that evaluated the effectiveness of the Brand Botswana coordinating office in creating brand awareness as well as altering perceptions of the target audiences. The purpose of Brand Botswana is to position Botswana to international audiences as an attractive place to visit, work and invest (www.bitc.com). This is achieved through various marketing programs highlighting the country's assets, including its people, culture, tourist attractions, business potential, exports and its reputation of good governance. The office also attempts to get local audiences to rally behind the brand and raise national pride levels so as to attract appreciation of the country by international communities. Assessment of brand building activities is helpful in understanding a brand's strengths and weaknesses with a view to focusing future efforts, hence this study. The paper articulates findings of the current perceptions and awareness levels of a public survey conducted in 51 administrative districts of Botswana, across 139 localities covering 1258 individuals. A general conclusion of the study was that 75% respondents were aware of the brand. Perception scores stood at 64% suggesting that the respondents seem not to be clear on the purpose of the brand hence not deriving meaning from it.

Keywords Botswana · Brand Botswana · Brand · Nation brand · Nation branding

T. Maswabi (✉)
Department of Marketing, University of Botswana, Gaborone, Botswana
e-mail: tshepo.maswabi@mopipi.ub.bw

N. Forcheh
Department of Statistics, University of Botswana, Gaborone, Botswana

R. Taolo
Outsourced Management Solutions, Gaborone, Botswana

© Springer International Publishing AG, part of Springer Nature 2018   47
F. J. Martínez-López et al. (eds.), *Advances in National Brand and Private Label Marketing*, Springer Proceedings in Business and Economics,
https://doi.org/10.1007/978-3-319-92084-9_7

1   Introduction

Although arguments are advanced that nations have always existed as brands (Fan 2006), nation branding remains a necessary tool for identity and differentiation as nations compete for tourists and investors. Due to globalization, a conscious branding strategy, strong brand identity and positive brand image are key tools for ensuring competitive advantage among nations (Anholt 2002; Jaffe and Nebenzahl 2006). In 2010, Botswana made a conscious decision to embark on nation branding to communicate its unique offering to the world. Like any other nation that embraced the nation branding exercise, the country established a brand coordinating office, Brand Botswana, to coordinate nation branding efforts.

Brand Botswana is a unit under Botswana International Trade and Investment Centre (BITC), an investment and promotional arm of the government of Botswana. BITC is currently the custodian of the national brand and takes responsibility and accountability over the development, implementation and monitoring of the nation brand strategies and plans. The overarching goal of the nation brand is to galvanize Batswana around a single identity, to stimulate stronger communities, culture and heritage and instil a greater sense of pride and community engagement. The nation brand also seeks to position Botswana among international audiences as an attractive place to visit, work and invest.

Since inception, Brand Botswana has been engaged in several initiatives aimed at creating awareness around the nation brand. Some of these included a public education campaign that covered 104 villages; a rural branding campaign which entailed branding local shopping outlets with the Brand Botswana logo; the pride campaign targeting the public through specific Botswana TV and Radio programs, newspapers, magazines and billboards; co-branding with Debswana (the country's leading diamond producer by value) for outdoor advertising as well as co-branding with Botswana's national airline-Air Botswana.

2   Problem Statement

Botswana has made positive steps towards nation branding through the establishment of a brand coordinating office. However, more than 5 years since its launch, the popularity and level of effectiveness of the brand remains unknown. However, Brand Botswana has not evaluated how it is doing in terms of realizing the above objectives. Not only are brand managers pressured to account for investment made on marketing activities but measuring effectiveness of marketing cum branding efforts is necessary to track the impact on targeted markets and refocus future marketing strategies if need be. Botswana's ultimate goal is to attract foreign audiences but it is equally important to engage the local community. The extent to which these rally behind the brand and raise national pride levels impacts on the international communities' appreciation of the country. Evaluation of the local community's awareness levels, comprehension of the intent of the brand including responses to the brand, satisfaction with as well as support for the brand is paramount for the brand office to plan for future marketing activities, hence the purpose of the study.

3 Objectives of Study

The study therefore sought to ascertain the following:

1. To gauge the level of awareness about Brand Botswana and the effectiveness of initiatives and programs undertaken to date to create the awareness on the country.
2. Establish the prevailing perceptions about Brand Botswana as an entity and about Botswana as a country.

4 Significance of Study

The results of this study will benefit the brand office as well as the government in that once the levels of awareness are known more targeted and focused programs will be developed to create more awareness, develop meaning for the brand and ultimately build a brand that resonates with the targeted audiences. Secondly, government may develop appropriate policies including prescribing new brand promotion initiatives. Furthermore, the significance is derived from the originality of the study and its contribution to knowledge on nation branding.

5 Literature Review

Scholars such as Fan (2006) have argued that nations have always branded themselves even without nation branding. Thus the definition of nation branding is still evolving and there appears to be no universally accepted definition and framework of nation branding. Various authors (Quelch and Jocz 2004; Fan 2006) describe the concept as concerned with a nation's whole image on an international stage. Some authors (Kaneva 2011; Keller 2008) conceptualised it as country branding, destination branding; country equity; public diplomacy. To Kotler, it is simply another term for country of origin effect or place marketing. Yet to others the concept of nation branding refers to a country's intangible assets without any explicit links with a product (Kleppe et al. 2002). According to Jaffe and Nebenzhal (2006) in nation branding the aim is to create a clear, simple, differentiating idea built around emotional qualities which can be symbolised both verbally and visually and understood by diverse audiences in a variety of situations. It therefore can be deduced from the various definitions that a nation brand is a unique multidimensional blend of elements that provide the nation with culturally grounded differentiation and relevance for all of its target population.

According to Anholt (1998) nation branding refers to a consistent and all-embracing national brand strategy which determines the most realistic, competitive and compelling strategic vision for the country, and ensures that this vision is supported, reinforced, and enriched by every act of communication between the country and the rest of the world. The main goal of nation branding is to promote the economic interest of a nation, targeting both domestic and foreign audiences with images, products and places, yet being mindful that the success of the brand is dependent on the consent and buy in of the domestic audience. Hence a country brand occurs when a substantial proportion of the population gets behind the strategy and lives it out in their everyday dealings with the outside world. For this local population to rally behind the brand, a relationship has to be cultivated which spurns from awareness. Keller (2008) identifies brand awareness as the corner stone of building strong brand. He defines awareness as the ability to easily recognize and recall a brand when given a brand element as a cue or when presented with a purchase occasion or situation. Just like companies, in order to remain relevant nations can either be innovative or offer products and services that are of quality to the rest of the world or can through marketing communications alter people's perceptions of their nation (Shrimp and Andrews 2013). Perception can be described as an act of recognising, organising and interpreting information hence through marketing communications; marketers can create awareness and alter customer perceptions. Nations employ various brand elements such as name, logos, taglines, jingles websites, as well as communication or promotional tools such public relations, direct marketing, personal selling, advertising, to promote themselves as brands (Keller 2008). Through branding, nations create identities and clearly define their positioning (Keller 2008). Not only do they have to come up with different brand identities but they also need to put in place supporting marketing programs to communicate such brand identities and position themselves relative to rivals in the target consumers' minds (Aaker 1991). Anholt avows that a country has got to market itself to be known.

6 Conceptual Framework

Acceptance and adoption of the country brand by its residents is a necessary condition for a country brand to succeed (Florek 2005; Fan 2006; Ruzzier et al. 2010). Their collective actions send signals about the country and contribute towards the formation of a country's image in the eyes of foreigners. Therefore, residents have to be converted from unaware sceptics to aware believers. Active participation and engagement are then necessary for them to live the brand promise.

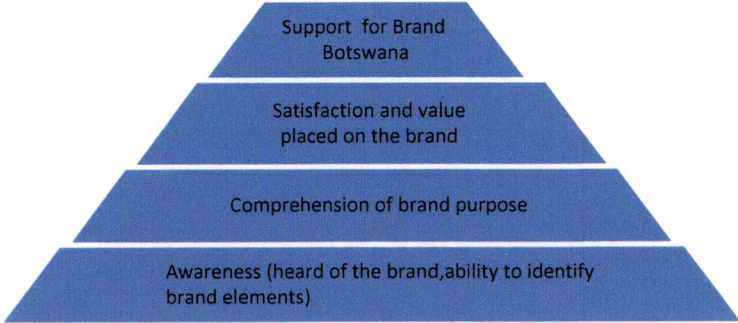

Fig. 1 Proposed model

Keller introduces an interesting concept albeit used for product branding, of customer based brand equity which is the differential effect that brand knowledge has on consumer responses to the marketing of that product. He asserts that ultimately a brand is what lies in the hearts and minds of consumers (Keller 2008). This is to say, brands are made by customers. Their perceptions hold true of brands and hence need to be influenced by brand managers. In an attempt to assist companies build unique and strong brands, Keller proposed a brand resonance model or brand equity pyramid that helps position brands and build brand equity. This model is a great brand positioning and equity building tool that assists brand managers to set relevant branding objectives, employ the best branding strategies as well as monitor their brand building efforts as they strive to build a brand loyal customer base.

Through this model Keller proposes four logical brand building steps necessary for any entity seeking to build a strong brand. Firstly an entity needs to create identity by clearly articulating the product class and needs to be satisfied by the product. Once customers have a clear understanding of what the product is all about and what needs it meets, then the entity must assist them derive meaning by linking the brand to tangible and intangible associations. Once customers derive a meaning (functional and emotional), then the entity must channel customers towards eliciting the right response through feelings and judgements. These positive responses will eventually lead to intense, active and loyal relationships with the brand. Keller's model provides the basis of our theoretical model (Fig. 1).

7 Methodology

The study adopted a mixed methods approach that combined qualitative and quantitative research methodologies. For the qualitative research, key informant interviews and focus group discussions were conducted with the Brand Botswana team, key stakeholders who included among others government, parastatals, private sector associations and the media. The main purpose of gathering qualitative information was to appreciate what key informants know and think of the brand, its objectives and effectiveness as well as factors that might be hindering its performance. The information gathered from key informants was also to be used to enhance the quantitative survey instrument. The quantitative survey targeted the general public as well as business community. This paper however, limits discussions to findings of the general public. As of the targeted date of the survey in 2015, both public education and rural branding had been conducted in 139 localities located in 15 administrative districts. First stage sampling was stratified according to districts. Probability proportional to size was used to determine the number of localities per district with at least one locality per district. In total, 40 villages and towns representing 29% of the targeted locations were sampled. An additional 11 villages and towns which had not participated in the public education or rural branding campaigns were also included in the sample. For the second stage, probability proportional to size was again used to determine number of respondents to be interviewed per selected locality with minimum sample size set at ten respondents. The measure of size was the population of the locality based on the updated 2014 sampling frame from Statistics Botswana. A total of 1258 adults were interviewed from the 51 localities. Interviews were held in high traffic areas such as malls where respondents were intercepted and interviewed. The fifth person was selected for possible interviewing.

The quantitative survey instrument included questions used to gather data on the profiles of respondents, sources of information about the brand, knowledge, awareness and support of the Brand. The specific items were informed from in-depth literature review as well as key informant interviews and focus group discussions. Awareness was measured by asking each respondent if they have ever heard of Brand Botswana. For those who had heard about it, a follow up question asked them to state about how long ago they had first heard of it. A second measure was obtained by aggregating responses given after asking respondents to state their knowledge of brand elements. Respondents were asked to indicate their knowledge level on each of the seven elements (name, Logo, colours, slogan, packaging, Url, Jingle) that make up the Brand Botswana as well as any other thing that they specifically know about the brand. Respondents who said they could recognise or know at least five brand elements were categorised as being "highly aware" of brand elements. Respondents who could not recognise any of the brand elements were categorised as having no knowledge, and the rest were categorised as being aware of the brand. The perception score was obtained by summing the number of correct responses to a list of ten questions relating to purpose of the brand. Respondents' feelings about the brand were gauged by asking how satisfied/dissatisfied they were with the Brand Botswana in general and whether they believe Brand Botswana was achieving its desired goals. A total of eight items relating to support of the Brand were used to gauge the level of support for the Brand. Respondents who strongly agreed to five or more of the items were classified as having a high level of support, while those that strongly disagreed to three or more items were classified as having a low level of support.

In order to estimate the effectiveness of initiatives, the study locations were classified according to type of brand promotion initiatives (public education campaign and/or business branding campaign) that had been conducted in the area. This led to four categories, namely (1) both campaigns conducted, (2) public education only, (3) business branding only and (4) neither campaign conducted. Chi-squared test of association were used to determine as to whether the level of awareness about Brand Botswana depended on type of initiative conducted in the area. Further, chi-squared tests were also used to determine the effect of initiatives on other brand building components, namely level of support for the brand, satisfaction with the brand in general, belief that the brand is achieving its aim and knowledge of the purpose of the brand. Analysis was also conducted to determine as to whether there was any significant association between the brand building blocks and sex of respondent, type of locality (urban/rural), main language and citizenship.

8   Findings

Table 1 presents a summary of test of association between brand building and potential predictive factors. A strong association ($p < 0.001$) was found between type of campaign in a locality and whether people in the locality heard of brand or not. However, the lowest level of awareness was in villages where business branding was done. Almost half (46.4%) of residents in localities where only business branding was done have never heard of the brand. The national proportion of those who have never heard of the brand was 27.6%. Type of campaign appear to have had an impact on three of the five brand building—namely respondents' satisfaction with brand in general ($p = 0.005$), belief that brand is achieving its goals ($p < 0.001$) and brand awareness elements ($p < 0.001$). Detailed analysis reveals that the lowest percentage of those satisfied (29.3%) was in villages which had only Business campaigns. About half the respondents from these villages also did not feel knowledgeable enough to respond. The situation was much better in villages that had public education campaigns with almost half (48.4%) being satisfied with the brand. High percentages of respondents in each type of location did not know whether or not the brand was achieving its intended purpose. However, among those that know, the majority felt that the brand was achieving its purpose. In areas where public education campaign was conducted about a third of respondents were highly aware of brand elements compared to just 18.6% among people in villages where only business campaign was conducted and 21.4% where no campaign was conducted. Further, the percentage who had no knowledge of brand elements was also much higher (42.1%) in villages where only business branding was conducted, compare to 22.8% where public education took place.

Males and females differed with respect to level of support ($p = 0.015$), satisfaction with the brand ($p = 0.005$) and belief in brand achieving its goals ($p < 0.001$). There were no differences between males and females with respect to level of

Table 1 Chi-squared test of association between brand building and independent factors

Brand Building Block	Type of campaign conducted in the locality		
	Chi-square	df	Sig.
Level of support of brand	11.8	6	0.068
Satisfied with the Brand Botswana in general	18.5	6	0.005
Belief Brand Botswana is achieving its desired goals	25.4	6	0.000
Know purpose of the brand	3.3	3	0.343
Aware of brand elements	29.0	6	0.000
	Sex		
Level of support of brand	8.4	2	0.015
Satisfied with the Brand Botswana in general	7.3	2	0.026
Belief Brand Botswana is achieving its desired goals	12.3	2	0.002
Know purpose of the brand	0.0	1	0.852
Aware of brand elements	2.3	2	0.317
	What language are you most comfortable communicating with?		
Level of support of brand	6.4	4	0.168
Satisfied with the Brand Botswana in general	79.9	4	0.000
Belief Brand Botswana is achieving its desired goals	91.9	4	0.000
Know purpose of the brand	1.4	2	0.496
Aware of brand elements	132.1	4	.000
	What is your country or region of citizenship?		
Level of support of brand	1.2	2	0.546
Satisfied with the Brand Botswana in general	2.6	2	0.272
Belief Brand Botswana is achieving its desired goals	1.9	2	0.380
Know purpose of the brand	0.9	1	0.334
Aware of brand elements	0.2	2	0.924
	Type of locality		
Level of support of brand	1.9	4	0.751
Satisfied with the Brand Botswana in general	16.3	4	0.003
Belief Brand Botswana is achieving its desired goals	19.4	4	0.001
Know purpose of the brand	2.6	2	0.269
Aware of brand elements	4.6	4	0.327

support and knowing the purpose of the brand. A significant association was found with respect to language that respondents were most comfortable with and satisfaction with brand in general ($p < 0.001$), belief in brand achieving its goals ($p < 0.001$) and awareness of brand elements ($p < 0.001$). As shown in Table 1, citizenship was not associated with any of the five brand building elements. Type of locality (Urban/Rural) affected satisfaction with brand in general ($p < 0.001$ and belief in brand achieving its goals ($p < 0.001$).

We now discuss the nature of association between brand building elements and the significant variables.

8.1   Brand Awareness Levels of Respondents

In quizzing the awareness levels of respondents, questions relating to their ability to recall and recognise the brand such as; have they heard of the brand and their ability to recall at least 5 brand elements were used. Table 2 (see Appendix) presents results by locality. The highest number (75%) of people highly aware and aware of the brand was recorded in towns followed by rural areas (71%) and cities (68%). The same pattern is depicted with more people with no knowledge (32%) recording a high number in cities, followed by rural (29%) areas and towns (24%). This could be an indication that the rural branding campaign had an effect in creating some level of awareness. More people showed high levels of awareness (503) where respondents were exposed to both the rural and public education campaigns as opposed to 124 that were exposed only to the public education campaign, 81 that were only exposed to rural branding and 164 that did not have exposure to any campaign (Table 3, see Appendix). There are no significant differences between males and females in terms of awareness with 71% being females and 70% being males who recorded a high level of awareness (Table 4, see Appendix). In terms of language majority (88%) who were highly aware or at least aware were comfortable receiving material in both Setswana and English followed by those who preferred only English and lastly those with a preference for vernacular (Table 5, see Appendix).

8.2   Brand Meaning

To ascertain as to whether respondents derived a meaning out of the brand questions relating to their ability to comprehend the intent of the brand were used such as their understanding of what the purpose of brand Botswana is /should be. More knowledge levels regarding the purpose of the brand are recorded in cities (72%) areas than in towns (66%) and rural areas (64%) (Table 2). More knowledge levels were recorded where both campaigns were rolled out than where there was a single campaign. However, one interesting observation is that a high (164) number of knowledgeable respondents were recorded in areas where there was no campaign than in areas where there was public education (127) or rural branding (84) (Table 3). There are no significant differences between males and females in terms of knowledge of the brand purpose (Table 4). There are also no significant differences between comprehension of purpose and language (Table 5).

8.3   Brand Responses (Judgements and Feelings)

In gauging how respondents felt or thought of the brand, questions such as general satisfaction with the brand as well as if respondents thought brand Botswana was achieving its purpose were posed. More people in cities believed that the brand is achieving its goals and are generally satisfied with it, as opposed to those in rural areas and towns. The brand enjoys more support in rural areas (30%) followed by towns (27%) and cities (26%) (Table 2). As with other brand building components, respondents who were exposed to both campaigns recorded a high level of satisfaction with the brand and agreed that the brand was achieving its intended purpose (Table 3). With regards to gender, more females were satisfied with the brand than males but insignificant differences were noted regarding whether the brand was meeting its goals. Majority of those generally satisfied and believed the brand was achieving its purpose preferred receiving materials in both English and Setswana (Table 4). Majority of those who did not believe the brand was not achieving its intent preferred English (13.9%) than Setswana (7%) or both (11.3%) forms of communication (Table 5).

8.4   Brand Relationship

The ultimate for any nation brand manager is a brand that resonates with residents who ultimately become its ambassadors. A number of questions were asked to ascertain if respondents have some form of relationship with the brand including; if given a second chance would they still choose Botswana as a country to live in, do they love the country, would they recommend it to someone, do they attend brand Botswana organised events etc. The level of support was found to be high in rural areas followed by towns and lastly cities (refer to Table 2). It was also found to be high were respondents were exposed to both types of campaigns, just like the rest of the brand building components (Table 3). In terms of gender, males were found to be more supportive than females (refer to Table 4). Not surprising as males attend community events more than women who are more often than not engaged in household chores. Regarding language, those highly supportive preferred material in both languages, followed by Setswana and English being the least preferred (Table 5).

9   Summary of Findings

It can generally be concluded that the Brand Office through the various marketing efforts has managed to create a high level of awareness especially in towns and rural areas. This is so because the Brand Office is situated in the capital city where creation of awareness will be easy as city residents are likely to encounter the brand and its activities via the BITC website, radio and TV, newspapers, public debates and events. For results to show a high level of awareness in towns and in rural areas as opposed to cities is commendable. However, as would be expected more people in cities have a better comprehension of the intent of the office than in towns and rural areas meaning that the brand Office should reach out more to those in rural areas regarding their intent. Again more people in cities believe the brand to be achieving its intent. However, more support for the brand is found in rural areas. This may be attributed to the use of the Kgotla system as an avenue for message dissemination and interaction largely attended by many in rural areas. No significant differences were noted in terms of gender and the various brand building components. Nevertheless males seem to be more supportive of the brand than females. More results were achieved where both campaigns were rolled out than single or no campaign. This echoes the importance of message consistency and frequency in communication that drives messages home and creates more awareness. The use of both English and Setswana for information dissemination seems to be referred across the different brand building components.

10 Conclusion

Although resonance (relationship) provides an important focus for brand building, the brand office is a step in the right direction as it has a achieved salience for the brand but needs to aggressively help targeted audiences derive a meaning out of the brand by clearly explaining the intent of the brand that will facilitate positive responses (eliciting national pride levels) to the brand and ultimately cause them to become part of the brand activities and active advocates for the brand.

Appendix

Table 2 Association between Brand building components and Locality of respondents

Locality respondent		Type of locality							
		City		Town		Rural		Total	
		Count	Percent	Count	Percent	Count	Percent	Count	Percent
Level of support of brand	Low	28	23.1	28	25.5	217	21.1	273	21.7
	Moderate	61	50.4	52	47.3	498	48.5	611	48.6
	High	32	26.4	30	27.3	312	30.4	374	29.7
	Total	121	100.0	110	100.0	1027	100.0	1258	100.0
Satisfied with the Brand Botswana in general	Dissatisfied	21	17.4	13	11.8	226	22.0	260	20.7
	Satisfied	68	56.2	53	48.2	419	40.8	540	42.9
	Dont know	32	26.4	44	40.0	382	37.2	458	36.4
	Total	121	100.0	110	100.0	1027	100.0	1258	100.0
Belief Brand Botswana is achieving its desired goals	No	19	15.7	7	6.4	84	8.2	110	8.7
	Yes	51	42.1	29	26.4	336	32.7	416	33.1
	Dont know	51	42.1	74	67.3	607	59.1	732	58.2
	Total	121	100.0	110	100.0	1027	100.0	1258	100.0
Know purpose of the brand	Dont know	34	28.1	37	33.6	364	35.4	435	34.6
	Know purpose	87	71.9	73	66.4	663	64.6	823	65.4
	Total	121	100.0	110	100.0	1027	100.0	1258	100.0
Aware of brand elements	Highly aware	27	22.3	27	24.5	289	28.1	343	27.3
	Aware	55	45.5	56	50.9	436	42.5	547	43.5
	No knowledge	39	32.2	27	24.5	302	29.4	368	29.3
	Total	121	100.0	110	100.0	1027	100.0	1258	100.0

Table 3 Association between Brand building components by type of Campaign

Components		Type of campaign conducted in the locality				
		Public education and business campaigns	Public education only	Business campaign only	No campaign	Total
Level of support of brand	Low	20.8	18.5	23.6	25.3	21.7
	Moderate	51.8	51.1	43.6	40.9	48.6
	High	27.3	30.4	32.9	33.9	29.7
	Total	100.0	100.0	100.0	100.0	100.0
Satisfied with the Brand Botswana in general	Dissatisfied	**22.2**	**17.4**	**20.0**	**19.5**	**20.7**
	Satisfied	**43.3**	**48.4**	**29.3**	**45.5**	**42.9**
	Dont know	**34.6**	**34.2**	**50.7**	**35.0**	**36.4**
	Total	100.0	100.0	100.0	100.0	100.0
Belief Brand Botswana is achieving its desired goals	No	9.7	9.2	2.9	8.9	8.7
	Yes	35.2	31.5	20.0	35.8	33.1
	Dont know	55.1	59.2	77.1	55.3	58.2
	Total	100.0	100.0	100.0	100.0	100.0
Know purpose of the brand	Dont know	33.8	31.0	40.0	36.2	34.6
	Know purpose	66.2	69.0	60.0	63.8	65.4
	Total	100.0	100.0	100.0	100.0	100.0
Aware of brand elements	**Highly aware**	**30.1**	**31.5**	**18.6**	**21.4**	**27.3**
	Aware	44.2	45.7	39.3	42.4	43.5
	No knowledge	25.7	22.8	42.1	36.2	29.3
	Total	100.0	100.0	100.0	100.0	100.0

Table 4 Association between Brand building components and Sex of respondent

Brand components		Sex				Total	
		Male		Female			
		Count	Percent	Count	Percent	Count	Percent
Level of support of brand	Low	129	22.7	144	20.9	273	21.7
	Moderate	251	44.2	359	52.1	610	48.5
	High	188	33.1	186	27.0	374	29.8
	Total	568	100.0	689	100.0	1257	100.0
Satisfied with the Brand Botswana in general	Dissatisfied	125	22.0	135	19.6	260	20.7
	Satisfied	220	38.7	319	46.3	539	42.9
	Dont know	223	39.3	235	34.1	458	36.4
	Total	568	100.0	689	100.0	1257	100.0
Belief Brand Botswana is achieving its desired goals	No	67	11.8	43	6.2	110	8.8
	Yes	177	31.2	238	34.5	415	33.0
	Dont know	324	57.0	408	59.2	732	58.2
	Total	568	100.0	689	100.0	1257	100.0
Know purpose of the brand	Dont know	195	34.3	240	34.8	435	34.6
	Know purpose	373	65.7	449	65.2	822	65.4
	Total	568	100.0	689	100.0	1257	100.0
Aware of brand elements	Highly aware	162	28.5	180	26.1	342	27.2
	Aware	234	41.2	313	45.4	547	43.5
	No knowledge	172	30.3	196	28.4	368	29.3
	Total	568	100.0	689	100.0	1257	100.0

Table 5 Association between Brand building components and language

Brand components		What language are you most comfortable communicating with?							
		Setswana		English		Both English and Setswana		Total	
		Count	Percent	Count	Percent	Count	Percent	Count	Percent
Level of support of brand	Low	172	22.6	24	30.4	75	18.5	271	21.7
	Moderate	367	48.2	33	41.8	206	50.7	606	48.6
	High	222	29.2	22	27.8	125	30.8	369	29.6
	Total	761	100.0	79	100.0	406	100.0	1246	100.0
Satisfied with the Brand Botswana in general	Dissatisfied	133	17.5	17	21.5	107	26.4	257	20.6
	Satisfied	280	36.8	37	46.8	220	54.2	537	43.1
	Dont know	348	45.7	25	31.6	79	19.5	452	36.3
	Total	761	100.0	79	100.0	406	100.0	1246	100.0
Belief Brand Botswana is achieving its desired goals	No	53	7.0	11	13.9	46	11.3	110	8.8
	Yes	186	24.4	32	40.5	195	48.0	413	33.1
	Dont Know	522	68.6	36	45.6	165	40.6	723	58.0
	Total	761	100.0	79	100.0	406	100.0	1246	100.0
Know purpose of the brand	Dont know	253	33.2	27	34.2	149	36.7	429	34.4
	Know Purpose	508	66.8	52	65.8	257	63.3	817	65.6
	Total	761	100.0	79	100.0	406	100.0	1246	100.0
Aware of brand elements	Highly aware	140	18.4	31	39.2	171	42.1	342	27.4
	Aware	325	42.7	26	32.9	190	46.8	541	43.4
	No Knowledge	296	38.9	22	27.8	45	11.1	363	29.1
	Total	761	100.0	791	100.0	406	100.0	1246	100.0

References

Aaker, D. A. (1991). *Managing brand equity*. New York: The Free Press.

Anholt, S. (1998). Beyond the nation brand: The role of Image and Identity in International Relations. *Journal of Public Diplomacy, 2* (2013):1, Art 1.

Anholt, S. (2002). *Branding and brand equity*. Cambridge, MA: Marketing Science Institute.

Botswana Investment Trade centre. http://www.bitc.co.bw

Fan, Y. (2006). *Branding the nation: What is being branded? Journal of Vacation Marketing, 12* (1), 5–14.

Florek, M. (2005). The country brand as a new challenge for Poland. *Place Branding, 1*(2), 205–214.

Jaffe, E. D., & Nebenzahl, I. D. (2006). *National image & competitive advantage – The theory and practice of place branding*. Denmark: Copenhagen Business School Press.

Kaneva, N. (2011). Nation branding: Toward an agenda for critical research. *International Journal of Communications, 5*(2011), 117–141.

Keller, K. L. (2008). *Strategic brand management: Building, measuring, and managing brand equity*. Upper Saddle River, NJ: Pearson/Prentice Hall.

Kleppe, I., Iversen, N., & Stensaker, I. J. (2002). *Country images in marketing strategies: Conceptual issues and an empirical Asian illustration. Brand Management, 10*, 61.

Quelch, J., & Jocz, K. (2004). *Positioning the nation-state. Place Branding, 1*(1), 74–79.

Ruzzier, M., Petek, N., & Konecnik Ruzzier, M. (2010). *The role of locals in implementing and living the country brand: I feel Slovenia*. Retrieved September 3, 2012, from http://www.majakonecnik.comlkonecnik/dokumenti/File/ruzzieretal_bmngmnt_2010.pdf

Shrimp, T. A., & Andrews, C. A. (2013). *Advertising, promotion and other aspects of integrated marketing communications*. Mason, Ohio: South-Western Cengage Learning.

Part II
Online Context and Digital Transformation

Flow and Consumer Behavior in an Online Supermarket

Doris Morales-Solana, Irene Esteban-Millat, and Alejandro Alegret Cotas

Abstract As a result of the business opportunities offered by the internet, there has been increased academic and professional interest in understanding the browsing behaviour and online purchasing habits of consumers in order to identify more effective organizational strategies. While it is a fact that the scientific community has made advances in the understanding of this phenomenon, there are still many questions to be answered in the area of mass consumption that require further research. In this sense, the general aim of this research is to extend knowledge of online consumer experiences, specifically mass-consumption flow states in digital environments. This will be the first time that an integrated flow model will be presented in this field.

Keywords Flow · Online consumer behavior · Online mass consumption · Online fast-moving consumer goods

1 Introduction

Flow is an element of study that has been extensively used in scientific literature to characterize behaviors of human beings in different environments. This concept was coined by Csikszentmihalyi (1975) and defined as the holistic sensation that people feel when they act with total involvement. In this research, flow is used to progress in the understanding of the behavior of digital consumers in the area of mass consumption. The first aim is to delimit the concept of online flow in the area of mass consumption, identifying its dimensions and antecedents, as well as the interactions that exist between them. In addition, the intention is to identify the main

D. Morales-Solana (✉)
Open University of Catalonian (UOC), Barcelona, Spain

I. Esteban-Millat · A. Alegret Cotas
EAE Business School, Open University of Catalonian (UOC), Barcelona, Spain
e-mail: iestebanm@uoc.edu; alejandro.alegret@campus.eae.es

© Springer International Publishing AG, part of Springer Nature 2018   65
F. J. Martínez-López et al. (eds.), *Advances in National Brand and Private Label Marketing*, Springer Proceedings in Business and Economics,
https://doi.org/10.1007/978-3-319-92084-9_8

consequences of flow state in the behavior of consumers in an online supermarket, confirming what they are and determining the relationship between them. To frame this research, a brief review of the literature on flow has been carried out. Likewise, studies on consumer behavior have been analyzed considering the historical background of consumer behavior and the different perspectives from which this discipline has been studied. All together, the aim is to verify the influence of flow state on consumer behavior in an online supermarket.

2   Online Flow

Flow is a cognitive state during which people are completely involved in something to the point of forgetting time and everything else but the activity itself (Csikszentmihalyi 1975). This concept was introduced in the study of online consumer behavior, confirming that companies that provide flow experiences to their users obtain benefits (Hoffman and Novak 1996). More specifically, flow has been especially used in the context of e-commerce (Koufaris 2002) for it being a key determining element of the behavior of online consumers that influences their revisit, attitude towards the brand, website usage, purchase intention and perceived web quality (Landers et al. 2015; Shim et al. 2015; Wang et al. 2015; Obadâ 2014; Liu and Shiue 2014).

Despite the strong interest in adapting the flow theory as an area of study in different online environments, the literature shows certain inconsistencies and conceptual discrepancies about its dimensions (Obadâ 2013). In addition, the constant evolution of the internet makes it necessary to continuously review the variables related to flow in order to shed light on this matter, and progress in the understanding of consumer behavior in this area. Thus, for example, it has been proven that users' perception of their skills to face the challenges found in the medium, which has been one of the most important antecedents of flow, does not affect at present their ability to experience online flow (Carlson and O'Cass 2011). It is suggested that anyone, regardless of their skill level, can experience this state during any e-commerce process (Carlson and O'Cass 2011).

Table 1 shows the main flow variables that are specific to the digital environment and used in recent years which, despite not being considered in many jobs (Gao et al. 2017; Bilgihan et al. 2015; Landers et al. 2015; Shim et al. 2015; among others), improve our knowledge about the flow experience.

On the one hand, the descriptions of some of these elements overlap semantically. Thus, for example, variables such as system quality and process feature include, among other aspects, ease of use in its conceptual description. On the other hand, some concepts are used in a way that is not only unclear and confusing but also lacks of empirical soundness, such as the website quality variable which includes multiple dimensions. In fact, there is no consensus in the literature on its definition and, although most studies postulate that website quality is a determining factor for

Table 1 New items of online flow

Element	Description	Authors
Website quality	Set of features that are related to the content, aesthetic, interactivity, personalization and convenience shown by the website and that allow us to judge its value	Fan et al. (2013)
Information quality	Attributes of the information on a website related to its accuracy, completeness, timeliness, relevance and sufficiency, and/or reliability, usefulness and inclusion of different types of opinion	Gao et al. (2015, 2017), Gao and Bai (2014), Zhou (2014), Zhou et al. (2010)
System quality	Aspects of the website system based on its reliability, speed, ease of use, browsing and visual appeal, and/or on its security and interactivity	Gao et al. (2015, 2017), Gao and Bai (2014), Zhou (2014), Zhou et al. (2010)
Process feature	Website features that are related to the ease of browsing, security, reliability, ease of use, accessibility, response time and interface	Ding et al. (2010)
Perceived complementarity	Aspects of the web design that are related to its ability to include new functions and services, providing additional values to Internet users	Gao and Bai (2014)
Design	Layout of the elements on a website that are related to the visual look of graphics and the musicality of sounds	Kim et al. (2010)
Transaction	Aspects of the website privacy related to the privacy and security of the information shared on it	Cho and Kim (2012)
Embodiment	Personification of a website through the use of avatars	Kim et al. (2013)
Scenario	Narrative structure of the website content	Kim et al. (2010)
Information/ Navigation	Set of website features that are related to the ease with which individuals can move through all its pages, the aesthetic, the information content and the design of transactions	Cho and Kim (2012)
Perceived content quality	Sensation of individuals about the content of a website that is perceived as valuable for its ability to meet their information needs	Shin (2012)
Perceived system quality	Impression of individuals about the quality of the website system and that has to do with stability, accessibility, reliability and security	Shin (2012)
Perception of website security	Belief of individuals that the web is secure to share personal and sensitive information	Cha (2011)

(continued)

Table 1 (continued)

Element	Description	Authors
Personalization	Ability of the website to adapt to the user in feel and look, functionality and inclusion of advertising	Kim and Han (2014), Rose et al. (2012)
Website communications performance	Website utilities related to updated and relevant information adapted to the needs of consumers	Carlson and O'cass (2011)
Website exchange performance	Transactions on a website such as secure purchase, payment of invoices and the possibility of making reservations	Carlson and O'cass (2011)
Navigation performance	Quick access and ease of use of a website	Landers et al. (2015)
Website aesthetic performance	Visual appeal and representation of the elements on a website	Carlson and O'cass (2011)
Website technical performance	Website features related to speed of transfer, speed of data processing and possibility of interacting	Carlson and O'cass (2011)
Media richness	Aspects of a website that define it as a rich, diverse and real-time online communications environment	Kim et al. (2013)
Ubiquity	Feature of the web environment that allows access from any place and at any time	Zhou (2012)
Interactive speed	Feature of the website related to speed of interaction	Rose et al. (2012)

customer satisfaction, these claims have not always been supported by empirical evidence (Éthier et al. 2006).

In addition, some authors suggest addressing the study of flow in specific areas of online consumption in order to better determine which elements facilitate the flow experience, and the relationships between them. In this way, research has been carried out on flow to study, for example, mobile shopping or certain more specific aspects such as instant messaging or website browsing through this electronic device (Gao et al. 2015; Gao and Bai 2014; Zhou 2014). The study of flow in the area of online banking, among others, is also noteworthy (Zhou 2012).

The above considerations allow us to define the objective of this research to address it, and contribute to the advancement of knowledge about online consumption experiences through the concept of flow and its application in mass consumption in general and, more specifically, in an online supermarket.

3 Digital Consumer Behavior

The emergence of the Internet in households and in people's daily lives impacts on the behavior of consumers, transforming commerce and turning people into users of information systems and digital consumers (Koufaris 2002). From the very moment that virtually all organizations adopt the Internet for commercial purposes, there are studies theorizing about how consumers can use it (Jarvenpaa and Todd 1997; Hoffman and Novak 1996) since this medium, the Internet, and its different manifestations such as e-commerce are providers of better opportunities for those companies (Kotha et al. 2001) that allow consumers to make decisions about online purchases even before visiting a physical store. Thus, some authors (Häubl and Trifts 2000; Winer et al. 1997; Hoffman and Novak 1996) point out that the purchase process in virtual environments shows significant differences with regard to shopping through traditional channels due to the high degree of interactivity of the medium and, more specifically, to the way in which consumers search for and evaluate the information about products (Degeratu et al. 2000).

In fact, e-commerce broadens the perspective about the behavior of traditional consumers by considering search, browsing, find, selection and comparison of products, aspects of the purchasing behavior. In this regard, there are authors (Taylor and Strutton 2010; Dennis et al. 2009) who define online consumer behavior as a complete web experience where the very nature of the medium gives greater control and interactivity to consumers, thus forcing distributors to manage two commercial spaces: the physical and the virtual one. The virtual space is managed through a website that can be designed to induce flow (Culache and Obadă 2014) through elements such as its performance, the type of communication provided, its technological capacity, the innovation it represents, its levels of security, the quality degree of its content, as well as the inclusion of moving images and three-dimensional elements (Carlson and O'Cass 2011). In response to these aspects, most users experience positive moods while browsing (Chen 2006) whether they seek utilitarian or hedonic benefits (Bilgihan et al. 2015).

Starting in 2000, and in the mass consumption sector, distributors such as large supermarket chains (Carrefour, Costco, Tesco and Dia, among others) begin to open online sales channels through increasingly appealing and operational websites for consumers. Later, in 2010, new purely digital competitors (Ulabox, Simply and TuDespensa) enter the food sector, even though there are consumers who do not perceive online shopping as the best alternative due to reasons such as reliability (Mintel 2016), website loading speed, cost of the service provided by digital retailers (Mintel 2016) such as transportation, and for being unable to evaluate the quality of some products (Degeratu et al. 2000). In relation to this, a study carried out by Nielsen (2015) concludes that the consumer purchasing process in this area has changed even for the purchase of fresh products and that, with the expansion and improvement of delivery services, together with the quality guarantee, the appeal of buying this type of products will increase (Nielsen 2017). Thus, future projections seem to be optimistic. In fact, a study carried out by Kantar Worldpanel (2017) foresees online mass consumption global sales reaching 170 billion dollars globally in 2025.

The literature on the behavior of mass consumption consumers indicates that consumers opt for online supermarkets to avoid the negative aspects of shopping in traditional stores (Roberts et al. 2003) such as the physical effort (Hansen 2006), and waste of time (Roberts et al. 2003). The convenience of being able to reduce the effort and time used to buy products are advantages perceived by digital consumers, and key for shopping in online supermarkets (Ramus and Nielsen 2005). Being able to find good offers, avoid impulse purchase and invasive sales (Ramus and Nielsen 2005) are other of this type of advantages identified in the literature (Roberts et al. 2003). However, even those digital consumers most committed to online supermarkets, when the circumstances that have led to the purchase in these types of establishments cease, can return to traditional supermarkets (Harris et al. 2017).

4   Online Flow Model

The review of the literature on online consumer behavior through the concept of flow reveals that most of the research that deals with the study of flow does so in a general context, with few research papers addressing it in specific areas of consumption. In this regard, the absence of studies about flow on consumption in online supermarkets is surprising. Likewise, it is observed that there is no consensus on the operability of the flow concept, nor on the definition of its dimensions or on the interaction between them. Additionally, there are significant contradictions between the results obtained by the different scientific papers presented to date. To shed light on these issues and progress in the study of consumer behavior, a theoretical model of flow in the specific field of online supermarkets is designed in this research.

Considering the relationships established and validated in flow models in digital environments, and the main theories and models developed in the research on consumer behavior, a conceptual flow model has been designed for an online supermarket context; relationships between all variables, indicated with causal arrows in Fig. 1, are positive:

With this model, we intend, ultimately, to represent the flow phenomenon in the specific area of an online supermarket, identifying those factors that determine its appearance, as well as its consequences. In addition, an empirical study of flow in an online supermarket is currently being carried out in order to verify the theoretical model proposed here and find out the relative weight of each one of its dimensions, antecedents and consequences.

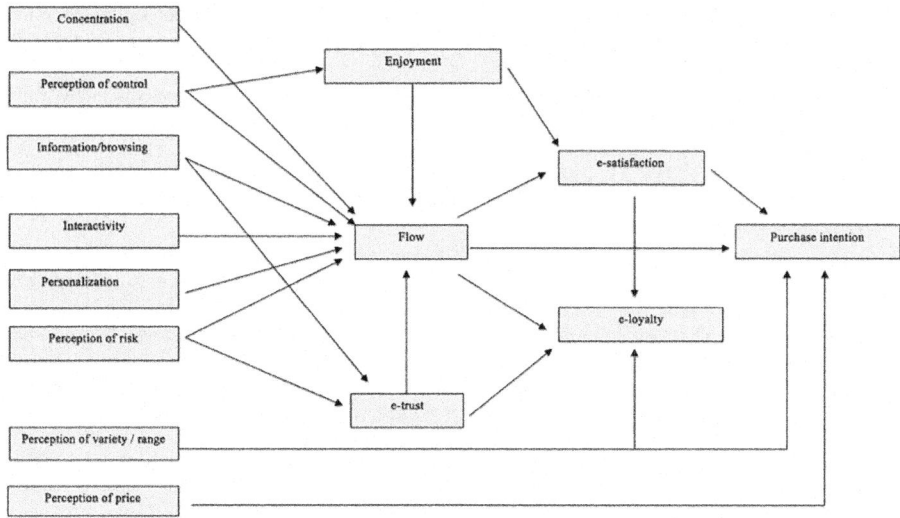

Fig. 1 Theoretical model of flow in the field of an online supermarket

References

Bilgihan, A., Nusair, K., Okumus, F., & Cobanoglu, C. (2015). Applying flow theory to booking experiences: An integrated model in an online service context. *Information and Management, 52*, 668–678.

Carlson, J., & O'Cass, A. (2011). Creating commercially compelling website-service encounters: An examination of the effect of website-service interface performance components on flow experiences. *Electron Markets, 21*, 237–253.

Cha, J. (2011). Exploring the internet as a unique shopping channel to sell both real and virtual items: A comparison of factors affecting purchase intention and consumer characteristics. *Journal of Electronic Commerce Research, 12*(2), 115–132.

Chen, H. (2006). Flow on the net–detecting web users' positive affects and their flow states. *Computers in Human Behavior, 22*(2), 221–233.

Cho, E., & Kim, Y. (2012). The effects of website designs, self-congruity, and flow on behavioral intention. *International Journal of Design, 6*(2), 31–39.

Csikszentmihalyi, M. (1975). *Beyond boredom and anxiety* (1a ed.). San Francisco, CA: Jossey-Bass.

Culache, O., & Obadă, D. (2014). Multimodality as a premise for inducing online flow on a brand website: A social semiotic approach. *Procedia – Social and Behavioral Sciences, 149*, 261–268.

Degeratu, A. M., Rangaswamy, A., & Wu, J. (2000). Consumer choice behavior in online and traditional supermarkets: The effect of brands name, price, and other search attribute. *International Journal of Research in Marketing, 17*(1), 55–78.

Dennis, C., Merrilees, B., Jayawardhena, C., & Wright, L. (2009). E-consumer behavior. *European Journal of Marketing, 43*(9-10), 1121–1139.

Ding, D., Hu, P., Verma, R., & Wardell, D. (2010). The impact of service system design and flow experience on customer satisfaction in online financial services. *Journal of Service Research, 13*(1), 96–110.

Éthier, J., Hadaya, P., Talbot, J., & Cadieux, J. (2006). B2C web site quality and emotions during online shopping episodes: An empirical study. *Information and Management, 43*, 627–639.

Fan, Q., Lee, J., & Kim, J. (2013). The impact of web site quality on flow-related online shopping behaviors in C2C e-marketplaces: A cross-national study. *Managing Service Quality, 23*(5), 364–387.

Gao, L., & Bai, X. (2014). An empirical study on continuance intention of mobile social networking services: Integrating the IS success model, network externalities and flow theory. *Asia Pacific Journal of Marketing and Logistics, 26*, 168–189.

Gao, L., Waechter, K., & Bai, X. (2015). Understanding consumers' continuance intention towards mobile purchase: A theoretical framework and empirical study – A case of China. *Computers in Human Behavior, 53*, 249–262.

Gao, L., Bai, X., & Park, A. (2017). Understanding sustained participation in virtual travel communities from the perspectives of is success model and flow theory. *Journal of Hospitality and Tourism Research, 41*(4), 475–509.

Hansen, T. (2006). Determinants of consumers' repeat online buying of groceries. *International Review of Retail, Distribution and Consumer Research, 16*(1), 93–114.

Harris, P., Dall'Olmo, F., Riley, D., & Hand, C. (2017). Online and store patronage: A typology of grocery shoppers. *International Journal of Retail and Distribution Management, 45*(4), 419–445.

Häubl, G., & Trifts, V. (2000). Consumer decision making in online shopping environments: The effects of interactive decision aids. *Marketing Science, 19*(1), 4–21.

Hoffman, D. L., & Novak, T. P. (1996). Marketing in hyper-media computer-mediated environments: Conceptual foundations. *Journal of Marketing, 60*(3), 50–68.

Jarvenpaa, S. L., & Todd, P. (1997). Consumer reactions to electronic shopping on the World Wide Web. *Journal of Electronic Commerce, 1*(2), 59–88.

Kantar Worldpanel. (2017). *El futuro del e-commerce.* Disponible en https://www.kantarworldpanel.com/es/Noticias/La-cesta-de-la-compra-online-crece-un-32-en-espana [Fecha de consulta: 10 de enero de 2018].

Kim, Y., & Han, J. (2014). Why smartphone advertising attracts customers: A model of web advertising, flow, and personalization. *Computers in Human Behavior, 33*, 256–269.

Kim, G., Oh, E., & Shin, N. (2010). An empirical investigation of digital content characteristics, value, and flow. *The Journal of Computer Information System, 50*(4), 79–87.

Kim, H., Suh, K., & Lee, U. (2013). Effects of collaborative online shopping on shopping experience through social and relational perspectives. *Information and Management, 50*, 169–180.

Kotha, S., Rindova, V. P., & Rothaermel, F. T. (2001). Assets and actions: Firm-specific factors in the internationalization of US Internet firms. *Journal of International Business Studies, 32*, 769–791.

Koufaris, M. (2002). Applying the technology acceptance model and flow theory to online consumer behavior. *Information Systems Research, 3*(2), 205–223.

Landers, V., Beatty, S., Wang, S., & Mothersbaugh, D. (2015). The effect of online versus offline retailer-brand image incongruity on the flow experience. *Journal of Marketing Theory and Practice, 23*(4), 370–387.

Liu, H., & Shiue, Y. (2014). Influence of facebook game player's behavior on flow and purchase intention. *Social Behavior and Personality, 42*(1), 125–134.

Mintel. (2016, March). *Online grocery retailing.* London: Mintel International Group Limited.

Nielsen. (2015). *Encuesta Nielsen sobre Comercio Conectado.* Disponible en http://www.nielsen.com/content/dam/nielsenglobal/latam/docs/reports/ComercioConectado_ES.pdf [Fecha de consulta: 28 de marzo de 2017].

Nielsen. (2017). *Lo que está disponible en tiendas en línea para la compra de comestibles. Estrategias omni-channel para alcanzar a los compradores en transición.* Disponible en http://www.nielsen.com/content/dam/nielsenglobal/latam/docs/reports/ComercioConectado_ES.pdf [Fecha de consulta: 30 de marzo de 2017].

Obadâ, D. (2013). Flow theory and online marketing outcomes: A critical literature review. *Procedia Economics and Finance, 6*, 550–561.

Obadă, D. (2014). Online flow experience and perceived quality of a brand website: InPascani.ro case study. *Procedia – Social and Behavioral Sciences, 149*, 673–679.

Ramus, K., & Nielsen, N. A. (2005). Online grocery retailing: what do consumers think. *Internet Research, 15*(3), 335–352.

Roberts, M., Xu, X. M., & Mettos, N. (2003). Internet shopping: The supermarket model and customer perceptions. *Journal of Electronic Commerce in Organizations, 1*(2), 32–43.

Rose, S., Clark, M., Samouel, P., & Hair, N. (2012). Online customer experience in e-Retailing: An empirical model of Antecedents and Outcomes. *Journal of Retailing, 88*(2), 308–322.

Shim, S., Forsythe, S., & Kwon, W. (2015). Impact of online flow on brand experience and loyalty. *Journal of Electronic Commerce Research, 16*(1), 56–71.

Shin, D. (2012). 3DTV as a social platform for communication and interaction. *Information Technology and People, 25*(1), 55–80.

Taylor, D., & Strutton, D. (2010). Has e-marketing come of age? Modeling historical influences on post-adoption era Internet consumer behaviors. *Journal of Business Research, 63*, 950–956.

Wang, L., Lee, C., Mantz, T., & Hung, H. (2015). Effects of flow and self-construal on player percepcion of brand personality in advergames. *Social Behavior and Personality, 43*(7), 1181–1192.

Winer, R., Deighton, J., Gupta, S., Johnson, E., Mellers, B., Morwitz, V., & Sawyer, A. (1997). Choice in computer-mediated environments. *Marketing Letters, 8*(3), 287–296.

Zhou, T. (2012). Examining mobile banking user adoption from the perspectives of trust and flow experience. *Information Technology and Management, 13*, 27–37.

Zhou, T. (2014). Understanding continuance usage intention of mobile internet sites. *Universal Access in the Information Society, 13*, 329–337.

Zhou, T., Li, H., & Liu, Y. (2010). The effect of flow experience on mobile SNS users' loyalty. *Industrial Management and Data Systems, 110*(6), 930–946.

KAM Effectiveness and Future Performance Risk for FMCG Companies. Underlying Risks of KAM

Pedro Rubio, María Eugenia Fabra, and Victoria Labajo

Abstract Research into the benefits of developing Key Account Management programs for FMCG manufacturers has been extensively performed, but not—considering the underlying risks—with the precision given by incorporating a significant quantitative sample. There is room for further research, particularly in cases where retailer concentration is high and where both customers' negotiation power and private labels' market share are growing: all of which increases the difficulties for suppliers aiming for success in innovation. Using structural equation modeling with a sample of 219 FMCG professionals involved in KAM, this paper seeks to verify the relationship between the development of KAM programs and the risks it implies for future performance. The conclusion should provide further reflection for scholars and FMCG manufacturers: are FMCG companies generating a future performance risk by focussing on KAM programs and reinforcing KAM effectiveness? If so, would it be possible for them to control the side effects of accelerating the strengthening of key accounts?

Keywords Key Account Management · KAM benefits · Customer power · Private label · KAM risks · FMCG

1 Introduction

In recent decades, interest in relationship marketing has focused the attention of marketing academics and managers on Key Account Management (KAM). These programs promise improved performance with the clients of large companies; they are considered to be a future investment in the most valuable clients in a portfolio, focusing efforts on win-win in the long term, on deals and on solutions. The fact that these selected customers are the fastest- growing, largest, and most strategic resource

P. Rubio (✉) · M. E. Fabra · V. Labajo
Universidad Pontificia Comillas, Madrid, Spain
e-mail: prubio@comillas.edu

© Springer International Publishing AG, part of Springer Nature 2018   75
F. J. Martínez-López et al. (eds.), *Advances in National Brand and Private Label Marketing*, Springer Proceedings in Business and Economics,
https://doi.org/10.1007/978-3-319-92084-9_9

prioritization for KAM programs of FMCG manufacturers reveals the programs to be a highly convenient, incontrovertible option for these firms. Taking the above into account, the authors have investigated what occurs when customer concentration is high and the market is maturing with strong private label (PL) development, as is currently occurring in the FMCG sector in all developed countries—including of course Spain. In this environment, "blind marriage" to the most demanding and powerful customers may translate into a risk which undermines the future performance of FMCG companies.

This paper seeks to provide a deeper understanding of the relationship between KAM effectiveness and the danger of accelerating risks on companies' future performance. Such a research framework provides insights for further reflection from scholars and FMCG manufacturers: are FMCG companies putting their future at risk when they focus on KAM programs and reinforce KAM effectiveness? If so, it would be possible for them to control the side effects of accelerating the strengthening of key accounts?

2 Background

The benefits of KAM programs are seen by academic literature as practically incontestable, with researchers primarily focussing their efforts on understanding the key factors of success (Anderson and Narus 1990; McDonald et al. 1997; Narayandas and Rangan 2004). Workman et al. (2003) is one of the flagship papers, using a quantitative SEM approach with a robust sample size in a field historically dominated by qualitative research. They concluded that KAM effectiveness is directly improving companies' market performance and profitability. On the other hand, they were unable either to assess the direction of causality or to rule out other constructs such as powerful customers; and, as a reviewer of one of the above-mentioned papers notes, the relationship the Key Account and the manufacturer KAM programs should be more formalized when powerful customers demand such programs. So, if these powerful customers are relatively less profitable than other clients, it may explain their findings.

One of the small voices of the literature to raise the possible risks of KAM is the qualitative research of Piercy and Lane (2006), which warns of customer portfolios which are increasingly difficult to manage. Unit margins were previously equal for customers, being based on the cost of the product, but now they depend on customer bargaining power, since the products, due to the evolution of technology and PLs, are increasingly substitutable. Piercy and Lane express the lack of logic in continuing to build stronger relationships with unattractive clients, particularly if this limits the option of allocating resources to other, more productive sites. This is why, in the case of FMCG companies, it seems reasonable to understand how to start funding alternative Go-to-Market growth strategies, by devoting already scarce resources to these strategies.

2.1 KAM Benefits

Key accounts or strategic accounts are a company's most valuable customers, and companies cannot afford to lose them without entering into serious difficulties (Zupancic 2008). Most authors agree on the long-term benefits generated by KAM (Anderson and Narus 1990; McDonald et al. 1997; Narayandas and Rangan 2004), and their findings add breadth and depth those discussed previously by other authors. There is in fact, both in the scientific literature and in the business world, a favorable current of opinion (one might almost say that it is axiomatic) regarding the enormous advantages for the results of suppliers and customers of developing KAM programs.

KAM initially emerged as a response to the pressures exerted on suppliers by globalization, the growing power of customers, the sophistication of purchases and the need to find new ways of working with the most important customers (Wengler et al. 2006). It promises to replace adversarial relations between buyer and seller with cooperation, teamwork when solving problems, and integration into a new model of buyer-seller interaction (Piercy and Lane 2006). In today' FMCG markets, there is natural selection of suppliers, along with the constant growth of PL branding and the difficulties of national brands' (NB) innovation in achieving success with increasingly large customers: customers are acquiring more negotiation power, becoming more sophisticated, and demanding customized solutions. The significance of these key clients is defined according to the Pareto rule (20:80), where 20% of the clients represent 80% of the income (Sheth and Parvatiyar 2002). This means that a minority of powerful clients control a majority percentage of suppliers' income and margins. Such a concentration of turnover with the most important customers may even be accelerated in developed and mature businesses, as with FMCG.

2.2 Customer Power and KAM Risks

The literature review indicates how those authors who defend the benefits of KAM philosophy have displaced from their analysis the subject of profit per account, since several works make it clear that these key accounts are to be perceived as an investment of the supplier in their own future, and that this requires the short-term sacrifice of profitability for long-term gain (Wang and Brennan 2014). Such confidence in long-term benefits is questioned, with several researchers warning that communicating their privileged status to a Key Account may be dangerous: the natural reaction to learning this would be to request higher discounts and more favourable conditions of purchase (Millman and Wilson 1999). The logical solution would be to select key clients wisely, but the reality is that the companies must develop these programs with companies whose turnover is highest (Piercy and Lane 2006). Piercy and Lane suggest that such weakness is inherent in the KAM model itself, since is leading companies to an excessive level of dependence on a small number of clients, and, since they are in the control of these large accounts, their strategic freedom is being compromised. In addition, as key accounts extend their market and negotiating power, the inevitable result will be a fall in prices and a progressive reduction in profits.

According to the report from the Spanish retail food sector in 2010, as published by the Spanish Government Antitrust Agency (CNC 2011), in a context increasingly concentrated in and dominated by a small number of supermarket and hypermarkets chains—as well as by the growth of PLs—the bargaining power of buyers is likely to reduce acquisition prices without reducing the amount purchased by them or the quantity exchanged in the market, since the mere threat of reducing purchases or changing suppliers may be enough in itself to improve terms of exchange.

McDonald et al. (1997) warn that a customer will only continue to buy from a supplier if its product continues to be more satisfying to consumers than its competitors'—even though their service as a supplier may be excellent. That is why innovation is crucial and why manufacturers must continue to add new value to customers and actively resist PL. Esade et al. (2015) highlight the role of innovation in increasing value, particularly in mature markets such as FMCG: categories with a high level of innovation outgrow fourfold those with low innovation. Nevertheless, Key Accounts in the Spanish retail sector do not even facilitate shopper access to manufacturer innovations by allocating shelf space to them (Kantar Worldpanel 2016).

2.3 KAM Effectiveness and Danger of Accelerating Risks on Future Performance

Despite successfully developing KAM programs, NB manufacturers may be putting at serious risk the future performance of the company. In order to highlight this, the following hypotheses have been tested with empirical data (Fig. 1):

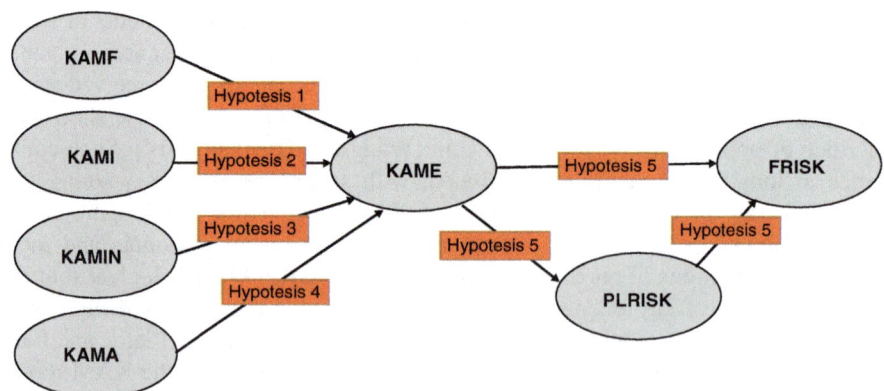

Fig. 1 Structural model proposed

- H1: KAM Formalization (KAMF) has a direct positive effect on KAM effectiveness (KAME).
- H2: KAM Activity intensity (KAMI) has a direct positive effect on KAM effectiveness (KAME).
- H3: KAM Top Management involvement (KAMIn) has a direct positive effect on KAM effectiveness (KAME).
- H4: KAM Access to Marketing and Sales resources (KAMA) has a direct positive effect on KAM effectiveness (KAME).
- H5: KAM effectiveness (KAME) has an indirect positive effect on Risk on future performance (FRISK) through Risk inherent in PL's strengthening (PLRISK).

The novelty of our study becomes clear when we incorporate into the KAM Effectiveness Model generalised by Workman et al. (2003) (a) the risks arising from the strategy of major retailers who have the strong support of their PL and (b) the difficulties encountered by manufacturers seeking to innovate.

3 Method and Data Analysis

Data to test the hypotheses were collected using a structured questionnaire sent out by email to executives involved in KAM in FMCG manufacturers operating in Spain. The number of valid answers received was 219. The structural model was diagrammed and run on IBM AMOS 25. Data analysis through confirmatory factor and discriminant validity analysis were conducted. In addition, the structural model was fitted to the data. Sample size and definition of variables allowed us to work with this type of model in terms of normality and continuity of data. The empirical analysis follows the two-stage process (Anderson and Gerbing 1988) of structural equation modelling (SEM): (1) Definition of a measurement model; (2) Definition of a structural model. The validation of the models has been carried out by using the Maximum Likelihood (ML) method.

A measurement model has been developed by adapting key constructs and items defined by Workman et al. (2003) derived from previous literature. See Table 1:

Based on confirmatory analyses (CFA), six constructs have been defined: KAM formalization (KAMF), KAM activity intensity (KAMI), KAM Top Management involvement (KAMIn), KAM access to Marketing and Sales resources (KAMA) as well as KAM effectiveness (KAME), Risk inherent in PL's strengthening (PLRISK) and Risk on future performance (FRISK) (Table 2).

Although the χ^2 fit index was statistically significant, the measurement model produced good fit ($\chi^2 = 634.837$; df $= 356$; χ^2/df $= 1.78$; IFI $= 0.840$; CFI $= 0.830$; RMSEA $= 0.060$). The standardized loadings were all significant ($p < 0.000$), awarding the convergent validity of the scales (Table 3).

The **structural model** presented strong goodness of fit: $\chi^2 = 650.991$; df $= 364$; χ^2/df $= 1.78$; IFI $= 0.834$; CFI $= 0.827$; RMSEA $= 0.060$. The results of running the structural model confirm the hypothesis set out in this paper (Table 4).

Table 1 Literature indicators and metrics

Construct	Scale/Metrics	Literature
KAM formalization	7-point scale with anchors 1 = strongly disagree; 7 = strongly agree;	Workman et al. (2003) adapted from Jaworski and Kohli (1993)
KAM activity intensity	7-point scale with anchors 1 = on the average; 7 = far more than the average	Workman et al. (2003)
KAM top management involvement	7-point scale with anchors 1 = strongly disagree; 7 = strongly agree;	Workman et al. (2003)
KAM access to MKT and sales resources	7-point scale with anchors 1 = very difficult; 7 = very easy	Workman et al. (2003)
KAM effectiveness	7-point scale with anchors 1 = very poor; 7 = excellent	Workman et al. (2003) adapted from Irving (1995)
Risk inherent in PL's strengthening	7-point scale with anchors 1 = strongly disagree; 7 = strongly agree;	Defined ad hoc
Risk on future performance	7-point scale with anchors 1 = strongly disagree; 7 = strongly agree;	Defined ad hoc

On the one hand, regarding H1–H4, the results confirm the findings of Workman et al. (2003). On the other hand, the effect of KAM effectiveness on Risk on future performance (H5) is mediated by the Risk inherent in the strengthening of the PL.

4 Discussion and Managerial Implications

Using a structural equation model (SEM), this paper demonstrates the relationship between the effective development of KAM programs and the risks on future performance for FMCG manufacturers, when adding in PL strengthening as a side effect of investing in KAM programs in companies which are developing and nurturing relationships with major customers. Underlying KAM there are threats to suppliers which include retailer negotiation power, PL development, and difficulties with innovation. The risks of serving key clients has not been sufficiently widely covered by the preceding literature, which has failed to provide significant quantitative sampling.

When FMCG manufacturers are focusing investment on KAM formalization, activity intensity, top management involvement and access to Marketing and Sales resources, these actions will lead them into KAM effectiveness, but also—if the strengthening of the PL and prioritization of scarce resources are not taken into account—into a dangerous situation. Based on our research, two questions arise which may help to mitigate this risk on companies' future performance:

Table 2 Mean, standard deviation, and correlations among constructs

	Mean	SD	Correlations						
			1	2	3	4	5	6	7
1 KAMF	5.26	1.29	(0.784)						
2 KAMI	4.95	1.55	0.197*	(0.801)					
3 KAMIn	5.13	1.47	0.218*	0.5**	(0.718)				
4 KAMA	5.03	1.30	0.39**	0.37**	0.412**	(0.732)			
5 KAME	5.14	1.10	0.257**	0.429**	0.499**	0.12	(0.600)		
6 PLRISK	5.32	1.33	0.13	0.199*	0.049	0.096	0.144	(0.760)	
7 FRISK	5.41	1.46	0.038	0.278**	−0.064	0.1	0.049	0.539**	(0.660)

*, ** Significant at the 5% and 1% levels correspondingly

Table 3 Standardized loadings

			Estimate
KAMF.1	<---	KAMF	0.923
KAMF.2	<---	KAMF	0.699
KAMI.1	<---	KAMI	0.605
KAMI.2	<---	KAMI	0.743
KAMI.3	<---	KAMI	0.574
KAMI.4	<---	KAMI	0.693
KAMI.5	<---	KAMI	0.606
KAMI.6	<---	KAMI	0.582
KAMIn.1	<---	KAMIn	0.365
KAMIn.2	<---	KAMIn	0.823
KAMIn.3	<---	KAMIn	0.787
KAMIn.4	<---	KAMIn	0.548
KAMA.1	<---	KAMA	0.628
KAMA.2	<---	KAMA	0.637
KAMA.3	<---	KAMA	0.651
KAMA.4	<---	KAMA	0.640
KAME.1	<---	KAME	0.594
KAME.2	<---	KAME	0.685
KAME.3	<---	KAME	0.515
PLRISK1	<---	PLRISK	0.461
PLRISK 2	<---	PLRISK	0.554
PLRISK 3	<---	PLRISK	0.516
PLRISK 4	<---	PLRISK	0.654
PLRISK 5	<---	PLRISK	0.625
PLRISK 6	<---	PLRISK	0.443
PLRISK 7	<---	PLRISK	0.641
PLRISK 1	<---	FRISK	0.473
PLRISK 2	<---	FRISK	0.702
PLRISK 3	<---	FRISK	0.733

Table 4 Structural model. Standardized regression coefficients of latent variables

			Standardized regressions coefficients of latent variable
KAMF	→	KAME	0.206**
KAMI	→	KAME	0.285**
KAMIn	→	KAME	0.402***
KAMIA	→	KAME	−0.225*
KAME	→	PLRISK	0.165*
KAME	→	FRISK	−0.012
PLRISK	→	FRISK	0.535***

*, **,*** Significant at the 10%, 5% and 1% levels correspondingly

- Can PL strengthening be overcome by manufacturer innovation?
- Are there alternative strategies, in terms of channels or clients' portfolio management, which could diversify those risks deriving from customer concentration?

Every company involved in a growing KAM program should at the same time also analyze alternative growth strategies or new business models. Manufacturers' own e-commerce systems may be among these, but to make it work within the FMCG sector, significant investment is required, from web design to delivery logistics (Kantar Worldpanel 2015). That is why FMCG companies can seem to be in a hurry to accelerate the digital Go-to-Market transformation—in order to start mitigating and diversifying as soon as possible the underlying risks of KAM, reassigning some of the investment devoted to such programs in their own e-commerce, so as to reach the final consumer.

The present contribution is limited mainly to the FMCG sector in Spain. Future research should extend to different countries, markets and sectors with equal or less maturity, with the aim of confirming the conclusions of this paper. Future lines of research should address the potential of manufacturer innovation in overcoming private label development as well as the current development and ongoing plans of digital Go-To-Market's own e-commerce systems, which are aimed at reaching companies' final consumers.

References

Anderson, J. C., & Gerbing, D. W. (1988). Structural equation modeling in practice: A review and recommended two-step approach. *Psychological Bulletin, 103*, 411–423.

Anderson, J. C., & Narus, J. A. (1990). A model of distributor firm and manufacturer firm working partnerships. *The Journal of Marketing, 54*(1), 42–58.

CNC. (2011). *Report on relations between manufacturers and distributors in the food sector.*

Esade, Ramón Llul & Promarca. (2015, September 17). *Conclusions of the Symposium on Innovation, variety and competition in the Consumer Goods Market, Madrid.*

Irving, E. (1995). *Marketing quality practices.* Unpublished dissertation, University of North Carolina, Chapel Hill.

Jaworski, B. J., & Kohli, A. K. (1993). Market orientation: Antecedents and consequences. *Journal of Marketing, 57*(July), 53–70.

Kantar Worldpanel. (2015). *Accelerating the growth of e-commerce in FMCG*, 2015 Edition.

Kantar Worldpanel. (2016). *Radar of innovation.*

McDonald, M., Millman, T., & Rogers, B. (1997). Key account management: Theory, practice and challenges. *Journal of Marketing Management, 13*(8), 737–757.

Millman, T., & Wilson, K. (1999). Processual issues in key account management: Underpinning the customer-facing organisation. *Journal of Business and Industrial Marketing, 14*(4), 328–344.

Narayandas, D., & Rangan, V. K. (2004). Building and sustaining buyer–seller relationships in mature industrial markets. *Journal of Marketing, 68*(3), 63–77.

Piercy, N., & Lane, N. (2006). The underlying vulnerabilities in key account management strategies. *European Management Journal, 24*(2), 151–162.

Sheth, J. N., & Parvatiyar, A. (2002). Evolving relationship marketing into a discipline. *Journal of relationship marketing, 1*(1), 3–16.

Wang, X. L., & Brennan, R. (2014). A framework for key account management and revenue management integration. *Industrial Marketing Management, 43*(7), 1172–1181.

Wengler, S., Ehret, M., & Saab, S. (2006). Implementation of key account management: Who, why, and how? An exploratory study on the current implementation of Key Account Management programs. *Industrial Marketing Management, 35*(1), 103–112.

Workman, J. P., Jr., Homburg, C., & Jensen, O. (2003). Intraorganizational determinants of Key Account Management effectiveness. *Journal of the Academy of Marketing Science, 31*(1), 3–21.

Zupancic, D. (2008). Towards an integrated framework of key account management. *Journal of Business and Industrial Marketing, 23*(5), 323–331.

Managing Online Anti-branding Consumer Behaviours: A Multiple Case Study Analysis in the Italian Landscape

Mario D'Arco and Vittoria Marino

Abstract This article seeks to contribute to the extant knowledge about branding in the digital era exploring why consumers assume adversely behaviours towards brands and how brand managers react when their brand is attacked. From the multiple case study analysis emerged that not every brand reacts at the same way. Specifically we noted the following four different strategies: (1) ignore; (2) apologize; (3) start a dialogue with trolls and haters; (4) change behaviour. Interestingly, (3) and (4) appeared more effective in mitigating consumers attacks. On the contrary (1) and (2) would be risky in some contexts.

Keywords Digital branding · Brand management · Anti-branding activities · Consumer empowerment · Brand hate

1 Introduction

At the dawn of the Internet, scholars began predicting a shift in power from the marketer to the consumer, suggesting a new form of consumer-brand relationship (Bernoff and Li 2008; Bruce and Solomon 2013; Hennig-Thurau et al. 2010; Labrecque et al. 2013). Empowered by social networking sites, blogs and wikis, consumers can share, co-create, discuss and modify their own perspective on companies and brands, a view that is often in conflict with the image a brand wishes to convey (Christodoulides 2009). Furthermore, consumers are able to influence other consumers' consumption activities on a level not previously seen (Kim and Johnson 2016). Consumers, in fact, are more likely to trust their peers rather than sponsored commercial messages (Kohli et al. 2015; Kim and Johnson 2016). With these changes in the marketing environment, brand managers are losing control over

M. D'Arco (✉) · V. Marino
Department of Management and Information Technology, Curriculum Marketing and Communication, University of Salerno, Fisciano, Italy
e-mail: mdarco@unisa.it; vmarino@unisa.it

© Springer International Publishing AG, part of Springer Nature 2018   85
F. J. Martínez-López et al. (eds.), *Advances in National Brand and Private Label Marketing*, Springer Proceedings in Business and Economics,
https://doi.org/10.1007/978-3-319-92084-9_10

their brands (Gensler et al. 2013). Therefore, they can no longer be considered the custodian of brand knowledge and brand image. Marketers and consumers build a brand together. This means that the brand, as Fournier and Avery explain (2011: 194), is a sort of *open source* cognitive construal "embedded in a cultural conversation in which consumers gain an equal, if not greater, say than marketers in what the brand looks like and how it behaves."

With so many new consumer capabilities, marketers need to verify if their beliefs and practices are still valid today and, if not for any reason, what they should change in brand building and management techniques. Therefore, this article seeks to contribute to the extant knowledge about branding in the digital era exploring how brands should strategically react to possible consumer-generated negative social media messages, actions such as online petitions or brand retaliation. To this purpose we conduct a multiple case study analysis. Specifically, each case develops around a central event that focuses on consumers' activities that are not aligned with the best interests of the brand.

The rest of the paper is organised as follows. First, we present a theoretical overview of the main issues pertaining brand management in the current marketing landscape. Thereafter, we illustrate our research methods and a detailed explication of data collection and analysis. Finally, we discuss the main theoretical and practical implications, as well as the study's limitations and ideas for future research.

2 Theoretical Background

2.1 Theories, Model and Frameworks

In order to explain the evolution of brand and branding in the digital era, scholars have adopted in their studies a certain number of theoretical frameworks, "that is a network, or 'a plane,' of interlinked concepts that together provide a comprehensive understanding of a phenomenon or phenomena" (Jabareen 2009: 51). For example, Hennig-Thurau et al. (2010) introduce a "pinball" framework to describe new media's impact on relationships with customers. Managing customer relationships is like playing pinball. Firms serve up a "marketing ball" (brands and brand-building messages) into a cacophonous environment which can interfere with the companies' marketing messages (such as bumpers do when playing pinball) and make it more complex to control brand images and relationship outcomes such as customer equity.

Singh and Sonnenburg (2012) using the metaphor of improvisation (improv) theater performances, offer a semantic framework to understand brands in the social media arena. Specifically, the authors underline that "brand owners and users in social media interact with one another in the same impromptu and uncontrolled fashion that characterizes improv theater" (Singh and Sonnenburg 2012: 190). This means that brand owners do not tell brand stories alone but co-create brand performances in collaboration with the consumers. The improv theater metaphor also shows that the audience roles in social media can vary during the performance from modest (spectator) to very overt (actor), depending on the degree of improvisation and tension offered by the brand. In particular, brand audience, according to their euphoric or dysphoric states, can assume the following roles: "fan", "evangelist", "critic", or "hacker".

Gensler et al. (2013) to illustrate the impact of social media on brand management develop a conceptual framework in which consumers are considered "pivotal authors of brand stories". The contents created by consumers using social media channels become central for the meaning of a brand. While firm-generated brand stories typically are consistent and coherent over time, consumer-generated brand stories are more likely to change over time and may represent a threat for brand's aspired identity. Thus, brand managers need to monitor and coordinate consumer-generated stories, as well as react to negative consumer-generated brand stories that harm the brand.

2.2 Anti-branding Phenomena

According to Krishnamurthy and Kucuk (2009), "consumer empowerment" and "consumer dissatisfaction" are the main antecedents of the anti-branding process. If consumer empowerment is a necessary condition to achieve consumer activism goals in markets, such as organize anti-branding sites, create a community, or post on social media negative product/service reviews, consumer dissatisfaction is the trigger. Consumer dissatisfaction can be transactional, related to the market practices, or ideological (Krishnamurthy and Kucuk 2009). All these three types of dissatisfaction might affect brand value, and be very harmful to companies. Furthermore, negative online word-of-mouth communication has considerable detrimental effects on consumer-based brand equity and thus leads to a significant brand equity dilution (Bambauer-Sachse and Mangold 2011).

Speaking of consumer dissatisfaction, in a recent study, Hegner et al. (2017) show that brand hate is triggered by three determinants, that is negative past experience that consumer had with a certain product/service of a brand; symbolic incongruity between consumers' self-concept and brand image; ideological incompatibility that consumer perceives on the base of illegal, immoral or antisocial activities performed by brands. Besides, the behavioural outcomes of brand hate are respectively brand avoidance; negative word-of mouth and brand retaliation. Hegner et al. (2017) also underline that ideological incompatibility has the strongest influence on brand hate, followed by symbolic incongruity and negative past experience.

2.3 Building the Brand in the Digital Era

The conventional perspective, introduced by Keller (1993), of brand as a firm-owned and controlled knowledge structure that can be built in consumers' minds through carefully coordinated marketing activities has no place in the digital era. Comparing the different theoretical frameworks introduced in the paragraph 2.1, emerges that branding on the internet exemplifies participation and co-creation of meaning and value. It is a continuous, social, and highly dynamic and interactive process between the firm, the brand, the consumers and other stakeholders (Merz et al. 2009). Therefore, branding isn't only, as depicted by Keller's Customer-Based Brand Equity model, about identifying key points of difference and building unique, favourable and strong brand associations in the mind of consumers. It isn't just an organizational activity, but an organic process that brings two parties—brand makers and brand users—closer together to co-create value (Ind et al. 2013).

Traditional branding, as underlined by Christodoulides (2009: 142), was "the exercise of a narcissist, the brand manager, who was preoccupied with creating a specific image for the brand, primarily through corporate communications shouting how wonderful the brand is, then passing on the desired image to consumers. Any voices diverging from this image had to be suppressed."

Nowadays, brands to achieve success in computer mediated environments need to stop conducting monologues like they used to do in the past using traditional media, and recognise the importance of listening consumers, find out what they talk about, understand them, get into that conversation, enable interactivity, build relationships. In conclusion, a brand can't be treated as a monolith anymore. Brand exemplifies an *open source* cognitive construal embedded in a cultural conversation (Fournier and Avery 2011). Thus, social media and other digital tools such as video sharing sites and community platforms enable open source branding by empowering consumers to produce and share contents with their peers about brand experiences in their everyday lives. This means that brands are more exposed to criticisms, parodies, sabotages and hateful behaviour.

3   Research Methodology

To contribute to the research about brand and branding in the digital era, we conduct a multiple case study analysis of events concerning consumers' activities that are not aligned with the best interests of the brand. Specifically, our objective is to understand why consumers assume such adversely behaviours and how brand managers react when their brand is attacked.

We preferred a case study analysis because this qualitative method can be utilised to investigate "a contemporary phenomenon within its real life context, especially when the boundaries between phenomenon and context are not clear evident and it relies on multiple sources of evidence" (Yin 1994, p. 13). Thus, this technique helps researchers to answer 'why' and 'how' questions, verify a theory or build new theoretical constructs, advance previous research in a specific field (Eisenhardt 1989; Eisenhardt and Graebner 2007).

Regarding the number of cases to include in a research project, we opted for a multiple cases study rather than a single case. The first and foremost step in the case study research design is the sampling logic. The sampling technique consists to choose cases that are likely to replicate or extend the emergent theory, from a minimum of four to a maximum of 10 (Eisenhardt 1989). We designed this study with literal replication logic (Yin 1994) in order to explain similarities as well as variance in root causes of and reactions to consumers brand attack. We used the following protocol to select our sample. First, the selection of a case was based on prior knowledge, such as information assimilated from the press and social media. Second, we searched information on Google using keywords such as "Epic fail", "Brand attack", "Consumer complaint". Third, on the base of our prior knowledge and web data collection, we selected interesting cases (e.g., contrasting and extreme cases; cases which belong to different industries) instead of typical, average cases in order to explore cause changes in the characteristics and specificities of the object study.

3.1 Case Description

In this paragraph we introduce the four identified case studies. Specifically, the attention is focused on the event that triggered the consumer attack.

Case A On August 24, 2017, Carpisa—an Italian manufacturer and retailer of luggage, handbags, wallets and accessories with over 600 direct stores worldwide—announced the contest campaign "Vinci con Carpisa" (Win with Carpisa) to win a month internship in their Marketing and Advertising Department. In order to participate to this challenge people aged between 20 and 30 needed to buy a women's bag of the new collection 2017/2018 and then submit for free a marketing plan using a dedicated landing page. This campaign produced among consumers and the internet users a profound sense of anger, irony and indignation, because they considered Machiavellian and immoral the idea behind the "competition", namely that the work is a "prize to be won" or that to get a job opportunity you have to "pay" something, in this case a bag.

Case B For Christmas 2017, the Danish jewellery brand Pandora launched on billboards at Milan's metro stations an ad that asked whether a woman would be happiest receiving an iron, pyjamas, an apron or a Pandora bracelet for Christmas. But rather than inspire customers, the ad prompted an outburst of negative comments and parodies, generated by the presence of sexism and gender stereotypes in the message of the advert. On social media the campaign was branded as outdated. A user posted on Facebook that not all women are housewives and that do exist female scientists too. Another user in order to express outrage wrote: "Welcome to the Middle Ages." Others called on the advert to be withdrawn.

Case C On August 27, 2017 Motta—an Italian brand operating in the food industry, owned by Bauli Group—launched a Tv advertising campaign for the breakfast snack Buondì. The first episode of Buondì's multi-subject campaign shows a smiling little girl who is asking to her mother a breakfast that combines lightness and greediness. The mother, who is happily adorning a table in the garden with flowers in bloom, replies: "Such kind of breakfast doesn't exist, my dear! Might an asteroid hit me if it does." In the next scene the mom is killed by an asteroid impact. This Tv ad immediately underwent many criticisms on social media. According to their moral principle, some consumers considered the spot "cruel", "terrible", "non educational", "non-ironic", "dangerous" and "sad for all those children who lost a parent".

Case D On November 2017, "Essere animali", an activist group, launched on Change.org an online petition addressed to the Marketing Director of Selex Group, the third-largest distributor in Italy with a number of branded products which exceeds 5000 (http://www.selexgc.it/interno.aspx?id=212&lng=1. 22 December, 2017). The objective of this petition was to invite Selex Group to stop selling foie gras in its stores. For animal activists foie gras production is controversial because ducks and geese are kept in small cages and force fed with pipes. As a consequence of this attack, Selex Facebook page was flooded with the following consumers' automated message: "Selex, fai la scelta giusta! Metti il Fois Gras #ViaDagliScaffali" (Selex, make the right choice! Take the Foi Gras #AwayFromTheShelves").

3.2 Data Collection and Analysis

Data were collected principally from Facebook and Twitter. To quickly capture content concerning the case A, B, C, D we used Ncapture, a web browser extension of the qualitative data analysis software NVivo. To carry out a detailed evaluation of the collected data, we applied the social media analytics procedure (Abrahams et al. 2015; Fan and Gordon 2014). Following this general schema social media content can be seen as consisting of the following components: linguistic features (i.e., unique words, phrases, noun phrases, or named entities), semantic features (i.e., words, topics and semantic relationships between linguistic entities), social features (i.e., the number of messages, posts, or comments), sentiment features (i.e., positive/negative valence of a post, user ratings), and its source (the author of the content).

With regard to data processing, the first step was to find out consumer anti-branding behaviours, thus we focused mostly on consumer-generated content's semantic features and sentiment features. According to the taxonomy introduced by Hegner et al. (2017), we analysed the determinants of brand hate. From the semantic and sentiment analysis emerged that in the cases A, B, C, D the main consumers' motivation to engage in anti-brand behaviour is related to ideological incompatibility.

The next step was to study how in the cases A, B, C, D the brand responded to the online attacks. From the analysis of the Case A emerged that Carpisa did not reply to those web users who disapproved the Contest "Vinci Con Carpisa". This excessive silence is perceived in a negative way. Some web users in fact make notice to the brand that they deserve the same attention of that given to the user who are asking for information about the product availability and price.

In the Case B the company issued a statement on its Facebook page in an attempt to explain the message behind the large billboard in the Milan's Subway. Addressed to "Pandora Lovers", the company wrote: "Many of you have seen our 2017 Christmas campaign, and the billboards across Italy. We note that the message has been misunderstood and want to explain it better. Pandora has always cared about women and this year we want them to find the perfect gift under the tree. How many of us receive presents we don't want? This initiative was borne out of research which showed that most women get the wrong gift at Christmas." But as the condemnation became more widespread, the company later stressed its point in another statement: "Our aim was to give a nod to the stereotypes we're all familiar with in an ironic and playful way, with the intention to make you smile and absolutely not to cause offense."

In the Case C the community manager of Buondì Motta Facebook page paid attention to every negative comments and replied to each one with the same ironical tone of voice of the Tv spot. For example in response to the comment: "Your irony is non educational. Change advertising agency. As a consumer, I feel offended" the community manager wrote: "There are many kinds of irony: we play on the absurd. How many times have you seen asteroids hit the earth?"

In the Case D the company published on its Facebook and Twitter page a very simple image containing a text message about the decision to stop selling foie gras.

Finally, for each one of the brand reaction strategies identified in the case A, B, C, D we assigned a verbal label in order to develop an initial taxonomy. The labels associated to each case are the following: ignore (Case A); apologize (Case B); start a dialogue with trolls and haters (Case C); change behaviour (Case D).

4 Conclusion and Implications

Previous research about branding in the digital era enables an exhaustive under-standing of the core mechanisms and risks of social media for brands, but does not explain the underlying mechanisms of strategies in reaction to consumers brand attack. Thus, the overall intent of this multiple case study exploratory research is to address this knowledge gap developing a preliminary analysis of the possible reaction strategies. From the analysis of the cases A, B, C, D we extrapolated an initial taxonomy of brand reaction strategies: (1) ignore; (2) apologize; (3) start a dialogue with trolls and haters; (4) change behavior. Interestingly, start a dialogue with trolls and haters and change behavior appeared more effective in mitigating consumers' attacks. React quickly and with the adequate tone of voice should represent a winning move in order to protect online reputation and brand credibility. The case of Buondì Motta shows that brand awareness might even increase, when social media users perceive the brand's reaction as fair, pertinent, and professional (i.e., a facebook user writes: " [...] Comunque grazie per le risposte a tutti. Va

benissimo parlare e scambiarsi le idee. I social servono anche a questo", "[...]
Anyway thanks to give an answer to everyone. It's good to talk and exchange
ideas. This is the real purpose of social media.").

Selex Group after having been attacked by social media users announced with an
image on Facebook and Twitter that they would change their marketing behaviour
and stop selling foie gras. This strategy immediately stopped the group of activists
who started commenting this post with positive statements such as "Complimenti
Selex per aver fatto la scelta giusta e aver tolto il Foie Gras dagli scaffali
#ViaDagliScaffali!" (Congratulations Selex for making the right choice and remov-
ing Foie Gras from the shelves #AwayFromTheShelves); "Grazie Selex per aver
fatto la scelta giusta. In qualità di clienti vigileremo che l'impegno sia rispettato
#ViaDagliScaffali" (Thanks Selex for making the right choice. As customers we will
ensure   that   the   commitment   made   will   continue   to   be   respected
#AwayFromTheShelves).

Ignoring negative consumer-generated content like in the Case A is less
recommended, because consumers accusations may spread rapidly across the web
and acquire credibility and authority if they are not contrasted.

Finally, a strategy that includes an apology as in the Case B should work if the
excuses are based on rational arguments. Pandora's excuses are not solid enough to
prevent a reputation damage to the respective brand. Pandora campaign is the result
of a superficial approach to marketing communication, there are no good excuses for
this mistake, as we can see from the following consumer comments: "Cara Pandora,
noi preferiamo i regali sbagliati ai messaggi sbagliati... i primi possono non essere
particolarmente graditi, i secondi sono veramente sgraditi, ritirate la campagna [...]"
(Dear Pandora, we prefer the wrong gifts to the wrong messages... the former may
not be particularly welcome, the latter are really unwelcome, remove the campaign
[...]); "Avreste fatto più bella figura a chiedere scusa per la caduta di stile senza
cercare giustificazioni che non stanno nè in cielo nè in terra! La vostra campagna è
estremamente offensiva sia per le donne (stereotipate "lava e cucina") che per gli
uomini (tutti trogloditi vero?)." [You would have done better to apologize for the fall
of style without seeking justifications that are neither Heaven nor Earth! Your
campaign is extremely offensive for both women (stereotyped as housewives) and
for men (all troglodytes, isn't it?)].

These findings have some managerial relevance and practical implications. First,
the analysis of the case studies emphasizes that the technology that was supposed to
empower marketers has empowered consumers (Fournier and Avery 2011). This
means that web users can communicate on social media their dissatisfaction and
anger to a vast audience and thereby be a threat for the brand. Second, the findings
highlight that brand managers need to start questioning traditional branding
approaches that put emphasis on mass media techniques. Specifically, in order to
build strong brand equity and driving sales, companies need to concentrate on a new
list of practices such as listening to consumers, monitoring social media, create
authentic brand narratives and engagement strategies, adopt content and online PR
activities.

To conclude, we recognize that this research has some limitations. First, it focuses only on Italian cases, therefore a suggestion for future inquiry is to extend the research to other countries, in order to verify if cultural differences exist both in the nature of consumers' attacks and brand reactions. Second, our findings are the results of observation of events and actions. In order to test the robustness of the findings, for future research we could utilise financial data to forecast the consequences of anti-branding phenomena and the effective validity of the strategies that could help the brand to mitigate consumers attack on social media.

References

Abrahams, A. S., Fan, W., Wang, G. A., Zhang, Z. J., & Jiao, J. (2015). An integrated text analytic framework for product defect discovery. *Production and Operations Management, 24*(6), 975–990.

Bambauer-Sachse, S., & Mangold, S. (2011). Brand equity dilution through negative online word-of-mouth communication. *Journal of Retailing and Consumer Services, 18*(1), 38–45.

Bernoff, J., & Li, C. (2008). Harnessing the power of the Oh-So-Social Web. *MIT Sloan Management Review, 49*(3), 36–42.

Bruce, M., & Solomon, M. R. (2013). Managing for media anarchy: A corporate marketing perspective. *Journal of Marketing Theory and Practice, 21*(3), 307–318.

Christodoulides, G. (2009). Branding in the post-internet era. *Marketing Theory, 9*(1), 141–144.

Eisenhardt, K. M. (1989). Building theories from case study research. *Academy of Management Review, 14*(4), 532–550.

Eisenhardt, K. M., & Graebner, M. E. (2007). Theory building from cases: Opportunities and challenges. *Academy of Management Journal, 50*(1), 25–32.

Fan, W., & Gordon, M. D. (2014). The power of social media activities. *Communications of the ACM, 57*(6), 74–81.

Fournier, S., & Avery, J. (2011). The uninvited brand. *Business Horizons, 54*(3), 193–207.

Gensler, S., Volckner, F., Liu-Thompkins, Y., & Wiertz, C. (2013). Managing brands in the social media environment. *Journal of Interactive Marketing, 27*(4), 242–256.

Hegner, S. M., Fetscherin, M., & van Delzen, M. (2017). Determinants and outcomes of brand hate. *Journal of Product & Brand Management, 26*(1), 13–25.

Hennig-Thurau, T., Malthouse, E. C., Friege, C., Gensler, S., Lobshat, L., Rangaswamy, A., & Skiera, B. (2010). The impact of new media on customer relationship. *Journal of Service Research, 13*(3), 311–330.

Ind, N., Iglesias, O., & Schultz, M. (2013). Building brands together: Emergence and outcomes of co-creation. *California Management Review, 58*(3), 5–27.

Jabareen, J. (2009). Building a conceptual framework: Philosophy, definitions and procedure. *International Journal of Qualitative Methods, 8*(4), 49–66.

Keller, K. L. (1993). Conceptualizing, measuring, and managing customer-based brand equity. *Journal of Marketing, 57*, 1–22.

Kim, A. J., & Johnson, K. K. P. (2016). Power of consumers using social media: Examining the influences of brand-related user-generated content on Facebook. *Computers in Human Behavior, 58*(1), 98–108.

Kohli, C., Suri, R., & Kapoor, A. (2015). Will social media kill branding? *Business Horizons, 58*(1), 35–44.

Krishnamurthy, S., & Kucuk, S. U. (2009). Anti-branding on the internet. *Journal of Business Research, 62*(11), 1119–1126.

Labrecque, L. I., vor dem Esche, J., Mathwick, C., Novak, T. P., & Hofacker, C. F. (2013). Consumer power: Evolution in the digital age. *Journal of Interactive Marketing, 27*(4), 257–269.

Merz, M. A., He, Y., & Vargo, S. L. (2009). The evolving brand logic: A service-dominant logic perspective. *Journal of the Academy of Marketing Science, 37*(3), 328–344.

Singh, S., & Sonnenburg, S. (2012). Brand performance in social media. *Journal of Interactive Marketing, 26*(4), 189–197.

Yin, R. K. (1994). *Case study research: Design and methods* (2nd ed.). Thousand Oaks, CA: Sage.

The Challenges of Digital Transformation for Fast-Fashion Brands: A Proposal for an Operational Tool to Measure Omni-Channel Integration

Marta Rey-García, Ana Regueiro Otero, and Vanessa Mato-Santiso

Abstract With the rise of mobile technologies and social networks, a new, growing segment of smarter, digitally-connected, price-minded consumers has emerged. These new consumers use multiple shopping channels to obtain the product or service they want, at the right time and at the desired price. This impact of digital transformation on retailing customers is particularly acute in the case of fast-fashion brands, and is forcing them to move from a multi-channel paradigm into an omni-channel one. In this new omni-channel context, the different channels fashion brands use tend to interact with each other, as they are simultaneously and indistinctly used by customers in any phase of the purchasing process, from browsing to point of sale and beyond. Furthermore, omni-shopping customers expect consistency and timeliness across both online and offline channels in terms of a seamless customer experience. They want to engage in a personal conversation with fashion brands through a flux of inadvertent and intentional interactions, that combine instrumental and expressive, individual and community dimensions, across a diversity of channels and touch points. This paper identifies the main challenges that fast-fashion retailers face when trying to turn the combination of multiple channels into truly integrated omni-channel strategies, and proposes a simple operational tool to assess the extent to which fast fashion companies are behaving under an omni-channel paradigm from the point of view of the consumer doing a purchase.

Keywords Omni-channel strategies · Fast-fashion brands · Multi-channel retailing · Measurement tool · Digital transformation · Purchasing process · Customer experience

M. Rey-García (✉) · A. R. Otero · V. Mato-Santiso
School of Economics and Business, University of A Coruña, A Coruña, Spain
e-mail: martarey@udc.es; vanessa.mato@udc.es

© Springer International Publishing AG, part of Springer Nature 2018   95
F. J. Martínez-López et al. (eds.), *Advances in National Brand and Private Label
Marketing*, Springer Proceedings in Business and Economics,
https://doi.org/10.1007/978-3-319-92084-9_11

1 Introduction

In recent years, increased digital density—the total number of people, things and processes with persistent connections to the Internet per unit of social activity (Káganer et al. 2013)—has transformed consumer behavior, with a growing number of smarter, digitally-connected, price-conscious consumers that use multiple shopping channels to obtain the product or service they want, at the right price, and at the right moment (Aubrey and Judge 2012). Retailing brands are reacting accordingly, under the broader, disruptive effects of digital transformation, understood as a deep social change, which encompasses both the behavior of people and organizations and the relationships between them and objects (Káganer et al. 2013). From the year 2000 onwards, with the peak of new digital and mobile channels and social networks, the concept of multi-channel emerges as the strategy where products or services are delivered or divided through at least two different channels (Katros 2000; Easingwood and Coelho 2003). Namely, multi-channel strategies by retailing brands are based on the management and use of several channels for sale, both offline and online. Under this paradigm, the objectives and the treatment of the information of the multiple channels are managed independently from each other.

However, we nowadays observe a transition towards an omni-channel paradigm, defined as the synergistic management of all the channels and touch points available with the stakeholders. Touch points are "short, unidirectional or bidirectional interactions, between consumers and companies, and the exchange may be more superficial or more intensive" (Verhoef et al. 2015, p. 176). Omni-channel strategies try to optimize consumer experience across channels and touch points taking into account that they interact with each other and are used interchangeably by consumers to take any action (Verhoef et al. 2015). An omni-channel strategy implies the full integration of the offline and online shopping experience, and it represents the ideal strategy to offer various channels regarding the latest developments of consumer behavior (Mirsch et al. 2016). Thus, omni-channel strategies also entail a huge opportunity for companies and brands to re-invent the physical store so that it actively contributes to driving growth. Instead of seeing e-commerce and online channels as a threat to the traditional retail networks, brands need to build a strategy that supports and leverages the physical channel as part of an integrated 'omni-channel ecosystem' (Aubrey and Judge 2012).

2 The Impact of Digital Transformation on the Strategy of Fast-Fashion Brands

The fast fashion industry is based on a business model that mainly consists of "keeping clothing styles up-to-date and prices down" (Caro and Martínez-De-Albéniz 2014, p. 59). Thus, fast fashion retailers compete on both price and product freshness. In this industry, consumers expect a high rotation in products (especially young people, who demand new products at least each week), low prices, and reduced waiting times, among other benefits. In particular, the value proposition of fast fashion is supported by two basic elements: a quick response in the production side, and a dynamic assortment planning with frequent changes. A fast fashion retailer that offers a quick response has a flexible supply chain and can order stock very frequently (not only before each season), taking advantage of any available information from current and potential consumers. However, these companies have higher production costs in comparison with traditional retailers (Caro and Martínez-De-Albéniz 2010).

Effects of digital transformation are already evident at every step of the value chain of fast fashion brands, starting with the design phase. Unlike the traditional model, the main goal of fast fashion companies is to respond to nascent demand trends, providing the products very rapidly in order to capture the maximum value from early-adopting, fashion-minded consumers. Due to the necessity of finding out the preferences of consumers and reacting to them in the shortest time possible, big data analysis of real-time, multi-channel browsing and sales information becomes a key mechanism for increased efficiency of the design and production phases, ultimately reducing time to market.

Secondly, digital transformation is revolutionizing production processes. The combination of digital and radio-frequency identification (RFID) technologies offers the greatest promise for guaranteeing product traceability across the supply chain and overall sustainability of fashion brands, improving consumer satisfaction (Garrido Azevedo and Carvalho 2012). On the one hand, reputational risks of global fashion brands have shot up due to increased digital density; on the other hand, sustainability is increasingly appreciated by fashion customers.

Finally, and moving downstream, the behavior of consumers and the way they purchase from fashion brands has changed completely in the digital age. On the one hand, purchase channels such as online private shopping clubs, online stores, and social media have rapidly gained ground. Fast fashion sales through the Internet have increased due to the growing penetration of the network, the increase in confidence in online transactions and the development of customized online offerings. Mobile apps, in particular, are booming. Therefore, online channels entail both a great opportunity and an enormous challenge for fast fashion brands (Deloitte 2013). On the other hand, the brick and mortar store is also undergoing its own process of digital transformation, taking advantage of new in-store digital technologies such as mobile payment, free-wifi, PDAs, beacons, sensors, virtual dressing rooms, virtual shopping assistants and personal shoppers, digital signage, augmented reality, virtual reality, interactive windows, near field communication, or virtual mannequins. According to Rey-García et al. (2017, pp. 317–318), the "effects of these disruptive innovations do not necessarily imply the death of the physical store, but may enhance its contribution to the creation of value for consumers".

3   The Challenge of Becoming Omni-Channel Fashion Brands

In recent years, and beyond the overall effects of digital transformation on the way of doing business around the world, a further wave of digitalization has been detected in marketing and retailing that entails specific challenges in the interface with end consumers (Leeflang et al. 2014). In the particular case of fast fashion retailers, the technological convergence of different digital technologies in mobile devices such as smartphones compounds with the transformation of the patterns of relationship between global brands and empowered, self-expressing customers and the relevant role of influencers—namely through social media and blogging—. Fashion consumers are forcing brands to move from a multi-channel to an omni-channel retailing model, where different online and offline channels are integrated and consumers seamlessly navigate across them in their information search and purchase processes (Verhoef et al. 2015), fulfilling both instrumental and expressive, individual and community dimensions. This new paradigm poses the following relevant challenges for fashion brands.

3.1   Distribution Systems

Becoming omni-channel may require integrated distribution systems to satisfy increasingly impatient customers. On the one hand, using an integrated distribution system instead of the two existing distribution systems—the retail distribution system and the consumer distribution system—may reduce the distribution cost by up to 44%. On the other hand, it may become necessary to use the same fleet of vehicles to distribute the products ordered through online channels and the products required by the stores (Abdulkader et al. 2018).

3.2   Information Systems

Omni-channel strategies require advanced data management in real time in order to understand behaviors and create predictive patterns with the information of consumer interactions. Taking advantage of the information provided by consumers over the Internet, including online customer reviews—the largest focus group-, is a key element to improve products based on consumer needs and overall customer experience. Information and communications technology (ICT) can help fashion retailers in analyzing data about consumer behavior to develop more effective omni-channel strategies from a consumer perspective (McCormick et al. 2014).

3.3   Interactive Contents and Social Media

According to a recent report for the Spanish fashion industry (Deloitte 2013), one of the main challenges fast fashion brands face consists of designing a omni-channel strategy that is consistent across the different online platforms where bidirectional interaction with customers takes place, such as social media, blogs or forums. On the one hand, it is necessary for consumers to experience a harmonious interaction through the different channels and to perceive that they are always interacting with the original brand, regardless of the channel or touch point (Deloitte 2016a). Consumers want to feel they engage in a personal conversation with brands, so that they express their values and preferences, while the fashion retailer listens to them and responds to their needs by providing engaging offerings. On the other hand, information contents and services must be consistent through different channels, so that a consumer can do any action through any channel and at any time (Beck and Rygl 2015), without having to enter the information multiple times. They must also be timely to avoid lost sales in the face of the impatience that characterizes omni-shoppers, including a post-sale service with an almost immediate response, building on information that was already collected, in response to queries or interaction prompts with consumers (Deloitte 2016a).

3.4   Physical Stores

In the new omni-channel ecosystem, the different channels interact with each other and they are simultaneously and indistinctly used in the information search process and in further steps of the purchasing process. Digitally transformed physical stores—those integrated with online channels and digital technologies—can improve both the performance across the different channels, as well as the consumers' overall shopping experience. Applying omni-channel strategies in physical stores therefore implies integrating its management with the other channels and touch points, under common objectives and shared information. For example, consumers may browse the physical store for product information, and simultaneously use their mobile devices to search for more information about similar products, offers available, as well as more attractive prices (Verhoef et al. 2015). Thus, the conventional divisions between interactive communication channels (bidirectional) and traditional mass communication channels (unidirectional), physical and virtual channels, become blurred.

3.5   Measurement and Evaluation

The increase in the variety of channel formats, coupled with the evolution from multi- to omni-channel strategies in the last decade, has made purchasing more convenient and comfortable for consumers; while at the same time making the selling process more difficult to control and manage for retailers. Selecting the right combination of metrics to identify the contribution of each channel at each step of the purchasing process, and at the same time quantify their overall contribution to conversion rates is essential to enable their integrated management. On top of specific metrics for e-commerce and for the physical store (e.g. conversion rates), multi-channel fashion brands must measure their digital and mobile influence factors. The digital influence factor is defined as the percentage of brick-and-mortar sales that is influenced by the use of any digital device by consumers (PCs, tablets, smartphones, wearables, or in-store digital technologies). The mobile influence factor is the percentage of off-line sales that is influenced by the usage of any mobile device with web access, smartphones included (Deloitte 2016b). Conversely, the contribution of physical stores to online sales should also be measured. Therefore, fashion brands should find the appropriate specific metrics that facilitate the analysis of performance across both the general objectives of the brand and each of its different channels (Ailawadi and Farris 2017).

4 Proposal of a Tool to Measure Omni-Channel in Fast Fashion Industry

In order to assess the extent to which fashion brands are adopting omni-channel strategies from the perspective of end consumers, we propose a simple measurement tool based on a "pseudo-purchase" or "mystery shopper" approach. It should be highlighted that, unlike consumer-satisfaction surveys, the mystery-shopping approach is used to measure the process rather than the outcomes of a service. The emphasis is on the service levels, focusing on activities and procedures that do or do not occur, rather than gathering opinions from consumers about the service experience (Wilson 2001). The proposed operational tool envisions omni-channel strategies as the latest evolutionary stage of multi-channel fashion brands. It tries to evaluate the extent to which the promise of a consistent purchasing experience regardless of the channel used is actually offered through a test of the occurrence and functioning of levels of service under different multi-channel scenarios.

The tool considers two channel types: online channel (website or mobile app) and offline channel (physical store). Thus, testing it to its full capacity requires user registration through the online interfaces. It then simulates four scenarios for a purchasing experience, depending on the combination of channels and online access devices that are utilized, that we consider critical to assess omni-channel integration:

1. Buying through the website, collecting at home and returning at the physical store
2. Buying through the mobile app, collecting at home and returning at the physical store
3. Buying at the physical store and returning through the website
4. Buying at the physical store and returning through the mobile app

Under each of these scenarios, the tool helps testing whether consumers can really carry out any action of the purchasing process (buying a product, returning a product, etc.) through any channel (offline, online) in a consistent way. In order to achieve that goal, it considers a series of channel-specific indicators (test questions) that measure different levels of service. These indicators help assess whether the action undertaken by consumers through different channels can result in similar benefits.

Online consumers cannot observe the true color or touch the product, thus, it is important that companies ensure that products sent are in perfect conditions and carefully presented, as well as keeping waiting time at a minimum. Thus, the indicators proposed for scenarios 1 and 2 emphasize product delivery and presentation conditions, waiting times and timely follow-up of online orders, while assuring the same consistency in the case of in-store returns. The idea is that uncertainty is reduced and physical aspects enhanced so that overall purchase experience is coherent with fashion brand positioning. By contrast, when buying in a physical store, consumers can touch the product, check whether it is in good conditions, and obtain it immediately. Thus, the indicators proposed for scenarios 3 and 4 focus instead on the extent to which the brick and mortar store integrates digital technologies to enhance customer experience while buying at the store, and allows clients to seamlessly commute to the digital realm after the sale and return the product with one single click. Regarding the measurement scale, a simple color-coding may be used to indicate whether the service is offered and is functioning correctly (green), the service is offered but does not correctly function or is poorly operationalized (orange), or the service is not offered (red). The basics of the operational tool are synthesized in Table 1.

Table 1 An operational tool for measuring the implementation of omni-channel strategies in fast fashion brands

Multi-channel combinations	Purchasing experiences	Omni-channel indicators
Click online, collect at home, return in-store	Scenario 1: Purchase through website, collect at home, return at the physical store	✓ Is an order confirmation sent by email? ✓ Is order delivery followed-up by email? ✓ Is waiting time acceptable? ✓ Does the product arrive in good conditions?
	Scenario 2: Purchase through mobile app, collect at home, return at the physical store	✓ Is the product carefully presented? ✓ Is the return procedure in the physical store agile? ✓ Is a return confirmation sent by email?
Buy at store, return online	Scenario 3: Buy at the physical store, return through the website	✓ Are there devices in the store that allow consumers to access the digital catalog of the collection?
	Scenario 4: Buy at store, return through mobile app	✓ Are there devices in the store that allow consumers to buy online? ✓ Is there free Wi-Fi connection in the store? ✓ If consumers ask for a product that is not available at the store, does the staff offer to buy it online? ✓ Can consumers manage their online orders from the physical store? ✓ Can consumers manage returns through the website or the mobile app? ✓ Is a return confirmation sent by email?

5 Empirical Testing of the Proposed Tool and Future Research

The tool will be tested under the two multi-channel combinations and four purchasing experience scenarios included in Table 1 for three fast-fashion retailing brands: Zara, Mango and H&M. More specifically, pseudo-purchases will be performed through their websites, mobile apps and comparable physical stores. The tool can thus be used to benchmark a fashion brand with its competitors and may be customized to include additional stages of the purchasing process, thus helping retailers to identify opportunities for improvement towards a true omni-channel integration. A natural extension is to include other phases or actions involved in the purchasing process with their corresponding multiple channel combinations (e.g. click online, collect at store, return online). In particular, it would be interesting to consider the browsing stage in further depth, as on the one hand, it is a complex process in itself that includes developing awareness about the product, searching for information on it, evaluating and selecting alternatives and, eventually, interacting with the product in a physical way. On the other hand, multiple channel combinations are also possible (e.g. browse in-store, click online; browse online, buy in-store...).

References

Abdulkader, M. M. S., Gajpal, Y., & ElMekkawy, T. Y. (2018). Vehicle routing problem in omni-channel retailing distribution systems. *International Journal of Production Economics, 196*, 43–55.

Ailawadi, K. L., & Farris, P. W. (2017). Managing multi-and omni-channel distribution: Metrics and research directions. *Journal of retailing, 93*(1), 120–135.

Aubrey, C., & Judge, D. (2012). Re-imagine retail: Why store innovation is key to a brand's growth in the 'new normal', digitally-connected and transparent world. *Journal of Brand Strategy, 1*(1), 31–39.

Beck, N., & Rygl, D. (2015). Categorization of multiple channel retailing in Multi-, Cross-, and Omni-Channel Retailing for retailers and retailing. *Journal of Retailing and Consumer Services, 27*, 170–178.

Caro, F., & Martínez-de-Albéniz, V. (2010). The impact of quick response in inventory-based competition. *Manufacturing and Service Operations Management, 12*(3), 409–429.

Caro, F., & Martínez-De-Albéniz, V. (2014). How fast fashion works: Can it work for you, too. *IESE Insight, 21*(21), 58–65.

Deloitte. (2013). *El sector de la moda en España. Oportunidades en el canal digital.* Accessed February, 2018 from http://www.deloitte.es/DQ/comunicados_electronicos/estudio_oportunidades_en_el_canal_digital/es_DQbyDeloitte_Estudio_de_moda_Julio2013.pdf.

Deloitte. (2016a). *En la búsqueda de la Omnicanalidad. El cliente en el centro nuevamente.* Accessed February, 2018 from https://www2.deloitte.com/content/dam/Deloitte/uy/Documents/technology/Articulo%20Omnicanalidad%20-%20reporte.pdf.

Deloitte. (2016b). *Navigating the new digital divide. A global summary of findings from nine countries on digital influence in retail.* Accessed February, 2018 from https://www2.deloitte.com/content/dam/Deloitte/global/Documents/Consumer-Business/gx-cb-global-digitaldivide.pdf.

Easingwood, C., & Coelho, F. (2003). Single versus multiple channel strategies: Typologies and drivers. *The Service Industries Journal, 23*(2), 31–46.

Garrido Azevedo, S., & Carvalho, H. (2012). Contribution of RFID technology to better management of fashion supply chains. *International Journal of Retail and Distribution Management, 40*(2), 128–156.

Káganer, E., Zamora, J., & Sieber, S. (2013). 5 skills every leader needs to succeed in the digital world Cinco habilidades del líder digital. *IESE Insight, 18* (ART-2412).

Katros, V. (2000). A note on internet technologies and retail industry trends. *Technology in Society, 22*(1), 75–81.

Leeflang, P. S., Verhoef, P. C., Dahlström, P., & Freundt, T. (2014). Challenges and solutions for marketing in a digital era. *European Management Journal, 32*(1), 1–12.

McCormick, H., Cartwright, J., Perry, P., Barnes, L., Lynch, S., & Ball, G. (2014). Fashion retailing–past, present and future. *Textile Progress, 46*(3), 227–321.

Mirsch, T., Lehrer, C., & Jung, R. (2016). Channel integration towards omnichannel management: A literature review. In *Proceeding of the 20th Pacific Asia Conference on Information Systems* (PACIS 2016).

Rey-García, M., Lirola-Walton, E., & Mato-Santiso, V. (2017). La transformación digital de la distribución comercial: La tienda física, de caja brick and mortar a nodo omnicanal. In J. A. Trespalacios Gutiérrez, R. Vázquez Casielles, E. Estrada Alonso, & C. González Mieres (Eds.), *Marketing insights: La respuesta del comercio a las tendencias de comportamiento social del consumidor* (pp. 297–320). Oviedo: Cátedra Fundación Ramón Areces de Distribución Comercial, Universidad de Oviedo.

Verhoef, P. C., Kannan, P. K., & Inman, J. J. (2015). From multi-channel retailing to omni-channel retailing: Introduction to the special issue on multi-channel retailing. *Journal of Retailing, 91*(2), 174–181.

Wilson, A. M. (2001). Mystery shopping: Using deception to measure service performance. *Psychology and Marketing, 18*(7), 721–734.

Does Culture Affect Consumer Behaviour, When Shopping On-Line?

Adnane Alaoui and Donata Vianelli

Abstract On-line retailers have to decide whether to standardize or adapt their marketing strategy to the foreign consumer markets. The objective of this article is not only to locate differences in on-line shopping behavior between English, Italian, and Chinese consumers, but also to explain these differences, through cultural dimensions. A discriminant analysis was conducted on English, Italian and Chinese consumers, based on eighteen behavioral variables, to illustrate the effect that a change of culture would have on a consumer's on-line shopping behavior. The behavioral variables were classified in a descending lexicographic order of their discriminating power, between these cultures. After running the discriminant analysis, a factorial analysis of the eighteen behavioral describers was also run, to organize the latter into a smaller number of factors that are mutually exclusive, and very exhaustive. Factorial analysis identified five distinct factors that point out differences between the three countries, underlining that on-line retailers cannot duplicate abroad their home marketing strategy, because the needs e-shoppers wish to fulfill diverge between these markets.

Keywords Culture · Cross-cultural · On-line shopping · Consumer behavior

1 Introduction and Literature Review

The global expansion of firms in general and retailers in particular, has been facilitated by the development of e-commerce technologies and the growth of consumer on-line shopping in different countries. This was achieved by overcoming

A. Alaoui (✉)
John Moores University, Liverpool, UK
e-mail: A.Alaoui@ljmu.ac.uk

D. Vianelli
University of Trieste, Trieste, Italy
e-mail: donata.vianelli@deams.units.it

© Springer International Publishing AG, part of Springer Nature 2018
F. J. Martínez-López et al. (eds.), *Advances in National Brand and Private Label Marketing*, Springer Proceedings in Business and Economics,
https://doi.org/10.1007/978-3-319-92084-9_12

geographical remoteness that is often perceived as a barrier to internationalization, through increasing the efficiency of the global supply chain, and strengthening the image of global brands across different countries (Lancioni et al. 2000; Gregory et al. 2007; Alon et al. 2016). From a marketing perspective, in recent years both manufacturers and retailers have had the possibility to become e-retailers, targeting consumers in different countries and selling their products through online stores. An increasing number of online shoppers accompanies the positive trend in the number of e-retailers. Some recent statistics show that in 2021, the number of global digital buyers will be over 2.14 billion people, up from 1.66 billion people shopping online in 2016 (Statista 2018a, b). However, despite the global growth of online shopping, one can still note a very pronounced divergence between countries, in terms of in the percentage of people that shop on-line. Asia has the highest number of internet users (almost 2 billions), but with a penetration rate of 49.7 only, followed by Europe (659.6 millions), Latin America/Caribbean (404.2 millions) and United States (320.0 millions) with a penetration rate of 80.2%, 62.4% and 88.1% respectively (Internet World Stats 2018). The European market is more heterogeneous, and differences between countries are significant. According to Eurostat (2018), the highest percentage of e-shoppers can be found in United Kingdom (82% of the population), followed by North European countries, while the lowest percentage can be found in Italy (32%), Bulgaria (18%), and Romania (16%).

Despite the increasing number of consumers doing online shopping, studies on this area are still limited and researchers have called for more research (Ashraf et al. 2017). This is particularly evident in a context of cross-cultural analysis of consumer behavior. In fact, in a context of e-shopping, e-retailers' strategies would not only be affected by the different adoption rates across different countries (Ashraf et al. 2014), but also by cultural differences that shape e-shoppers' behavior. More specifically, when considering the role of national cultures on technology adoption, two of the Hofstede strongest statements are related to uncertainty avoidance and individualism/collectivism. Hofstede (2001) defines uncertainty avoidance as a dimension that reflects the extent to which the members of a culture feel threatened by ambiguous or unknown situations; individualism is defined as the degree of interdependence a society maintains among its members: in individualist societies people are supposed to look after themselves and their direct family members, while collectivistic societies are strongly connected with a group (extended family, friends, colleagues, etc.). According to Choi and Geistfeld (2004), in a context of online-shopping higher levels of uncertainty avoidance may result in higher levels of perceived risk, reducing the likelihood to adopt online shopping as a medium to acquire products. Similarly, greater collectivism may facilitate the use of e-commerce, because the in-group collectivistic approach may lead to sharing opinions and information, decreasing the perceived risk associated with shopping online.

In conclusion, on-line retailers must decide whether to standardize or adapt their marketing strategy to the foreign consumer markets, when considering going global, as the adaptation/standardization dilemma plays a central role in the internationalization of retailing (Alon et al. 2016). The objective of this article is not only to locate differences in on-line shopping behavior between English, Italian, and Chinese consumers, but also to explain these differences, through cultural dimensions such as Hofstede's cultural indexes and Wursten and Fadrhonc's (2012) regional clusters.

2 Research Methodology

A discriminant analysis was conducted on English, Italian and Chinese consumers, based on eighteen behavioral variables, in order to illustrate the effect that a change of culture would have on a consumer's on-line shopping behavior. Concerning the analysis, the behavioral variables were classified in a descending lexicographic order of their discriminating power, between these cultures. After running the discriminant analysis, a factorial analysis of the eighteen behavioral describers was also run, to organize the latter into a smaller number of factors that are mutually exclusive, and very exhaustive.

With respect to sampling, 1161 respondents were analyzed, more specifically, 443 Italian consumers, 250 British consumers, and 468 Chinese consumers. A mixed method was used in the sampling procedure, as a non-probabilistic method was used in selecting English participants through convenience sampling, while a probabilistic procedure was adopted in both Italy and China, namely cluster sampling. The samples collected were calibrated to ensure they were demographically balanced, so that a difference in the results between the countries studied would more likely be due to a cultural difference than to a demographical difference. Finally, the questionnaire was written originally in English, and then translated to both Italian and Chinese.

We decided to investigate these countries for two reasons. First, China, Italy and England provide a diverse set with varying levels of Hofstede's cultural dimensions. Individualism in China has a score of 20 (being a collectivistic society), while in Italy and England the score is 76 and 89 respectively, showing the presence of a highly individualistic culture. Please note that in most of our interpretation, we are not making a distinction here between the North and the South of Italy, as they are similar with respect to all cultural indicators (Wursten and Fadrhonc 2012), except for individualism, where the former is more individualistic than the latter. Concerning uncertainty avoidance, China is more similar to England, with a score of 30 and 35 respectively, while Italy has a score of 76. Not only the selected countries are culturally different, but they also have a different degree of maturity of online shopping, as pointed out in the introduction. The second reason for studying these three countries is the fact that they belong to different geographic clusters, as England is part of the "Contest" cluster, China is part of the "Family" cluster, Northern-Italy is part of the "Solar" cluster, and Southern-Italy is part of the "Pyramid" cluster (Wursten and Fadrhonc 2012), which suggests potential cultural differences.

The research objective is both "descriptive", because the study describes consumers' on-line shopping behavior in each culture, and "causal", because it investigates the cause-to-effect relationships between culture and on-line shopping behavior. The variables/questions introduced in this study were selected based on their aptitude to point-out the effect of culture on on-line shopping behavior, as will be developed under the "findings" section. The research approach adopted is a survey that uses a questionnaire as an instrument. Four types of scales were used to measure eighteen behavioral variables. The *first* one is a Likert scale to measure respondents' opinions, where "5" stands for "strongly Agree" and "1" for "strongly disagree", and was used for instance to measure the variable "Knowledge of a specific Brand would increase my confidence in buying it online", which falls under the second factor as can be seen on Table 1. The *second* scale measures the likelihood of an event happening, where the probability of the event of interest occurring ranges from 0 to 100%, and was used for instance to measure the variable "How Likely would you be influenced by Family when shopping online?", which falls under the third factor as can be seen on Table 1. Then, the *third* type of scale is built on a polarized continuum, where "5" and "1" are the positive and the negative ends respectively, and was used for instance to measure the variable "What product quality are you Expecting from an On-Line Purchase?", where "5" and "1" meant "High" and "Low" Product Quality, respectively. Finally, the *fourth* type of scale is built on a continuum from "1" to "4" where respondents were given four choices of answers, and "4" stands for the highest answer possible, while "1" stands for the lowest, as is the case for the variables "How much do you spend on average for online shopping per month" (Under first Factor—see Table 1), "What is your expectation for delivery time?" (Under fourth Factor—see Table 1), or "How often do you shop online?" (Under First Factor—see Table 1). A respondent that has code "3" for his/her answer to the latter question for instance would mean that s/he shops more frequently on-line than a respondent that has code "2".

3   Findings

Factorial analysis revealed that five distinct factors of on-line shopping behavior were being compared between the markets stated above (Table 1).

Indeed, the First factor "Usage of, and familiarity with on-line shopping" differentiated between English and Chinese consumers. For instance, for the variable "To what extent people prefer on-line shopping to physical stores" (PreOnli), as $Mean_{PreOnli - England} = 3.42 > Mean_{PreOnli - China} = 2.73$, on a scale, from "1" to "5" (1 = Strongly prefer physical stores, and 5 = Strongly prefer on-line shopping). This result is supported by the literature; As England is part of the *Contest* cluster that is characterized by a high level of masculinity, it values decisiveness at the expense of dialog and "growing insight" (Wursten and Fadrhonc 2012); as a result, English consumers would appreciate limiting the human interaction with the vendors (by shopping on-line), more than Italian and Chinese consumers would, as the latter fall under societies with an average rather than high level of Masculinity.

Concerning the second factor that is "Trust & Product Quality Expectation, when Shopping On-Line", it differentiates between Italian consumers on one side, and

Table 1 Group means and ANOVA's P-values

Factors/Variables	England	China	Italy	ANOVA
First Factor: Usage of, and familiarity with, on-line shopping				
Number of years of online shopping	2.25	1.75	2.02	0.000
How often do you shop On-Line?	2.59	2.35	2.60	0.000
To what extent do you prefer online shopping?	3.42	2.73	2.47	0.000
How much do you spend on average for online shopping per month	2.29	1.92	1.73	0.000
Second Factor: Trust and product quality expectation, when shopping on-line				
When shopping online, how confident are you that your payment information is secure?	3.13	2.99	3.42	0.000
Knowledge of a specific Brand would increase my confidence in buying it online	3.05	3.05	4.00	0.000
What product quality are you Expecting from an On-Line Purchase?	3.29	3.47	3.68	0.000
Third Factor: Influencers of on-line shoppers				
How Likely would you be influenced by Family when shopping online?	0.57	0.37	0.22	0.000
How Likely would you be influenced by Friends when shopping online?	0.63	0.52	0.40	0.000
How Likely would you be influenced by Social Media when shopping online?	0.59	0.35	0.37	0.000
To what extent are you influenced by online advertising?	3.23	2.51	1.87	0.000
Fourth Factor: Purchase and post-purchase elements of on-line shopping				
How much time does it take you to choose a product when shopping online?	2.71	2.51	2.80	0.001
What is your expectation (acceptable standard) for delivery time?	3.27	2.01	3.24	0.000
How difficult is it to return a product Purchased On-Line?	3.42	2.71	3.06	0.000
Fifth Factor: Perceived competitive advantages of on-line shopping				
How Likely would you Shop On-Line mainly to Save Money?	0.47	0.27	0.51	0.000
How Likely would you Shop On-Line mainly to have a Wider Brand Variety?	0.61	0.45	0.40	0.001
How Likely would you Shop On-Line mainly to Save Time?	0.69	0.62	0.57	0.101
How Likely would you Shop On-Line mainly for its ease in comparing products?	0.44	0.35	0.40	0.109

Chinese and English consumers on the other side", through its variables namely, "payment security", and "how knowledge of a brand, encourages its purchase on-line" (BrdKno), as Mean $_{BrdKno\text{-}Italy}$ = 4.00 > Mean $_{BrdKno\text{-}England}$ = 3.05 $\cong$ Mean $_{BrdKno\text{-}China}$ = 3.05 on a scale, from "1" to "5" (1 = Strongly Disagree, and 5 = Strongly Agree). Considering the literature the Italian culture is characterized by high Uncertainty Avoidance Index (UAI), therefore one would expect Italian consumers to have a lower trust in the payment system than both Chinese and English consumers, that are part of cultures with a low UAI (Wursten and Fadrhonc 2012). Surprisingly, our results show the opposite, as Italian consumers are more confident about on-line payment security than English or Chinese consumers are, which suggests further investigation to explain this discrepancy that could be due to a non-cultural factor. On the other hand, Italian look for branded products more than English or Chinese consumers, to decrease uncertainty about online shopping, which fits our expectation.

The third factor that is "Influencers of on-line shoppers", also differentiates between English and Chinese consumers, through its variables namely, "Family's influence"(Family), "Friends' influence", "on-line advertising's influence on on-line shoppers", and "social-media's influence". For instance, the probability that a consumer from each country would choose family as a mean of influence was: $Mean_{Family - England} = 57 \% > Mean_{Family - China} = 37\%$. In this case as well, results require further analysis, as China is part of the *Family* clusters that is characterized by a high Power Distance Index (PDI), where older people are respected and there opinion heard (Wursten and Fadrhonc 2012), therefore, it is expected that Chinese consumers would score higher on this variable than English consumers, since they would value more their parents/family's opinion when shopping, which is not the case from our results! Is the new generation of Chinese consumers changing a 1000 years old culture?

Concerning the fourth and the fifth factor, the results are split: According to the discriminant analysis procedure, there are variables that differentiate between English and Chinese consumers, such as the variable "difficulty to return products purchased on-line", that falls under the fourth factor that is, "Purchase and Post-purchase elements of on-line shopping" (see Table 1). The other variable that differentiates between English and Chinese consumers is "variety as a competitive advantage", that falls under the fifth factor that is, "perceived competitive advantages of on-line shopping" (see Table 1). Contrarily, other variables of the fourth and the fifth factors differentiate between Chinese consumers on one hand, and Italian and English consumers on the other hand, such as the variables "time required to choose a product on-line" (Choosing) and "expected delivery time" that fall both of them under the fourth factor, and "opportunity to save money" (Save), that falls under the fifth factor (see Table 1). Indeed, $Mean_{Save-China} = 27\% < Mean_{Save-England} = 47\% \cong Mean_{Save-Italy} = 51\%$, while $Mean_{Choosing-China} = 2.51 < Mean_{Choosing-England} = 2.71 \cong Mean_{Choosing-Italy} = 2.80$. These results can be explained through cultural indexes. For instance, the variable "Choosing", was studied in this paper based on the following logic: The *Solar* or the *Pyramid* clusters that Northern and southern Italians belong to respectively, tend to have a higher UAI than in the *Contest* or *Family* clusters, that host the English and the Chinese cultures, respectively (Wursten and Fadrhonc 2012). Since expressing emotions is more common in societies with a high UAI (Wursten and Fadrhonc 2012), one would expect Italian consumers to be more involved emotionally when shopping, and to pursue a hedonic objective from their shopping experience, while the English and Chinese consumers would be expected to be more utilitarian and interested in acquiring the product only. As a result, the latter should decide about their purchase in a shorter time than the Italians would. Hence, our results confirm our expectation.

On the other hand, the variable "Save" that falls under the fifth factor, and differentiates Chinese consumers from English and Italian consumers, can be explained by the fact that China is part of the *Family* clusters that is characterized by a high level of Collectivism, which makes Chinese consumers are more "Face-conscious", meaning that they fear "losing face" (Wursten and Fadrhonc 2012). As a result, Chinese consumers would be less likely to admit shopping on-line in order to save money, as a such declaration may make them lose face. This would explain why China scores the least on this question, compared to English and Northern-Italian consumers (where our respondents come from), that both tend to have a higher level of Individualism.

It is interesting to note from the findings above, that with respect to certain variables, English consumers are more similar to Chinese than to Italian consumers, such is the case for the variable "BrdKno" for instance (see numbers under second factor). While with respect to other variables, Italians consumers are more similar to Chinese than to English consumers, such is the case for the variable "PreOnli" among other variables, as can be seen from the numbers stated above. These results question the assumption, and go against the expectation that countries that share a geographical proximity would have a relatively similar consumer behavior.

Finally, there are variables that were not found to be significant in differentiating between the cultures stated above, such as the "opportunity to save time" (Save-Time), or the "ease to compare products" (ComProd), as the main reasons for shopping on-line, which both fall under the fifth factor that is, the "perceived competitive advantages of on-line shopping". In fact, the probability that a consumer from each country would believe that the variable "ComProd" is a main competitive advantage of on-line shopping, is as follows: $Mean_{ComProd-England} = 44\% \cong Mean_{ComProd-Italy} = 40\% \cong Mean_{ComProd-China} = 35\%$, while the numbers for the variable "Save-Time" are as follows: $Mean_{SaveTime - England} = 69\% \cong (Mean_{SaveTime - Italy} = 57\% \cong Mean_{SaveTime - China} = 62\%)$. These results mean that all three cultures agree on the importance of "saving time" as a competitive advantage of shopping on-line over shopping at a physical store, while most consumers in these cultures do not view the "ease to compare products" as a main competitive advantage of on-line shopping.

Another task the Discriminant analysis accomplishes is the prediction of people's group membership based on their answers to the survey. In other words, by merely examining a person's answers to the questionnaire, one could predict whether the respondent is English, Chinese or Italian. This is equivalence to claiming that after this Discriminant analysis, it is possible to know what to expect as a behavior, from people belonging to each of these three cultures, with respect to the eighteen variables considered. The results show that 80.2% of respondents were classified correctly, as English, Chinese or Italian, simply by scrutinizing the type of answers they have provided in the survey. This is a good hit ratio, as it increases the prediction accuracy by 47.2% compared to allocating people randomly to either group, which would have resulted in a 33.33% chance of being part of either group of consumers, as this study considers three groups namely, English, Chinese or Italian consumers. This prediction accuracy can be extended to the whole population, and not remain restricted to respondents in the sample. To do so, a Leave-One-Out validation method was used, and revealed that the accuracy for people out of the sample will remain as high as 78.9%, which is still an increase of the prediction accuracy by 45.9% compared to allocating people randomly (33.33% accuracy).

4 Conclusions and Practical Implications

On-line retailers cannot duplicate abroad their home marketing strategy, as most of the needs e-shoppers wish to fulfill could diverge between markets. The fundamental factors differentiating consumer's online shopping behavior in different countries, must be identified and taken into consideration when setting e-retailing strategies for a foreign market, in order to decide about the degree of adaptation needed. While several of the variables studied clearly applied to all product categories, a couple of these variables could be the subject of future research to unveil to what extent the latter could be industry specific. Nevertheless, both some specialized retailers, and department stores with wide assortments, would value the results of this research as it depicts divergences as well as similarities between the cultures studied, which draws the line for where standardization of the on-line marketing strategies should stop, and where adaptation should start.

References

Alon, I., Jaffe, E., Prange, C., & Vianelli, D. (2016). *Global marketing: Contemporary theory, practice and cases.* New York: Routledge – Taylor & Francis.

Ashraf, A. R., Thongpapanl, N., & Auh, S. (2014). The application of the technology acceptance model under different cultural contexts: The case of online shopping adoption. *Journal of International Marketing, 22*(3), 68–93.

Ashraf, A. R., Thongpapanl, N., Menguc, B., & Northey, G. (2017). The role of M-commerce readiness in emerging and developed markets. *Journal of International Marketing, 25*(2), 25–51.

Choi, J., & Geistfeld, L. V. (2004). A cross-cultural investigation of consumer e-shopping adoption. *Journal of Economic Psychology, 25*(6), 821–838.

Eurostat. (2018). *E-commerce statistics for individuals.* Retrieved January 17, 2018 from http://ec.europa.eu/eurostat/statistics-explained/index.php/E-commerce_statistics_for_individuals

Gregory, G., Karavdic, M., & Zou, S. (2007). The effects of e-commerce drivers on export marketing strategy. *Journal of International Marketing, 15*(2), 30–57.

Hofstede, G. (2001). *Culture's consequences: Comparing values, behaviors, institutions and organizations across nations* (2nd ed.). Thousand Oaks, CA: Sage.

Internet World Stats. (2018). *Internet users statistics in 2017.* Retrieved January 17, 2018 from http://www.internetworldstats.com/stats.htm

Lancioni, R. A., Smith, M. E., & Oliva, T. A. (2000). The role of the internet in supply chain management. *Industrial Marketing Management, 29*(1), 45–56.

Statista. (2018a). *Number of digital buyers worldwide from 2014 to 2021*. Retrieved January 17, 2018 from https://www.statista.com/statistics/251666/number-of-digital-buyers-worldwide/
Statista. (2018b). *Global markets with the highest online shopping penetration rate*. Retrieved January 17, 2018 from https://www.statista.com/statistics/274251/retail-site-penetration-across-markets/
Wursten, H., & Fadrhonc, T. (2012). International marketing and culture. *Itim International*, 1–9.

Consumer Motivations for Click-and-Collect and Home Delivery in Online Shopping

Maria-Jose Miquel-Romero, Marta Frasquet-Deltoro, and Alejandro Molla-Descals

Abstract Multichannel retailers are implementing cross-shopping options such as click-and-collect with the objective of better serving their customers. When consumers shop online to multichannel retailers they usually can choose between home delivery or click-and-collect (delivery at a nearby store). In this paper we investigate the consumers' motivations behind this choice. Our results reveal that click-and-collect is explained by higher hedonic orientation whereas home delivery is explained by convenience orientation. Immediate gratification, and perceived delivery risk do not play a significant role in the choice.

Keywords Online shopping · Click-and-collect · Home delivery · Consumer motivations · Cross-channel

1 Introduction

The retail sector has undergone a digital revolution characterized by the addition of online channels to the traditional physical channels. Integrating offline and online channels has become a competitive priority for retailers if they want to reap the benefits of the digital economy (Herhausen et al. 2015). Cross-channel integration offers customers the possibility to combine offline and online channels during a shopping journey, giving rise to patterns such as webrooming (search online and purchase offline), showrooming (search offline and purchase online), or click-and-collect (purchase online and collect in store) (Verhoef et al. 2007, 2015). Literature has devoted enough research to analyse both consumer and channel factors that affect consumer's choice of channels for searching and purchasing, but the choice of

This research has been financed by the Spanish Ministry of Economy and Competitiveness (Project ref.: ECO2017-83051-R. Agencia Estatal de Investigación).

M.-J. Miquel-Romero (✉) · M. Frasquet-Deltoro · A. Molla-Descals
Faculty of Economics, University of Valencia, Valencia, Spain
e-mail: maria.j.miquel@uv.es; marta.frasquet@uv.es; alejandro.molla@uv.es

© Springer International Publishing AG, part of Springer Nature 2018   115
F. J. Martínez-López et al. (eds.), *Advances in National Brand and Private Label Marketing*, Springer Proceedings in Business and Economics,
https://doi.org/10.1007/978-3-319-92084-9_13

delivery method in online shopping has received very little attention. The *last mile* or *golden mile*, as it is named, is extremely problematic for retailers, as it is the process of the entire logistics chain in ecommerce that is more expensive, more inefficient, and has greater environmental impact (Brown and Guiffrida 2014). On this regard, as Hübner et al. (2016) highlight, retail research requires an overall view of the distribution concepts for direct-to-customer and store deliveries in omni-channel retailing, as this overall picture is still missing in the literature.

In the current context, in which the customer has access to combine different channels during the shopping process, the analysis of customer motivations seems relevant. Motives, together with perceptions, learning and beliefs, are the psychological factors influencing the individual's shopping choices (Schröder and Zaharia 2008). This paper analyses how consumer motivations, namely convenience orientation, hedonic orientation, immediate gratification and perceived delivery risk, influence the selection of the delivery method. To provide a deeper knowledge, individual's online experience is considered as a moderator of that influence.

2 Literature Review and Hypotheses Proposal

The term convenience was first introduced by Copeland in 1923 to refer to those goods that customer purchases frequently and that are easily accessible at stores, resulting in low risk or low involvement purchasing (Brown 1989). Parallel to this product attributes-oriented approach to the concept, a service attributes-oriented direction was also considered (Berry et al. 2002). This last approach is focused mainly on time-saving and effort minimization when delivering service to customers (Seiders et al. 2000, 2007). In the online setting, convenience is considered one of the main motivations explaining online purchase adoption (Beauchamp and Ponder 2010; Jiang et al. 2013).

Convenience has also been related to purchase orientations. In 1986, Morganosky defined the convenience-oriented consumer as *the one that seeks to accomplish a task in the shortest time with the least expenditure of human energy* (p. 37). More recent research suggests that convenience shoppers prefer online purchasing, as it offers time and effort savings, flexibility and reduction in aggravation (Schröder and Zaharia 2008; Girard et al. 2003). Linking this issue with the delivery method in an online purchase, we could suggest initially that convenience oriented online shoppers will perceive click-and-collect as less convenient than home delivery, as the first one is more related with traditional offline purchase that requires more time and effort. With consumers being faced with increasing time constraints, home delivery provides benefits to them from saving of time that would otherwise be spent driving to a store and back (Bhatnagar et al. 2000). However, due also to those time constraints that sometimes force individuals to be away from home till late, click-and-collect could also be considered a convenient option, mainly bearing in mind the extensive hours that many stores have today. Literature in consumer behaviour suggests that convenience is a context-dependent perception (Jih 2007), therefore both delivery options could be perceived as convenient. So:

H1 There is a positive relationship between individual's convenience orientation and (H1a) the probability of choosing click-and-collect and (H1b) the probability of choosing home delivery in an online purchase.

Earlier research focused on general shopping motives shows that consumers shop not only for practical or utilitarian motives, but also for social interaction and enjoyment (Tauber 1995). These social and enjoyment shopping motives, named in literature as "hedonic" or "recreational" motives, include looking for social experiences outside the home, communicating with others, status and authority, emotional and social need for an interesting and enjoyable shopping experience (Arnold and Reynolds 2003; Tauber 1995).

Research has related the use of non-store channels for purchasing to consumers who enjoy shopping less, being the utilitarian shopping motive (i.e. accomplishing a task) of more influence than the hedonic one (Childers et al. 2001). In the same line, Balasubramanian et al. (2005) suggest that when consumers shop for socialization and relaxation, the "atmospherics of the shopping environment" becomes a main driver of channel choice (p. 14). In fact, shopping at a store provides greater social interactions and entertainment, favouring hedonic experiences often unavailable through other non-store channels (Dholakia et al. 2005). Frasquet et al. (2015) show that hedonic oriented shopper will prefer offline to online shops for the search, purchase and post-sales stages of shopping, as they value the increased opportunities for enjoyment offered by the store. Based on this reasoning and placing our attention in the selection of the delivery method when buying online, we hypothesize:

H2 (H2a) There is a positive relationship between the individual's hedonic orientation and the probability of choosing click-and-collect in an online purchase. However, (H2b) there is a negative relationship between the individual's hedonic orientation and the probability of choosing home delivery.

Immediate possession refers to the instantaneous delivery of products or services (Rohm and Swaminathan 2004) and it is linked with one type of utility habitually attributed to channel intermediaries in favor of consumers: possession utility. Rohm and Swaminathan (2004) stated that consumers motivated by immediate possession will choose a conventional retail store format, rather than an online one. In the case of traditional brick-and-mortar retailers, the possession utility is provided immediately, as the consumer has direct access to the product; however, in online shopping this utility is delayed; consequently, online shopping results in delayed gratification derived from delayed possession. In 1987 George identified that one of the negative factors for in-home electronic shopping via videotext was elimination of instant gratification. However, as far as we know, no author has researched the influence of the motivation of immediate gratification on the delivery method chosen by online shoppers. We believe that those online shoppers motivated by immediate gratification will prefer click-and-collect, as the logistics to the store is perceived as straightforward option; however, the journey to the home of the buyer can be perceived as a longer process, not only because of the distance and time involved, but also because other agents (such as delivery companies) intervene, which can delay even more the process. So, we suggest:

H3 (H3a) There is a positive relationship between individual's immediate gratification orientation and the probability of choosing click-and-collect in an online purchase. However, (H3b) there is a negative relationship between the individual's immediate gratification orientation and the probability of choosing home delivery.

Perceived risk has been traditionally researched when examining factors influencing consumer's selection of various shopping media, highlighting that consumers perceive more risk in in-home shopping, as online purchase is, than in in-store shopping (Donthu and Garcia 1999; Schoenbachler and Gordon 2002). Baisch (1993) classifies risk of in-home shopping in four types, referring to the delivery-related risk as the customer uncertainty regarding his lack of influence on the delivery process, e.g., on the delivery time, and on the correctness, completeness and quality of the delivery. Analyzing the purchase situation, Schröder and Zaharia (2008) identified that online customers have a significant lower delivery-related risk aversion than store-oriented customers. Focusing our attention in the delivery method and taking into consideration the previous results, it is reasonable to suggest that those online shoppers with lower risk delivery perception will prefer home delivery as they will not be so much afraid of the product not arriving in due time and condition. On the other hand, collecting the products in the store offers more guarantees of timely delivery and the possibility to solve the potential problems with the product easier and quicker, as store personnel will be there to support the customer. Accordingly:

H4 (H4a) There is a positive relationship between individual's delivery risk perception and the probability of choosing click-and-collect in an online purchase. However, (H4b) there is a negative relationship between the individual's delivery risk perception and the probability of choosing home delivery.

But we can find support in literature about the influence of online experience on the perceived risk of online channels: the risk lessens as experience of online shopping increases (Miyazaki and Fernandez 2001; Vijayasarathy and Jones 2000). On the same idea, we suggest that online experience will moderate the relationship between delivery risk perception and delivery method, so:

H5 The influence of individual's delivery risk perception on the probability of (H5a) choosing click-and-collect and (H5b) choosing home delivery, in an online purchase will be higher for those shoppers with less online shopping experience, than for those with higher online experience.

3   Methodology

A structured questionnaire with 7-point Likert scales was designed and used to gather the information required to test the hypotheses. The target population were multichannel shoppers in the apparel product category living in Spain. We got a final sample of 702 respondents. Participants belonged to a nationwide online panel managed by a professional market research institute. All the scales were taken from literature and adapted to the specific research problem. Convenience and hedonic orientation as well as risk delivery perception scales were taken from Schröder and Zaharia (2008) (5, 3 and 2 items respectively); a three-item scale adapted from Rohm and Swaminathan (2004) measured immediate gratification orientation. The dependent variables were measured with two single items capturing the likelihood to choose click-and-collect and to choose home delivery in the next online purchase. Online shopping experience was measured with an open question asking for years and months.

4   Results

Before testing the hypotheses, psychometric properties of the scales were assessed, exceeding all of criteria the minimum threshold suggested by relevant literature. The theoretical model summarizing the proposed hypotheses was estimated separately for each independent variable, probability of click-and-collect and probability of choosing home delivery. Structural Equation Modelling using a robust methodology, in EQS 6.1 was performed. Results are shown in Table 1.

Surprisingly, results from Table 1 suggests that the consumer's motivations considered are not, in general, good predictors of the delivery method consumer

Table 1 Hypothesis testing

Hypotheses		Structural relationship	β	t value	Contrast
Click-and-collect	H1a	Convenience Orient. ⇨ (+) Click-and-collect	−0.08	−1.68^{ns}	Rejected
	H2a	Hedonic Orientation ⇨ (+) Click-and-collect	0.14	2.64**	Accepted
	H3a	Immed. Gratif. Orient. ⇨ (+) Click-and-collect	−0.06	−0.79 ^{ns}	Rejected
	H4a	Delivery Risk Percep. ⇨ (+) Click-and-collect	0.03	0.38 ^{ns}	Rejected
Home delivery	H1b	Convenience Orient. ⇨ (+) Home delivery	0.12	2.34*	Accepted
	H2b	Hedonic Orientation ⇨ (−) Home delivery	−0.05	−0.87^{ns}	Rejected
	H3b	Immed. Gratific. Orient. ⇨ (−) Home delivery	0.00	0.02 ^{ns}	Rejected
	H4b	Delivery Risk Percep. ⇨ (−) Home delivery	0.01	0.07 ^{ns}	Rejected

Click-and-collect: S-B χ2 (45 d.f.) = 115.71 (p < 0.000); BBNFI = 0.93; BBNNFI = 0.93; CFI = 0.95; IFI = 0.95; MFI = 0.95; RMSEA = 0.04

Home delivery: S-B χ2 (45 d.f.) = 110.34 (p < 0.000); BBNFI = 0.93; BBNNFI = 0.94; CFI = 0.96; IFI = 0.95; MFI = 0.95; RMSEA = 0.04

* = $p < 0.05$; ** = $p < 0.01$; ns non significant

will choose in online shopping. Those individuals more hedonic oriented will have a higher probability to choose click-and-collect; accordingly, H2a is accepted. Moreover, those individuals more convenience oriented will be more likely to choose home delivery, so, H1b is accepted. The rest of the hypotheses are rejected; our results show that immediate gratification orientation as well as delivery risk perceptions do not play any role in the delivery method chosen.

In order to test H5 (analyzing the moderating role of online experience on the relationship between delivery risk perception and delivery method), two multigroup analysis (MGA) were conducted (Byrne 2006), one for each delivery method. The total sample was divided into two groups of individuals according to their online experience, using the median (25 months) as a criterion. For both delivery methods, the first step of the analysis procedure showed that in none of both groups (low online experience—high online experience) the relationship between perceived delivery risk and the probability of choosing click-and collect/home delivery was significant, having no sense the analysis of the $\chi 2$ statistical variance (due to space limitations as well as lack of interest of the results, statistical information about the MGA has not been included). Accordingly, H5 is rejected.

5   Discussion

The main purpose of this study was to examine the relationship between consumer motivations and the choice of click-and-collect and home delivery for getting the products when purchasing online. For retailers implementing an omnichannel strategy, logistics gets more complex as they have to manage the traditional shipping to stores, with direct shipping to customers' homes that shop online. By implementing click-and-collect, retailers can take advantage of the experiential component of the store visit, as our results show that hedonic orientation explains the choice of the click-and-collect delivery method. This result is in line with previous findings about the store-oriented shopper having higher hedonic and social interaction orientation (Rohm and Swaminathan 2004), or hedonic orientation being related to the use of offline channels (Frasquet et al. 2015). Our results also show that convenience oriented shoppers are more likely to choose home delivery, thus avoiding going to the store to pick up the goods ordered online. This is in accordance with the findings of Rohm and Swaminathan (2004), regarding the convenience shopper who has a low physical store orientation and does not seek social interaction. It is surprising that perception of delivery risk does not influence the selection of the delivery channel. Perhaps the higher perceived risk associated with the online channel for purchasing (Schoenbachler and Gordon 2002) also includes in advance the delivery risk, and due to that, once the individual chooses the online channel the risk delivery diminishes. This could justify our results, as Schröder and Zaharia (2008) identified that online customers have a significant lower delivery-related risk aversion than store-oriented customers.

As a conclusion of our research, we suggest that more research is needed on this topic, as just two relationships were identified as significant. Motivations traditionally relevant for explaining the purchase channel selection are not, in general, of application on delivery method chosen when purchasing online. Moreover, based on the results, considerations on experience on each delivery method (instead of online shopping experience in general), or the type of product to buy among others could be analyzed as moderators for getting a deeper knowledge on the topic.

References

Arnold, M. J., & Reynolds, K. E. (2003). Hedonic shopping motivations. *Journal of Retailing, 79* (2), 77–95.

Baisch, M. (1993). *Die Risikowahrnehmung in "Non-Store"*- Kaufsituationen, Wien. Cited by Schröder and Zaharia (2008) op. cit.

Balasubramanian, S., Raghunathan, R., & Mahajan, V. (2005). Consumers in a multichannel environment: Product, utility, process utility, and channel choice. *Journal of Interactive Marketing, 19*(2), 12–30.

Beauchamp, M. B., & Ponder, N. (2010). Perception of retail convenience for in-store and online shoppers. *The Marketing Management Journal, 20*(1), 49–65.

Berry, L. L., Seiders, K., & Grewal, D. (2002). Understanding service convenience. *Journal of Marketing, 66*(3), 1–17.

Bhatnagar, A., Misra, S., & Rao, H. R. (2000). On risk, convenience, and internet shopping behavior. *Communications of the ACM, 43*(11), 98–105.

Brown, L. G. (1989). The strategic and tactical implications of convenience in consumer product marketing. *Journal of Consumer Marketing, 6*(3), 13–19.

Brown, J. R., & Guiffrida, A. L. (2014). Carbon emissions comparison of last mile delivery versus customer pickup. *International Journal of Logistics Research and Applications, 17*(6), 503–521.

Byrne, B. M. (2006). *Structural equation modeling with EQS: Basic concepts, applications and programming* (2nd ed.). Mahwah, NJ: Erlbaum.

Childers, T. L., Carr, C. L., Pecj, J., & Carson, S. (2001). Hedonic and utilitarian motivations, for online retail shopping behaviour. *Journal of Retailing, 77*(4), 511–535.

Dholakia, R. R., Zhao, M., & Dholakia, N. (2005). Multichannel retailing: A case study of early experiences. *Journal of Interactive Marketing, 19*(2), 63–74.

Donthu, N., & Garcia, A. (1999). The internet shopper. *Journal of Advertising Research, 39*(3), 52–58.

Frasquet, M., Mollá, A., & Ruiz, E. (2015). Identifying patterns in channel usage across the search, purchase and post-sales stages of shopping. *Electronic Commerce Research and Applications, 14*(6), 654–665.

George, R. J. (1987). In-home electronic shopping: Disappointing past, uncertain future. *The Journal of Consumer Marketing, 4*(4), 47–56.

Girard, T., Korgaonkar, P., & Silverblatt, R. (2003). Relationship of type of product, shopping orientations, and demographics with preference for shopping on the internet. *Journal of Business and Psychology, 18*(1), 101–120.

Herhausen, D., Binder, J., Schögel, M., & Herrmann, A. (2015). Integrating bricks with clicks: Retailer-level and channel-level outcomes of online–offline channel integration. *Journal of Retailing, 91*(2), 309–325.

Hübner, A., Holzapfel, A., & Kuhn, H. (2016). Distribution systems in omni-channel retailing. *Business Research, 9*(2), 255–296.

Jiang, L. A., Yang, Z., & Jun, M. (2013). Measuring consumer perceptions of online shopping convenience. *Journal of Service Management, 24*(2), 191–214.

Jih, W. K. (2007). Effects of consumer-perceived convenience on shopping intention in mobile commerce: An empirical study. *International Journal of E-Business Research, 3*(4), 33–48.

Miyazaki, A., & Fernandez, A. (2001). Consumer perceptions of privacy and security risks for online shopping. *The Journal of Consumer Affairs, 35*(1), 54–61.

Morganosky, M. A. (1986). Cost- versus convenience-oriented consumers: Demographic, lifestyle, and value perspectives. *Psychology and Marketing, 3*(1), 35–46.

Rohm, A. J., & Swaminathan, V. (2004). A typology of online shoppers based on shopping motivations. *Journal of Business Research, 57*(7), 748–757.

Schoenbachler, D. D., & Gordon, G. L. (2002). Multi-channel shopping: Understanding what drives channel choice. *Journal of Consumer Marketing, 19*(1), 42–53.

Schröder, H., & Zaharia, S. (2008). Linking multi-channel customer behavior with shopping motives: An empirical investigation of a German retailer. *Journal of Retailing and Consumer Services, 15*(6), 452–468.

Seiders, K., Berry, L. L., & Gresham, L. G. (2000). Attention, retailers! How convenient is your convenience strategy? *Sloan Management Review, 41*(3), 79–89.

Seiders, K., Voss, G. B., Godfrey, A. L., & Grewal, D. (2007). SERVCON: Development and validation of a multidimensional service convenience scale. *Journal of the Academy Marketing Science, 35*(1), 144–156.

Tauber, E. M. (1995). Why do people shop? *Marketing Management, 4*(2), 58–60.

Verhoef, P. C., Neslin, S. A., & Vroomen, B. (2007). Multichannel customer management: Understanding the research-shopper phenomenon. *International Journal of Research in Marketing, 24*(2), 129–148.

Verhoef, P. C., Kannan, P. K., & Inman, J. J. (2015). From multi-channel retailing to omni-channel retailing: Introduction to the special issue on multi-channel retailing. *Journal of Retailing, 91*(2), 174–181.

Vijayasarathy, L. R., & Jones, J. M. (2000). Print and internet catalog shopping: Assessing attitudes and intentions. *Internet Research: Electronic Networking Applications and Policy, 10*(3), 191–202.

Part III
Branding

Does the Commercial Format Influence the Effect that Store Brands' Equity Has on Loyalty to the Retailer?

Natalia Rubio, Nieves Villaseñor, and Mª Jesús Yagüe

Abstract This paper proposes a theoretical model that investigates the formation of store brands equity (SBs) and its influence on the loyalty to the retailer considering the role that the commercial format chosen by the retailer (supermarkets versus hypermarkets) can have in this process. The results obtained reveal one important data regarding the proposed modelling between both groups. While the formation process of store brands' equity is identical for supermarkets and hypermarkets, store brands' equity as source of retailer loyalty is significantly more important for supermarkets. Important implications for management are derived from the results obtained. For supermarkets' managers, generate preference for their own brands is a key issue, and, without underestimating the importance of a proper management of their own brands for hypermarkets' managers, they should focus on the implementation of other marketing tools to generate loyalty to the retailer, such as a pleasant in-store experience, purchase convenience and a wide assortment.

Keywords Store brands' equity · Retailer loyalty · Supermarkets · Hypermarkets

1 Introduction

According to data from the Spanish Association of Large Distribution Companies (2017), supermarkets accounted the 64.7% of the market share in 2017 (compared with 56.6% in 2009) due to the evolution of consumer behavior, which has sought greater recurrence in their food purchases, as well as proximity and convenience, while hypermarkets have reduced their market share from 19.1% in 2009 to 16.3% in 2017. Therefore, in this situation of growth of the supermarkets in comparison to hypermarkets, it is appropriate to consider what role the store brand plays.

N. Rubio (✉) · N. Villaseñor · M. J. Yagüe
Autónoma University of Madrid, Madrid, Spain
e-mail: natalia.rubio@uam.es; nieves.villasenor@uam.es; maria.yague@uam.es

© Springer International Publishing AG, part of Springer Nature 2018   125
F. J. Martínez-López et al. (eds.), *Advances in National Brand and Private Label Marketing*, Springer Proceedings in Business and Economics,
https://doi.org/10.1007/978-3-319-92084-9_14

Although there are works that indicate that only the socio-demographic characteristics of consumers explain their loyalty to different commercial formats (Kaswengi and Diallo 2015), the main objective of this research is to verify which commercial format favors in a greater degree the relevance of own brands to generate store loyalty. This analysis has a great importance for commercial management.

The decisions made with respect to their own brands form a vitally important part of the day-to-day activity of the retail chains. There are a great many academic studies into the positive effects that favourable perceptions of SBs have on a retailer's results. For example, there is empiric evidence that loyalty to SBs not only increases loyalty towards the retailer (González-Benito and Martos-Partal 2012), but also increases the brand equity of the establishment marketing it (Bigné et al. 2013) and encourages the transfer of favourable perceptions between SBs that are differently positioned as regards price (Palmeira and Thomas 2011) as well as among the various product categories (Erdem and Chang 2012). This, in turn, has a positive impact on the margin and profitability obtained by distributors, and their negotiating power. Likewise, highly valued SBs favour the relationship with consumers as they generate satisfaction and identification with the former (Rubio et al. 2015) thanks to their ability to reflect the identity of those who buy them (Goldsmith et al. 2010). However, no studies have been found which analyse the formation of store brands' equity and its effect on customer loyalty comparing various commercial formats. Thus, as principal objective this research measures the impact that store brands' awareness and store brands' image have on store brands' equity through store brands' loyalty, and how store brands' loyalty influences retailers' loyalty intentions comparing supermarkets and hypermarkets.

2 Literature Review

2.1 Store Brands' Equity

Adapting Aaker's brand equity model (1991) and reviewing the literature around store brands, store brands' equity can be conceptualized as the differential value provided by private labels to consumers based on a comparison between brand alternatives (Calvo-Porral and Levy-Mangin 2014). Private label awareness may have an impact on the recall or recognition of private labels by consumers. So, the stronger private label awareness in consumers minds, the more consumers are likely to purchase (Vahie and Paswan 2006). Originally, private labels had a clear orientation to price. Nevertheless, this initial positioning has evolved to give rise to a varied offer of good value for money. Thus, private labels are increasingly perceived as brands with a quality comparable to manufacturer brands. Good value for money and perceived quality are two characteristics of store brands' image and give consumers a good reason to purchase store brands (Rubio et al. 2014). Finally, private label loyalty is conceptualized as the tendency to continue a relationship with a store brand. Store brands' loyalty has a direct and positive role in affecting their equity (Choi and Huddleston 2014). Hence, the following hypothesis are proposed:

H1 The store brands' awareness is positively related with store brands' loyalty

H2 The store brands' image is positively related with store brands' loyalty

H3 The store brands' loyalty is positively related with store brands' equity

Although there exist works defending the loyalty to the retailer favours attitude and loyalty towards the commercialized store brands (De Wulf et al. 2005), another research stream, the present paper among them, indicates a relationship in the opposite direction (Bigné et al. 2013; Collins_Dodd and Lindley 2003; Gonzalez-Benito and Martos-Partal 2012). Therefore, we propose:

H4 The store brands' equity is positively related with loyalty towards retailer

2.2 The Moderating Effect of the Retailing Format

The store formats are conceptualized as different competing categories of store types that provide specific benefits to meet the needs of different customer types and shopping situations. In Europe, discount stores, supermarkets, and hypermarket formats dominate the grocery retailing and in the Spanish market should be highlighted the importance of supermarkets and hypermarkets. Conventional supermarkets could be defined as self-service stores offering a wide range of products, being 400–1000 m^2 in size and carrying 15,000 items. On the other hand, hypermarkets mostly differ from conventional supermarkets in size, since they are between 1000 and 5000 m^2 in size, carrying larger product assortments, usually 80,000 items. That is, hypermarkets use the diversity in their assortment as the main selling proposition (Calvo-Porral et al. 2016).

Store format seemed to be one important characteristic organizing consumer perceptions and is the basic level of categorizing grocery stores. The associations of supermarkets included personal attention, accessibility, nearness and high prices. Hypermarkets were associated with the great amounts of goods, special offers, and a lot of walking and searching. Convenience was associated with both formats, but the perception of convenience is likely to be different in small versus big stores. Supermarkets were perceived as convenient because they are near and they allow quick and easy shopping. Conversely, hypermarkets were viewed as convenient because a lot of goods can be purchased at one shopping trip and brought home easily by car (Uusitalo 2001). But it is not clear if at the store brands' level, consumers perceive hypermarkets and supermarkets as similar.

The study by Martinez-Ruiz et al. (2012) about the purchase preferences that consumers prone to the store brands manifest in relation to commercial formats forms the basis of the research proposal of this work. Their results indicate that private label-prone consumers are more aware of the availability of the store brands, to the extent that they consider it a separate factor when considering their loyalty to the store, as well as part of the economic value proposition offered by the grocery retailer; and are less aware of the levels of customer attention provided by the distributor. Added to this, due to the smaller assortment of supermarkets, compared with hypermarkets, the products' perceived quality influences in higher degree customer loyalty for supermarkets (Calvo-Porral et al. 2016). Thus, store brands' equity could be one of the main drivers of customer-loyalty in the supermarket industry.

In contrast, national brand-prone consumers exhibit less awareness of the availability of the store brands, which represents a mere variety attribute. In hypermarkets, the influence of products' perceived quality on customer loyalty is lower than that for supermarkets. Hypermarkets can enhance customer loyalty around confidence benefits and, consequently, the provision of this relational benefit can serve as a switching barrier to other retailing formats (Martinez-Ruiz et al. 2012). Therefore, in the case of hypermarkets, it is expected to prove that the role of store brands' equity has less importance as the main antecedent of customer loyalty.

There is previous evidence in the literature on store brands that support the moderating effect that the commercial format play in the relationship between store brands' equity and the loyalty to the retailer. Thus, the variety of products sold, the purchase convenience, the level of prices and the quality of the service configure the image of the commercial chain that affects the store brands' equity (Beristain and Zorrilla 2011), and the consumers' attitude towards the chain (Semeijn et al. 2004). In consumer products, the assortment variety is a determining factor in the choice of the commercial format (Baltas and Papastathopoulou 2003; Carpenter and Moore 2006), taking into account the comparison between discount stores, hypermarkets and supermarkets (Hansen et al. 2006). It is also a sector strongly conditioned by price competition. Zielke (2010) states that the level of prices and the value for money paid favour the choice of supermarkets over other commercial formats. Both characteristics are associated with the preference for store brands (Rubio et al. 2015), so it can be assumed that the store brands' equity influence loyalty to the chain to a greater extent in the case of supermarkets. However, in the case of hypermarkets, characterized by a more varied assortment and greater presence of leader brands, the influence of the store brands' equity on the loyalty to the chain is less effective.

H5 The commercial format has a positive moderating effect on the influence of store brands' equity in the retailers' loyalty intentions, being the effect stronger in the case of supermarkets compared to hypermarkets.

Figure 1 shows the theoretical model for this research.

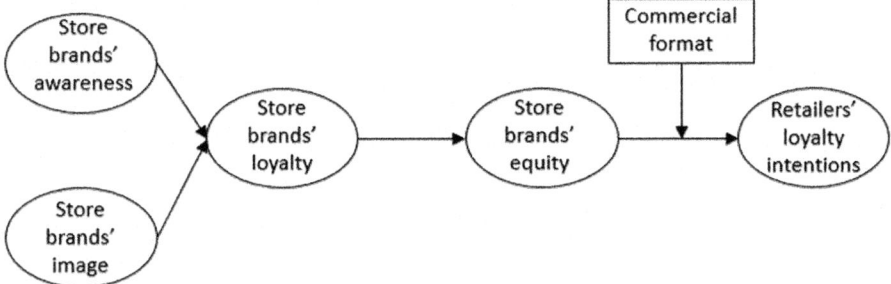

Fig. 1 Theoretical research's model

3 Methodology

To verify the proposed model and hypothesis, and empiric study was carried out. The study is based upon information compiled from those who are responsible for purchasing household consumer products, mainly women (73.45%), residents in Spain, with ages between 18 and 70, who work outside the home (59.57%), with secondary or university education (71.43%) and 2–4 members in the household (84.51%). The telephone survey is used as a technique for gathering information. The respondents buy in any of the eight chains of hypermarket and supermarket Mercadona, Eroski, Carrefour, Auchan and/or El Corte Inglés, which are present in the Spanish market. A randomized stratified sample by means of simple allocation was used to obtain the same response percentage for each of the commercial chains. 742 valid surveys were obtained. These retail groups are chosen because they are dominating the Spanish market at present, with the following market shares: Mercadona with 24.1%, Eroski Group with 5.6%, Carrefour Group with 8.6%, Auchan Group with 3.7%, and finally, El Corte Inglés Group with 3.9% of market share.

The items used to measure the concept proposed stem from the adaptation of previously used and validated scales found in the academic literature. Specifically, to measure store brands awareness, store brands image, store brands' loyalty and store brands equity, the items used were taken from the work by Calvo-Porral and Levy-Mangin (2014). Lastly, for loyalty towards the retailer, the scale by Zeithaml et al. (1996) was adapted.

4 Results

4.1 Analysis of the Measurement Model

First, we carried out an analysis of the measurement model, and then followed with an analysis of the structural model. Confirmatory factor analyses were employed using AMOS. The confirmatory factorial analysis results show that all standardized loading are significant, which reveals the strong convergent validity. In relation with the analyses of internal consistency and reliability, Cronbach alpha, composite reliability coefficients and analysis of the extracted variance exceeded were calculated. We obtained acceptable values for all these measures. The results obtained for the structural modelling adjustment indicate a proper fit for the model.

4.2   Causal Relationship Model

The adjustment obtained for the model in Fig. 1 is satisfactory ($\chi2 = 287.22$; g.l. $= 140$; $\chi2$/g.l. $= 2.05$; CFI $= 0.985$; GFI $= 0.962$; AGFI $= 0.943$; NFI $= 0.972$; IFI $= 0.985$; RMSEA $= 0.038$) and it confirms all of the hypotheses proposed. Figure 2 shows the parameters obtained.

In the case of the multigroup analysis based on the commercial format, there are no significant differences between supermarkets and hypermarkets in the proposed relationships for the formation of store brands' equity (see Figs. 3 and 4), which is natural given that in both types of formats the same store brands are commercialized. Although, as indicated by the H_5, the relationship between store brands' equity and loyalty to the retailer is significantly stronger in the case of supermarkets. This

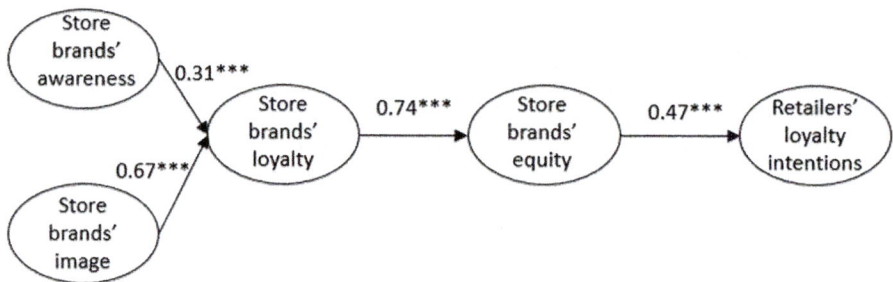

Fig. 2 Results of the empirical model

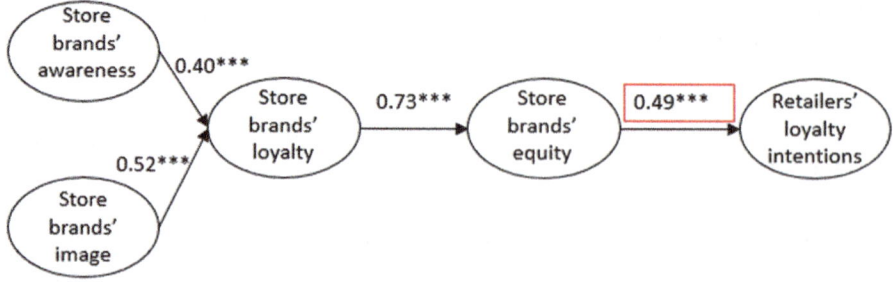

Fig. 3 Empirical model for supermarkets

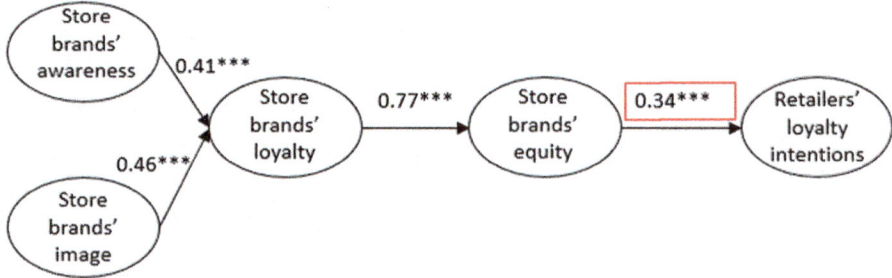

Fig. 4 Empirical model for hypermarkets

research has calculated the critical ratios for the differences between structural parameters to obtain the structural relationships which show significative differences in their effects' magnitude.

It can be explained by the fact that the store brands have a greater presence in the assortment of supermarkets (store brands exceed 35% of sales in supermarkets, compared to values such as 27.5% or 22.3% in the case of Carrefour and Alcampo hypermarkets (Kantar Worldpanel 2017), which would explain that store brands' preference is a more important motivation to generate loyalty to the retailer among the customers of the supermarkets.

5 Conclusions and Recommendations

This work has addressed the process of building store brands' equity and its effect on the customers' loyalty to the commercial chain considering a strategic decision of the distributors that greatly conditions the purchasing behaviour of its customers, and its business results: the commercial format chosen (supermarket or hypermarket). As a research question, it has been considered whether the choice of the commercial format has a moderating effect on the causal relationships established between the dimensions that make up the store brands' equity (brand awareness, brand image and brand loyalty) and loyalty towards the retailer, with no significant differences in the process of creating store brands' equity between supermarkets and hypermarkets (store brands' awareness and image increase store brands' equity through store brands' loyalty in both formats). But, supermarkets get a significantly stronger influence between store brands' equity and the customers' loyalty to the retailer. This means that the achievement of private label portfolios that benefit from brand equity is a strategic objective that is more relevant to supermarkets. Their store brands' portfolios require more marketing efforts compared to hypermarkets.

Additionally, useful recommendations can be extracted for the management of the store brands' portfolio depending on the commercial format. Supermarkets managers are advised to focus their marketing actions on generating awareness for their store brands' portfolio (giving free trials of their own brands in the store, through merchandising actions that favor their own brands) and generating a positive image of their own brands (quality and good value for money) to preserve the loyalty of its customers as an antecedent of its perceived own brands' equity. For hypermarkets, given that their store brands do not exert such a significant influence on the loyalty of its customers, it is recommended to direct the resources towards other marketing variables such as the store's quality service (ex. wide assortment of products and leading brands, facilities for purchasing in terms of payment, extensive schedules), as well as improving in-store's shopping experience (e.g. pleasantly decorated store) and improving omnichannel experience.

This study has its limits, which could be taken into account for future research. The data obtained refers to the consumer market of Spain. It would be convenient to consider other countries, other sectors and other distributors.

References

Asociación Nacional de Grandes Empresas de Distribución. (2017). Disponible en http://www.anged.es/wp-content/uploads/2018/01/resumen-indicadores-comercio-anged-enero18.pdf

Baltas, G., & Papastathopoulou, P. (2003). Shopper characteristics, product and store choice criteria: A survey in the Greek grocery sector. *International Journal of Retail and Distribution Management, 31*(10), 498–507.

Beristain, J., & Zorrilla, P. (2011). The relationship between store image and store brand equity: A conceptual framework and evidence from hypermarkets. *Journal of Retailing and Consumer Services, 18*(6), 562–574.

Bigné, E., Borredá, A., & Miquel, M. J. (2013). El valor del establecimiento y su relación con la imagen de marca privada: efecto moderador del conocimiento de la marca privada como oferta propia del establecimiento. *Revista Europea de Dirección y Economía de la Empresa, 22*(1), 1–10.

Calvo-Porral, C., & Lévy-Mangin, J. P. (2014). Determinants of store brands' success: A cross-store format comparative analysis. *International Journal of Retail and Distribution Management, 42*(7), 595–612.

Calvo-Porral, C., Faíña Medín, J. A., & Montes-Solla, P. (2016). Relational, functional benefits and customer value in large retailing: A cross-format comparative analysis. *Journal of International Food and Agribusiness Marketing, 28*(2), 132–148.

Carpenter, J. M., & Moore, M. (2006). Consumer demographics, store attributes, and retail format choice in the US grocery market. *International Journal of Retail and Distribution Management, 34*(6), 434–452.

Choi, L., & Huddleston, P. (2014). The effect of retailer private brands on consumer-based retailer equity: Comparison of named private brands and generic private brands. *The International Review of Retail, Distribution and Consumer Research, 24*(1), 59–78.

Collins-Dodd, C., & Lindley, T. (2003). Store brands and retail differentiation: The influence of store image and store brand attitude on store own brand perceptions. *Journal of Retailing and Consumer Services, 10*(6), 345–352.

De Wulf, K., Odekerken-Schröder, G., Goedertier, F., & Ossel, G. V. (2005). Consumer perceptions of store brands versus national brands. *The Journal of Consumer Marketing, 22*(4), 223–232.

Erdem, T., & Chang, S. R. (2012). A cross-category and cross-country analysis of umbrella branding for national and store brands. *Journal of the Academy of Marketing Science, 40*(1), 86–101.

Goldsmith, R. E., Flynn, L. R., Goldsmith, E., & Stacey, E. C. (2010). Consumer attitudes and loyalty towards private brands. *International Journal of Consumer Studies, 34*(3), 339–348.

González-Benito, Ó., & Martos-Partal, M. (2012). Role of retailer positioning and product category on the relationship between store brand consumption and store loyalty. *Journal of Retailing, 88* (2), 236–249.

Hansen, K., Singh, V., & Chintagunta, P. (2006). Understanding store-brand purchase behavior across categories. *Marketing Science, 25*(1), 75–90.

Kantar Worldpanel. (2017). *Balance y Perspectivas Gran Consumo*. Disponible en http://www.marketing4food.com/kantar-worldpanel-balance-y-perspectivas-gran-consumo-2017/

Kaswengi, J., & Diallo, M. F. (2015). Consumer choice of store brands across store formats: A panel data analysis under crisis periods. *Journal of Retailing and Consumer Services, 23*, 70–76.

Martínez-Ruiz, M. P., Jiménez-Zarco, A. I., & Izquierdo-Yusta, A. (2012). The effects of the current economic situation on customer satisfaction and retail patronage behavior. *Total Quality Management and Business Excellence, 23*(11–12), 1207–1225.

Palmeira, M. M., & Thomas, D. (2011). Two-tier store brands: the benefic impact of a value brand on perceptions of a premium brand. *Journal of Retailing, 87*(4), 540–548.

Rubio, N., Oubiña, J., & Gómez-Suárez, M. (2015). Understanding brand loyalty of the store brand's customer base. *Journal of Product and Brand Management, 24*(7), 679–692.

Rubio, N., Oubiña, J., & Villaseñor, N. (2014). Brand awareness–brand quality inference and consumer's risk perception in store brands of food products. *Food Quality and Preference, 32*, 289–298.

Semeijn, J., Van Riel, A. C., & Ambrosini, A. B. (2004). Consumer evaluations of store brands: Effects of store image and product attributes. *Journal of Retailing and Consumer Services, 11* (4), 247–258.

Uusitalo, O. (2001). Consumer perceptions of grocery retail formats and brands. *International Journal of Retail and Distribution Management, 29*(5), 214–225.

Vahie, A., & Paswan, A. (2006). Private label brand image: Its relationship with store image and national brand. *International Journal of Retail and Distribution Management, 34*, 67–84.

Zeithaml, V. A., Berry, L. L., & Parasuraman, A. (1996). The behavioral consequences of service quality. *The Journal of Marketing, 60*(2), 31–46.

Zielke, S. (2010). How price image dimensions influence shopping intentions for different store formats. *European Journal of Marketing, 44*(6), 748–770.

Private Label Sourcing Negotiation: Premium PL from Dual Brander

S. Chan Choi

Abstract As private labels become proliferated, retailers are introducing premium PLs that replace marginal national brands. We examine a special case of tiered private label sourcing, in which a premium PL is supplied by the manufacturer of the corresponding NB (dual brander), and an economy PL is supplied by a dedicated PL supplier. In our model, the NB's wholesale and retail prices are determined by the traditional bilateral Nash game. However, the premium PL's wholesale price is determined through a profit-sharing negotiation between the channel members. From an equilibrium-negotiation solution, we derive profit implications of NB's brand equity, the retailer's reputation, and the intrinsic quality of the NB. Interestingly, even if the retails holds a strong negotiation power, we find it optimal for the retailer leave some chips on the table for the NB manufacturer.

Keywords Premium private label · Equilibrium · Negotiation · Distribution channel

1 Introduction

Retailers can procure private labels from several sources including national brand manufacturers, dedicated private label manufactures (often overseas or regional), and own manufacturing facilities.[1] In the first case, the supplier utilizes its expertise and excess capacity to supply PLs, which is known as contract manufacturing or dual branding from the manufacturer's perspective. In the other cases, the suppliers are dedicated to manufacturing PLs for single or multiple retailers. In PL-sourcing, who produces the PL plays an important role for the retailer's margin and ultimately profit (ter Braak et al. 2013). It is natural to assume that the intrinsic quality of a PL supplied by a NB manufacturer is closer to that of the corresponding NB compared

---

[1]Private Label Manufacturers Association 2015 (http://plma.com/storeBrands/facts2015.html).

S. Chan Choi (✉)
Rutgers Business School – Newark & New Brunswick, Piscataway Township, NJ, USA
e-mail: chanchoi@rutgegs.edu

© Springer International Publishing AG, part of Springer Nature 2018
F. J. Martínez-López et al. (eds.), *Advances in National Brand and Private Label Marketing*, Springer Proceedings in Business and Economics,
https://doi.org/10.1007/978-3-319-92084-9_15

135

with the quality of an imitation PL supplied by a third-party dedicated PL manufacturer. In this paper, we are interested in studying effects of such sourcing-based quality differentiation on the distribution channel's prices and profits.

PLs have been traditionally undifferentiated at the wholesale level (Chen et al. 2010); and at the retail level, consumers generally consider PLs as value substitutes of the corresponding national brands. More recently, however, retailers began introducing multi-tier PLs, in which premium PLs are positioned between national brands and economy PLs (Keller et al. 2016). They are differentiated in the value-price dimension. It is reported that some retailers are even dropping lower-tier national brands in favor of overstuffing their shelves with their store brands. Some premium PLs such as Costco-Starbucks are co-branded between the retailer and NB manufacturers, thereby increasing the value of the PL offerings (Narula and Conroy 2010). In an empirical study, ter Braak et al. (2013) found that higher tier PLs command larger retail margins, which is moderated by the type of suppliers (dual branders vs. dedicated PL suppliers).

This paper models a retailer's problem of procuring its private labels from multiple sources with differentiated value-price combination. One of the key features of our model is the retailer's relative negotiation power in relation to the NB manufacturer in the PL production contract. We examine effects of the manufacturer's brand equity, the retailer's reputation, and the quality advantage of the premium PL over the economy PL on the profitability of the channel members. Among a number of findings, the most interesting one is that as the retailer's negotiation power increases, its profit first increases but then eventually decreases. An implication is that, although the retailer may be able to extract a larger incremental profit from the premium PL by exercising its superior negotiation power, it may get hurt from sub-optimal equilibrium price of the corresponding NB when it pushes too much.

2   The Game Scenario

Our simplified market structure has three players: the NB manufacturer, the dedicated PL manufacturer, and the retailer.[2] Prior to the introduction of the premium PL, the NB manufacturer supplies the key product to the retailer. The retailer also carries its own economy PL, which is supplied by a dedicated PL manufacturer at a fixed wholesale price. The NB manufacturer and the retailer plays a Nash game of bilateral monopoly in determining the NB's wholesale price and the retail margin. The retailer uses a product line pricing to maximize the combined profit. The economy

---

[2]In reality, a retailer may carry more brands in a product line such as a premium-tier and a 2nd-tier NBs as well as standard-tier (imitation) PLs. However, in order to focus on the effect of a dual branding manufacturer, this paper chooses the most parsimonious representation of the market. Building and examining a more comprehensive model with multiple-tier NBs and PLs and various strategic scenarios would be a fruitful future extension.

PL manufacturer is a passive participant in the game since its transfer price is not strategic as assumed in most analytical models (Sethuraman 2009).

Suppose the retailer is considering adding a premium PL to its product line. On the other hand, the NB manufacturer has excess capacity that can be utilized for the PL production. Its raw materials, design, manufacturing process, etc. will be the same as those of the NB. Therefore, the intrinsic quality of the premium PL is same as that of the NB. However, the product will carry the retailer's name instead of the manufacturer's.

The NB is the main business item for the NB manufacturer who determines the wholesale price of the NB in reaction to its retail price (and the resulting demand) set by its retailer. Supplying the PL is a side business for the NB manufacturer, whereas the retailer has much discretion and leverage to choose its PL suppliers. Therefore, we assume the transfer price of the premium PL is determined by a negotiation process. If an agreement is reached, it will be in the form of profit sharing in a ratio of (τ : 1) between the manufacturer and the retailer. Thus, a smaller value of τ means more negotiation power of the retailer. The presence of the existing economy PL is shown to be a factor for more retailer power (Ailawadi and Harlam 2004; Meza and Shudhir 2010). In determining the transfer price of the premium PL, the smart channel members consider the consequences in the resulting Nash equilibrium prices for the NB. For computational tractability, our model does not consider competition from other retailers or substitute national brands. The NB manufacturer's profit comes from the sales of the NB and its own PL to the retailer. The retailer's profit comes from the retail sales of the NB, premium PL, and the economy PL.

3   The Model

As discussed above, there are two manufacturers and one retailer in our simplified version of the distribution channel. The NB manufacturer produces the national brand product and charges a wholesale price (w_1) to the retailer. The PL manufacturer is a dedicated supplier of a private label to the retailer. It may be owned by the retailer or is a small contract manufacturer. Because the economy PL supply market condition is typically close to perfect competition (Kumar and Steenkamp 2007), their wholesale prices are usually fixed and close to marginal cost (Sayman and Raju 2007). Therefore, we normalize this economy PL's wholesale price to zero in our model. Prior to introducing the premium PL, the retailer determines the retail prices of both the NB (p_1) and PL (P_3) for maximum combined profit. The NB manufacturer and the retailer play a bilateral vertical Nash game in respective pricing, and the dedicated PL manufacturer is a non-player.

Now the retailer wants to introduce a premium PL with price p_2, and finds that the first manufacturer has some excess capacity. The quality of the product from the excess capacity is expected to be the same as the original NB because they are produced from the same raw materials, using the sane facility, and with the same technology. The only difference is the package that reveals only the retailer's name.

The NB manufacturer has a strong incentive not to dilute its own brand equity by associating his brand with the PL. Therefore, for the NB manufacturer, if it choose to be a dual supplier, the PL becomes a side business for extra revenue. For this premium PL, the transfer pricing assumed to be determined by a negotiation of profit sharing. As the retailer has more negotiation power over the NB manufacturer, the transfer price (w_2) becomes lower.

Therefore, the rule of the game follows the following steps:

1. The NB manufacturer and the retailer agrees that the transfer price of the premium PL will be based on its profit sharing negotiation in a ratio of ($\tau : 1$). A smaller value of τ means larger retailer's negotiation power.
2. A Nash game: Simultaneously, the NB manufacturer sets its wholesale price for the NB (w_1), and the retailer determines retail margins (m_1, m_2, m_3) of the three products: one NB and two PLs. At this stage, the wholesale price of the premium PL is considered as an external parameter.
3. Using the resulting equilibrium solution for (w_1, m_1, m_2, m_3), the premium PL's transfer price w_2 is determined to split the resulting profit from that product based on the ratio agreed in Step 1.

Given the resulting three retail prices, consumers compare perceived values of the three products to choose one. They can also choose not to buy any, if none of them offers positive utility. The consumer perceived value of these products can be decomposed into three components: the manufacturer's brand equity (e_M), the retailer's store reputation (e_R), and the intrinsic quality of the product made by the NB manufacturer (q_M). A national brand sold in a retail store has all three components. A premium PL supplied by the (hidden) national brand manufacturer lacks the NB brand equity but has the same product quality as the NB's. The retailer also adds the store reputation component. An economy PL supplied by a dedicated PL manufacturer has only the store reputation component. Mathematically, perceived values of the NB, premium PL, and economy PL can be expressed as $v_1 = e_M + e_R + q_M$, $v_2 = e_R + q_M$, and $v_3 = e_R$ respectively. As such, the product's value perceived by a typical consumer is the highest for the NB and the lowest for the economy PL. Demands of these three products are derived applying a popular model of vertical differentiation in economics.

Consumer surpluses for each of these products are then expressed as $u_1 = \theta v_1 - p_1$, $u_2 = \theta v_2 - p_2$, and $u_3 = \theta v_3 - p_3$, respectively, where θ is a parameter representing individual willingness to pay for a unit perceived value of a product. This parameter is also related with individual price sensitivity that are associated with store loyalty/retailer reputation (Koschate-Fischer et al. 2014). For tractability, however, we treat them as independent parameters. As in typical vertical differentiation models, θ is assumed to follow a uniform distribution between zero and one. Demand for each of the three products can be derived by equating pairs of the three utilities. The following equations are the resulting demand functions for the NB, premium PL, and economy PL, respectively:

$$D_1 = 1 - \frac{m_1 - m_2 + w_1 - w_2}{e_M},$$
$$D_2 = \frac{m_1 - m_2 + w_1 - w_2}{e_M} - \frac{m_2 - m_3 + w_2}{q_M}, \quad (1)$$
$$D_3 = \frac{m_2 - m_3 + w_2}{q_M} - \frac{m_3}{e_R}.$$

Profits for the NB manufacturer and the retailers are respectively

$$\Pi_M = w_1 D_1 + w_2 D_2, \quad (2)$$
$$\Pi_R = m_1 D_1 + m_2 D_2 + m_3 D_3.$$

4 Nash Equilibrium–Negotiation Solution

The manufacturer determines wholesale price w_1 for his own maximum profit, and the retailer determines m_1, m_2, and m_3 in product line pricing for maximum total profit. Recall that the transfer price of the premium PL w_2 is determined by a profit sharing negotiation. We first derive the Nash price equilibrium between the two players by solving the following for simultaneous equations (Step 2):

$$\frac{\partial \Pi_M}{\partial w_1} = 0, \frac{\partial \Pi_R}{\partial m_1} = 0, \frac{\partial \Pi_R}{\partial m_2} = 0, \frac{\partial \Pi_R}{\partial m_r} = 0.$$

The Nash equilibrium solution as functions of w_2 is as follows:

$$w_1 = \frac{e_M}{3} + w_2,$$
$$m_1 = \frac{1}{6}(2e_M + 3(e_R + q_M - w_2)), m_2 = \frac{1}{2}(e_R + q_M - w_2), m_3 = \frac{e_R}{2}. \quad (3)$$

It is worth noting that the retail margin of the economy PL (hence its retail price) is not affected by any other strategic factors but the retailer's own reputation. In other words, the economy PL's optimal pricing is independent of wholesale and retail prices of the NB or the premium PL. This is a property of the model in which the economy PL manufacturer is a non-strategic participant.

The next step (Step 3) in our game is to predict respective incremental profits from the addition of the premium PL in the product line:

$$\pi_M = w_2 D_2 \text{ and } \pi_R = m_2 D_2. \quad (4)$$

Substituting (3) in (4) yields the following incremental profits:

$$\pi'_M = \frac{(q_M - 3w_2)w_2}{6q_M} \text{ and } \pi'_R = \frac{(q_M - 3w_2)(e_R + q_M - w_2)}{12q_M}. \tag{5}$$

Since the negotiated profit sharing ratio in Step 1 is $(\tau : 1)$, we solve the equation $\pi'_M = \tau \pi'_R$ with respect to w_2, which results in the following transfer price of the premium PL:

$$w_2^* = \frac{\tau(e_R + q_M)}{2 + \tau}. \tag{6}$$

Substituting (5) into (3) results in the following equilibrium wholesale prices and retail margins:

$$w_1^* = \frac{e_M}{3} + \frac{\tau(e_R + q_M)}{2 + \tau}, w_2^* = \frac{\tau(e_R + q_M)}{2 + \tau},$$
$$m_1^* = \frac{(2 + \tau)e_M + 3(e_R + q_M)}{3(2 + \tau)}, m_2^* = \frac{e_R + q_M}{2 + \tau}, m_3^* = \frac{e_R}{2}. \tag{7}$$

Substituting the equilibrium-negotiation solution (7) into the demand functions (1) and profit functions (2), we obtain

$$D_1^* = \frac{1}{3}, D_2^* = \frac{2(1 - \tau)q_M - 3\tau e_R}{6(2 + \tau)q_M}, D_3^* = \frac{\tau(e_R + q_M)}{2(2 + \tau)q_M}. \tag{8}$$

and

$$\Pi_M^* = \frac{-9\tau^2 e_R^2 - 9(-2 + \tau)\tau e_R q_M + 2q_M\left((2 + \tau)^2 e_M + 9\tau q_M\right)}{18(2 + \tau)^2 q_M},$$
$$\Pi_R^* = \frac{(\tau e_R - 2q_M)(e_R + q_M)}{(2 + \tau)^3 q_M}. \tag{9}$$

5   Results

Examining these equilibrium solutions with respect to changes in parameters (τ, q_M, e_M, and e_R), we obtain the following results:

1. The retail price of the economy PL is dependent only on the retailer's reputation. It is independent of the quality, price, or brand equity of the other two products.
2. The retail prices of the NB increases as the NB manufacturer's brand equity, the retailer's reputation, and as the intrinsic quality of the NB increases. However, the retail price of the premium PL depends only on the last two factors.
3. The retail prices of the NB and the premium PL increases as the retailer's bargaining power increases.

4. Assuming the potential market size is constant, the market share (hence the demand) of the NB is constant at one-third of the potential market.[3]
5. At equilibrium, the three brands cover only half the potential market. Under our model assumption, the only way to capture the lower-end market is to introduce a brand of even a lower quality.[4]
6. As the NB's brand quality increases, both profits increase.
7. As the retailer's reputation increases,

   (a) The NB manufacturer's profit increases only if the NB's quality is sufficiently high.
   (b) The retailer's profit increases.

8. As the retailer's bargaining power increases,

   (a) The NB manufacturer's profit first decreases then increases.
   (b) The retailer's profit increases and then decreases.

Among these results, perhaps the least expected one is 8(b). We found that even in the case where the retailer has a strong negotiation power over the manufacture, it is advantageous for the retailer not to exercise the full extent of the power. By pushing the NB manufacturer too much in profit-sharing negotiation, the retailer may end up with a lower total profit because the price of the NB becomes suboptimal. Instead, it is better for the retailer to leave some chips on the table for the NB manufacturer who supplies the premium PL.

6 Conclusion

Multi-tier PLs have been widely reported and analyzed in managerial and empirical papers. To the author's knowledge, however, this paper is the first attempt to model multi-tier PLs in an analytical model. Also, this paper deviates from stylized bilateral equilibrium models in which all pricing decisions are determined by the same mechanism such as Nash equilibrium. In this paper, the wholesale price for the premium PL is determined by a profit-sharing negotiation. In the negotiation process, both players are considered strategic in that they foresee the consequences of the negotiation reflected in the subsequent equilibrium price in a bilateral monopoly game. Not only does this approach result in a meaningful product line pricing solution for the manufacturer, but also it reflects a more realistic behavioral assumption in the multi-tier private label context.

---

[3] At equilibrium, the optimal strategy for the highest quality product (NB) is to adjust its wholesale price such that the resulting demand stays constant.

[4] The results in #4 and #5 are due to the property of a uniform distribution of individual willingness to pay per unit quality parameter θ.

Also, this paper is the first to decompose the value of the products by their source: NB's brand equity, its intrinsic quality, and the retailer reputation. It is logical to model the value of the three products derived from these three components. This approach allows analyzing the effects of the three value components on respective channel member's profit. As these three value components are marketing metrics that can be influenced by marketing mix variables, our results can be further developed to measure ROIs of these marketing decisions.

References

Ailawadi, K., & Harlam, B. (2004). An empirical analysis of the determinants of retail margins: The role of store-brand share. *Journal of Marketing, 68*(1), 147–165.

Chen, J., Narasimhan, O., John, G., & Dhar, T. (2010). An empirical investigation of private label supply by national label producers. *Marketing Science, 29*(4), 738–755.

Keller, K. O., Dekimpe, M. G., & Geyskens, I. (2016). Let your banner wave? Antecedents and performance implications of retailers' private-label branding strategies. *Journal of Marketing, 80*(July), 1–19.

Koschate-Fischer, N., Cramer, J., & Hoyer, W. D. (2014). Moderating effects of the relationship between private label share and store loyalty. *Journal of Marketing, 78*(69), 69–82.

Kumar, N., & Steenkamp, J.-B. E. M. (2007). *Private label strategy.* Cambridge, MA: Harvard Business School Press.

Meza, S., & Sudhir, K. (2010). Do private labels increase retailer bargaining power? *Quantitative Marketing and Economics, 8*(3), 333–363.

Narula, A., & Conroy, P. (2010). *The battle for brands in a world of private labels.* Deloitee. Available at: https://www2.deloitte.com/insights/us/en/deloitte-review/issue-7/the-battle-for-brands-in-a-world-of-private-labels.html

Sayman, S., & Raju, J. S. (2007). Store brands: From back to the future. In N. K. Malhotra (Ed.), *Review of marketing research* (Vol. 3, pp. 132–151). New York: M.E. Sharpe.

Sethuraman, R. (2009). Assessing the external validity of analytical results. *Marketing Science, 28* (4), 759–781.

ter Braak, A., Dekimpe, M. G., & Geyskens, I. (2013). Retailer private-label margins: The role of supplier and quality-tier differentiation. *Journal of Marketing, 77*(July), 86–103.

The Impact of Pricing on Consumer Decision-Making for and Evaluations of Premium Private Labeled Brands in Grocery Retailing

Sascha Steinmann, Katharina-Maria Fonferek, and Hanna Schramm-Klein

Abstract We investigated the effects of adding a premium private label product to a choice set of two competing products (a premium brand and a traditional private label). Furthermore, our results show that the manipulation of the pricing of the premium private label influences consumer choice and evaluation of specific product attributes of all products in the choice set.

Keywords Pricing · Premium private label · Product evaluation · Consumer decision-making

1 Introduction

Highly intense competition, strong concentration tendencies, and a low return on sales in growing sales areas characterized the grocery retailing for a long time. To deal with these issues as well as to differentiate themselves from competitors many retailers have introduced private labeled products in their assortment (Kumar and Steenkamp 2007; Koschate et al. 2014). The associated products are commonly positioned in lower price segments and quality levels are often not far below those of national brands (De Wulf et al. 2005; Pauwels and Srinivasan 2004). Furthermore, premium positioned private labels are characterized by their capacity for innovation and superior quality, which gives the consumer a high-added value and hence, might positively influence a retailer's brand image (Ailawadi et al. 2008). Introducing premium private labeled brands in the assortment will increase the customers choice set in several product categories. From the perspective of the retailer it is therefore of crucial relevance to be aware of how the introduction of a new (premium) private label will be reflected in choice probabilities and market shares (Geyskens et al. 2010). For example, the results of Huber et al. (1982) and Doyle et al. (1999) have

S. Steinmann (✉) · K.-M. Fonferek · H. Schramm-Klein
Chair of Marketing and Retailing, University of Siegen, Siegen, Germany
e-mail: steinmann@marketing.uni-siegen.de

© Springer International Publishing AG, part of Springer Nature 2018
F. J. Martínez-López et al. (eds.), *Advances in National Brand and Private Label Marketing*, Springer Proceedings in Business and Economics,
https://doi.org/10.1007/978-3-319-92084-9_16

143

shown that adding a new product to a choice set can result in a shift of preference to one specific product in the expanded set of alternatives. This effect is called the asymmetrically dominance effect (ADE) or attraction effect. Hence, from a retail perspective it is of relevance to position the introduced premium private label in a way that it will dominate the premium brand in a specific product category and not the traditional private label of the retailer. With regard to the positioning and the consumers' perception of the introduced premium private labeled brand, pricing is of crucial importance. Food retailers with their own premium private labels might focus on enhancing the quality aspect, but at the same time they might be interested in attracting price-conscious customers. An inappropriate pricing could have a negative impact on the consumers' perceptions of the quality of premium private labels, which will negatively influence the preference for the premium private labeled brand (Geyskens et al. 2010).

To investigate the impact of pricing on consumer choice and product evaluations in the context of premium private labels and to answer the question what other product attributes are relevant to a purchase decision of a premium private label product we conducted an experimental study. Within this study, a premium private labeled product was added to a choice set of two products in the product category fruit spreads (traditional private label and premium brand). In three different experimental conditions, we manipulated the price of the premium private labeled product and the caused effects on the valuation of the premium private label compared to a traditional private label and a premium brand were analyzed.

2 Theoretical Background

From a research perspective, the question arises how the customer can come to the shopping decision for the premium private label products. The normative decision theory assumes that regardless of a new purchase option (here: premium private labeled product), the choice probability for the previous decision remains (Independence of Irrelevant Alternatives) or, based on the existing two purchase options, the choice should be proportionally adjusted (Regularity) (Paramesh 1973).

Previous research has discovered compromise, attraction and similarity effects which show that the previous mentioned assumptions of the classical economic standard theory often will not hold due to an influence of several contextual factors (Doyle et al. 1999; Huber et al. 1982; Simonson 1989). Basically, making a decision implies the existence of a choice of more than one option. This means that a decision for Option A is initially a decision against Option B. This decision is justified on the basis of individual preferences and interests of the decision maker. By convention, A is clearly preferred to B. By adding a third option in a choice set of two existing options, without a dominant option, individuals might chose a compromise in the decision-relevant determinants (Simonson 1989). Accordingly, under specific contextual conditions there might be a balance of properties; the added option could represent the compromise, in a trade-off between the existing options (Simonson

1989). For our study, we mainly focus on the impact of the pricing of the added option—the premium private labeled product—to the alternatives under consideration. If the price of the premium private labeled product is closer to the premium brand in the choice set, the new option—the premium private labeled product—should as well be evaluated as more similar to the premium brand. Hence, the choice probability of the premium brand should be influenced due to the introduction of the premium private labeled product. If the price of the new option is closer to the traditional private label, this should mainly have an effect on the choice probability of the traditional private label, while the choice probability of the premium product should remain stable (Simonson and Tversky 1992).

However, the findings of Sinhaa and Batrab (1999) show that price consciousness as well as value consciousness are as well of relevance in the context of consumer decision-making for private labels in different product categories. According to Burton et al. (1998) consumers may view private label products positively because of the relatively low prices (i.e., price consciousness), or because of a strong desire to maximize the ratio of quality received to the price paid (i.e., value consciousness), or view them negatively because they use the price as an indicator of product quality (e.g., price-quality associations). The findings of various studies (Lichtenstein et al. 1993; Petroshius and Monroe 1987) have shown that the price for a product has an impact on its evaluation. Plassmann et al. (2008) have shown that the evaluation of product attributes and emotions changed by manipulating the price of the product. Because of the fact that the perception of quality is indistinct precise, customers use product attributes that signal quality in the context of product evaluation. The fact that customers associate the quality of a product with the price suggests that the product-attributes evaluation of the premium private label should be more positive when the price for the premium private label is close to the premium brand.

3   Experimental Study: Measures and Procedure

We used three different brands from the product category "fruit spreads (strawberry)" as product stimuli in our experimental study (private label, premium private label, and premium brand). We used the official retail price of the premium brand (2.19 €) as well as the official retail price of the traditional private label (1.19 €) at the time of our study as price information for the participants in all experimental conditions. To manipulate the participants' perception of the relation between price and quality of the premium private labeled brand, we used a higher price (price adjustment towards the premium brand) and in a further experimental condition, a lower price (price adjustment towards the private label) was determined in an experimental condition. The prices used for the price adjustments were determined in a preliminary study. Accordingly, for the price adjustment of the premium private label towards the private label a price of 1.49 € was chosen. For the price adjustment towards the premium brand, a price of 1.69 € was determined. Furthermore, in a third experimental condition we used the official retail price of the premium private labeled product at the time of our study (1.59 €). We also considered a control group, where the participants had to evaluate and make their choice only between the premium brand and the traditional private label. The findings of the control group were used to determine expectation values for brand choice for the premium brand and traditional private label.

At the outset of the experiment, participants could inspect the product details (price, packaging design, quantity, nutritional information, etc.) of the fruit spreads of the considered brands. Furthermore, they were able to taste the fruit spreads, so that the flavor of the fruit spreads could be considered by the subjects to assess the brands. Following this first step, the participants were surveyed with a standardized questionnaire. In this case, they were asked to evaluate the different brands based on individual product characteristics and attributes (e.g. package design, quantity, taste) and establish a ranking of their preference for the fruit spreads. All of the items used for the measurement of the different constructs were measured on a five-point rating scale (e.g. $1 = I$ totally disagree $- 5 = I$ totally agree). Finally, the participants had to answer questions regarding their satisfaction with the different brands.

Overall, $n = 120$ consumers participated in the experiment and were randomly assigned to one of the three experimental groups or the control group (age: $M = 24.48$ (2.9) years, 40% female). The brands used in the experiment were mostly well known by the participants. Thus, nearly 95% of the participants were familiar with the fruit spread of the premium brand. Almost 70% of the subjects knew the traditional private label and 46.7% of them stated that they have already bought this at least once.

4 Key Findings

To study the effects of the experimental conditions, it was necessary to determine the choice probabilities for the traditional private label as well as for the premium brand based on the preference judgments of the participants in the control group (CG). The findings of the control group show a strong preference for the traditional private label (67.9%) in relation to the premium brand (32.1%). Using these choice probabilities, we were able to analyze how these choice probabilities will be influenced by the introduction and the price manipulation of the premium private labeled brand in the participants choice set. Overall, our results show significant difference regarding the choice probability of the traditional private label in each of the three experimental conditions compared to the CG. In each experimental condition, the preference for the traditional private label decreased significantly due to the introduction of the premium private label. Interestingly and contrary to our expectations, in the experimental group with the price adjustment of the premium private label close to the premium brand, the difference between the choice probabilities was highest. In this situation, the choice probability of the traditional private label was reduced by more than 45%.

Equally surprising are the results in the experimental group with the price adjustment of the premium private label towards the traditional private label. We obtain substantial changes regarding the choice probability of the traditional private label and the premium brand compared to the control group. Basically, it was not surprising that in this experimental situation, the premium private label has the highest choice probability in comparison to the other situations. Moreover, in this experimental condition, we obtained the highest choice probability of the traditional private label (50%), although this again deviates from the value from the control group (almost −17%). 25% of the participants had a strong preference for the premium private label as well as for the premium brand.

The findings in the experimental condition, in which the official retail price is specified for the premium private label, show a change in the choice probabilities of the traditional private and for the premium brand as well. In this condition, the highest choice probability is determined for the premium private label. The traditional private label suffers in this situation a loss of about 34% compared to the control group and is chosen with a share of 33.3% of the participants. Interestingly, in this situation the premium brand loses the largest proportion compared to the other experimental groups and was chosen by 16.7% of the participants.

Moreover, the findings of several ANOVAs show significant differences regarding, e.g., the participants' assessment of value for money, the price level, the quality, packaging design, as well as the taste of the different fruit spreads between the experimental conditions. For example, adjusting the price of the premium private label towards the premium brand in the choice set had a strong negative impact on the evaluation of the different attributes of the traditional private label, e.g., on the evaluation of packaging design ($F = 2.808$, $p < 0.05$, $\eta^2 = 0.067$). Furthermore, in this experimental condition, the participants perceived the traditional private label as less imaginative ($F = 3.324$, $p < 0.05$, $\eta^2 = 0.083$) and less innovative ($F = 3.212$, $p < 0.05$, $\eta^2 = 0.079$) compared to the conditions with a lower price for the premium private labeled brand. These findings indicate that the higher the price of the premium private label, the worse the traditional private label is evaluated.

5   Discussion and Conclusions

The findings indicate that pricing is a sensitive component of a successful brand management of premium private labels, as it has a significant effect on consumer perceptions and evaluations of the related products. This concerns not only the decision to purchase or not purchase a premium private label, but also the evaluation of the product as well as of further alternatives in the choice set. At the same time, the pricing for the premium private label has a significant influence on the perception of other brands in the same product category. Moreover, the results of our study indicate that under specific contextual conditions the assumptions of the classical economic standard theory do not hold if a new option—the premium private labelled product—is added to a choice set of two existing product alternatives (traditional private label and premium brand).

As we only considered one premium private labelled product and two well-known brands in one specific product category, it is questionable whether our results can be transferred to other product categories or unknown brands. Because of this limited external validity, future research is needed to study the identified effects with different brands, including unknown and/or fictive brands, in different product categories to deepen the understanding of the underlying processes with regard to the effects on consumer-related outcome variables under study. It should also be of interest to investigate the potential role of the retail format in the context of consumer decision-making for (premium) private labels, e.g., in hard discount consumers might expressly seek for private labels, while in other formats (e.g., retailers with a broad assortment) consumers might be more likely to prefer recognized brands as the first option.

In our experimental study, we only considered a choice set consisting out of three alternative products. In a real retail setting the variety of product alternatives in a single product category is usually much more complex compared to our experimental setting, meaning that consumers might base their decision on a comparison between more product alternatives. Furthermore, in a retail store further contextual factors should also influence decision-making, e.g. background music, or advertising at the point of sale. Besides, there might be several other aspects that potentially will influence consumer decision-making for (premium) private labels, e.g., the image of the retailer or consumer price consciousness. One might conclude that the image of the retailer should act as a moderator between the pricing and consumer choice. In follow-up research, these and the previously mentioned issues should be addressed.

Moreover, the sample size of the present study was relatively small. As the sample size determines the amount of error inherent to the results of statistical testing, the effects of an experimental treatment are more difficult to identify in small samples. Hence, future research is advised to conduct similar experimental studies with larger sample sizes, which will strengthen the statistical power of the analysis and potentially help to identify more significant effects of the experimental factor on the constructs under investigation.

Last but not least, previous research in retailing and consumer behaviour shows several important differences in preferences for private labels with respect to consumer demographics and culture. Hence, the impact of pricing on the evaluation and consumer decision-making for private labels could also be influenced by culture. Therefore, cross-cultural studies could provide insights on how the pricing should be adjusted according to the preferences and requirements of the potential and actual customers based on the cultural background of the target groups in different international markets.

References

Ailawadi, K. L., Pauwels, K., & Steenkamp, J.-B. E. M. (2008). Private-label use and store loyalty. *Journal of Marketing, 72*(6), 19–30.

Burton, S., Lichtenstein, D. R., Netemeyer, R. G., & Garretson, J. A. (1998). A scale for measuring attitude toward private label products and an examination of its psychological and behavioral correlates. *Journal of the Academy of Marketing Science, 26*(4), 293–306.

De Wulf, K., Odekerken-Schröder, G., Goedertier, F., & Van Ossel, G. (2005). Consumer perceptions of store brands versus national brands. *Journal of Consumer Marketing, 22*(4), 223–232.

Doyle, J. R., O'Connor, D. J., Reynolds, G. M., & Bottomley, P. A. (1999). The robustness of the asymmetrically dominated effect: Buying frames, phantom alternatives, and in-store purchases. *Psychology and Marketing, 16*(3), 225–243.

Geyskens, I., Gielens, K., & Gijsbrechts, E. (2010). Proliferating private-label portfolios: How introducing economy and premium private labels influences brand choice. *Journal of Marketing Research, 47*(5), 791–807.

Huber, J., Payne, J. W., & Puto, C. (1982). Adding asymmetrically dominated alternatives: Violations of regularity and the similarity hypothesis. *Journal of Consumer Research, 9*(1), 90–98.

Koschate-Fischer, N., Cramer, J., & Hoyer, W. D. (2014). Moderating effects of the relationship between private label share and store loyalty. *Journal of Marketing, 78*(2), 69–82.

Kumar, N., & Steenkamp, J.-B. E. M. (2007). *Private label strategy: How to meet the store brand challange.* Boston: Harvard Business School Press.

Lichtenstein, D. R., Ridgway, N. M., & Netemeyer, R. G. (1993). Price perception and consumer shopping behavior: A field study. *Journal of Marketing, 30*(2), 234–245.

Paramesh, R. (1973). Independence of irrelevant alternatives. *Econometrica, 41*(5), 987–991.

Pauwels, K., & Srinivasan, S. (2004). Who benefits from store brand entry? *Marketing Science, 23* (3), 364–390.

Petroshius, S. M., & Monroe, K. B. (1987). Effect of product-line pricing characteristics on product evaluations. *Journal of Consumer Research, 13*(4), 511–519.

Plassmann, H., Doherty, J. O., Shiv, B., & Rangel, A. (2008). Marketing actions can modulate neural representations of experienced pleasantness. *Proceedings of the National Academy of Science of the United States of America, 105*(3), 1050–1054.

Simonson, I. (1989). Choice based on reasons: The case of attraction and compromise effects. *Journal of Consumer Research, 16*(2), 158–174.

Simonson, I., & Tversky, A. (1992). Choice in context: Tradeoff contrast and extremeness aversion. *Journal of Marketing Research, 29*(3), 281–295.

Sinha, I., & Batra, R. (1999). The effect of consumer price consciousness on private label purchase. *International Journal of Research in Marketing, 16*(3), 237–251.

Influence of PL Equity on Store Loyalty: A Comparative Analysis Between Spain and the U.S.

José Luis Ruiz-Real, Juan Carlos Gázquez-Abad, Irene Esteban-Millat, and Francisco J. Martínez-López

Abstract This research aims to know the influence of PL equity on consumers' store loyalty, both in Spain and in the U.S., for different types of assortment. We considered assortments with different size and structure (only PL and mixed) and developed an online experiment with a sample of 2800 consumers (1400 in each country). ANOVAs show differences between Spain and the U.S. regarding the influence of PL equity on store loyalty. We also find significant differences in Spain when retailers offer mixed assortments, both small and large, and the high equity NB represents only one third. These results suggest several recommendations for retailers, depending on the country and the type of assortment they choose.

Keywords Private label · Retailing · Assortment · Store loyalty · High equity

1 Introduction

Achieving customer loyalty is a strategic issue for retailers and a relevant long-term competitiveness factor. Loyal customers make more purchases at the same store, tend to be less sensitive to prices and, consequently, less likely to look for alternatives and store switching (Knox and Denison 2000). Therefore, retailers seek lasting relationships with their customers and consider consumer loyalty strategies a priority (Kotler 1994). However, there are many difficulties to achieve customer loyalty.

J. L. Ruiz-Real (✉) · J. C. Gázquez-Abad
School of Economics and Business, Agrifood Campus of International Excellence ceiA3, University of Almería, Almería, Spain
e-mail: jlruizreal@ual.es; jcgazque@ual.es

I. Esteban-Millat
School of Economics and Business, Open University of Catalonia, Barcelona, Spain
e-mail: iestebanm@uoc.edu

F. J. Martínez-López
Business School, University of Granada, Granada, Spain
e-mail: fjmlopez@ugr.es

© Springer International Publishing AG, part of Springer Nature 2018   151
F. J. Martínez-López et al. (eds.), *Advances in National Brand and Private Label Marketing*, Springer Proceedings in Business and Economics,
https://doi.org/10.1007/978-3-319-92084-9_17

Currently, cross-buying behavior among consumers between different stores, and even between different retail formats, is common (Rhee and Bell 2002). This is due, among other questions, to profound changes in retailing sector, in which there is a strong segmentation of the market and a great diversity of commercial formats (Sirohi et al. 1998).

In this environment, assortment appears as an element of strategic importance for retailers to have customer loyalty. Specifically, two factors seem to have a prominent role: (1) the size of the assortment, and (2) its composition, with the important penetration that the private label (PL) has had in recent years, which has led to its consideration as high or low equity. The concept of high and low brand value, traditionally applied exclusively to national brands (NB), is now also used in PLs, with the development of products with better image and higher quality, such as functional products or PL of Premium category (e.g. Tesco Finest, Deluxe by Lidl). Faced with this situation, it is no longer possible to treat PLs as a homogenous group of brands in relation to their quality and image among consumers (Szymanowski and Gijsbrechts 2012). The strong expansion of the PL in recent years by retailers is evident, which has led to important changes in the composition of their assortments. Even part of the literature argues that PL loyalty has a direct effect on loyalty to the retailer (Gómez and Okazaki 2007).

However, different patterns of consumer behavior may be expected depending on the characteristics of the market (Youn et al. 2001). So, we analyze the possible differences between Spain and the U.S., given the clearly different characteristics of these markets (PL market share in Spain in 2017 was 41%, considerably higher than in the U.S., 16.6%). In addition, the assortment (in terms of size and composition) may be a determining factor to consumer behavior. Thus, this paper analyzes the influence of PL equity on consumer loyalty towards the store, both in Spain and in the U.S., considering assortments with different size and structure (PL only and mixed-assortments). An online experiment was developed in both countries. Results show significant differences between Spain and the U.S., and even in the Spanish market, depending on the type of assortment.

2   Literature Review and Hypotheses

Store loyalty has been measured differently by previous studies, but usually following a multidimensional approach, and also considering both behaviors and attitudes (Smith et al. 2003). Thus, we can explain it as a behavioural response of consumers towards a certain brand or store, over time, which implies patterns of repetition of purchase, and relative volume of purchase in the same place (Dunn and Wrigley 1984). Dick and Basu (1994) explain store loyalty by adding attitudinal elements, such as affection towards a specific brand or store. It has been also found a direct relationship between consumers' perception of assortment variety and their intention to be loyal to the store (Verhoef et al. 2007).

Brand equity is defined as the added value that a name or a brand brings to a specific product, store or retailer (Farquhar 1989). Chandon et al. (2000) distinguish between high and low equity brands. A brand has high equity if consumers react more favourably to a product when the brand is identified, than when it does not. Brand equity is a relevant element to generate competitive advantages not based on price; thus, a high brand equity means that consumers have strong and positive associations related to that brand, perceive the brand as high quality and develop loyalty towards it. On the other hand, the main reason for buying a brand with low equity is its low price. To measure the brand equity in the field of marketing, various methods are used, which include concepts such as level of awareness, sales volume, market share or consumer's quality perception (Keller 2003). As consumers are more committed to high equity brands than low equity ones, they are likely to value those assortments that have a high proportion of high equity brands (Kahn and Lehmann 1991). Anyway, retailers offer both types of brands, high and low equity, in their assortments, so their customers can meet heterogeneous needs (Hoch et al. 1999).

With respect to the *capacity of PL to generate store loyalty*, there are different streams in the literature. On the one hand, there are those who consider that PL buyers have a very high awareness of value and, therefore, have a greater sensitivity to prices (Hoch et al. 1999), which leads them to search for alternatives and be less loyal to the retailer and to the store (Hansen and Singh 2008). On the other hand, there are those who understand that PL brings exclusivity to retailers, which allows them to generate loyalty towards the chain (Ailawadi et al. 2008) and increases store loyalty, among other advantages (Steenkamp and Gielens 2003). A positive image of the PL helps companies be more competitive and encourages consumers to repurchase the same PL and, therefore, to repurchase at the same store (Porter and Claycomb 1997). Corstjens and Lal (2000) even recommend retailers to introduce high equity PL in their assortments, due to its ability to generate store loyalty.

3 Methodology and Results

We developed a controlled online experiment with a sample of 2800 individuals belonging to two large consumer panels in Spain and the U.S., owned by IRI Worldwide. On the Spanish panel, 1400 individuals (59.7% female, 40.3% male) ranged in age from 24 to 65 (average 41.75), and on the U.S. panel, also 1400 individuals (73% female, 27% male) were aged 24 to 79 (average 52.9), all of them responsible for buying food products, cleaning and personal care products at their homes. IRI panel is statistically representative of the population of both countries, both in terms of socio-demographic variables (gender, age, income level, education level, family size), and geographical distribution. The experiment has been replicated exactly in both countries, only differing the brands in the assortments.

In this experiment, two relevant aspects of the assortment variety were considered: size and composition. With respect to the first, three different assortment sizes

Table 1 ANOVA analysis (Spain)

Assortment	F	Sig.
PL only	1688	.195
Small and 1/3 high equity NB	5728	.017
Small and 2/3 high equity NB	1681	.196
Large and 1/3 high equity NB	4765	.030
Large and 2/3 high equity NB	1370	.243

are considered: one brand; four brands (small), and ten brands (large). The definitions of "small" and "large" assortments are based on previous experiments (Chernev 2003). As for the composition of the assortment, this included either only PL (assortments with a single brand), or mixed assortments, with PL and NB (assortments with 4 and with 10 brands). Additionally, assortment varied according to the PL brand equity (high-equity vs. low-equity) and the proportion of NB high equity (one third, or two thirds). In total, therefore, ten different scenarios were shown to consumers during the experiment. The experiment was conducted in four product categories, classified according to the typology developed in Dhar et al. (2001).[1]

Within each condition, brands presented in Spain and the U.S. were classified and selected according to their market share in each country and the rating given by IRI to each brand. From this information, we selected Hacendado (food products) and Bosque Verde (personal care and cleaning products) (Mercadona) and Great Value (Walmart) as high-equity PLs in the Spanish and the U.S. experiment, respectively; Auchan (Alcampo) and Kroger (food products) and Home Sense (personal care and cleaning products) (Kroger) were used as low-equity PL in the Spanish and the U.S. markets, respectively. Individuals were randomized to the different scenarios. The final number of individuals for each type of variety was 35. Considering that the experiment was carried out in four product categories, the total number of individuals for each type of assortment combination was 140. Therefore, we worked with a total sample of 1400 individuals both in Spain and in the U.S. After viewing an online presentation of the assortment, respondents filled out a questionnaire that assessed several aspects. To analyze customer loyalty we used a single-item, five-point scale (Rossiter 2002) on which respondents assessed the probability of switching to another store for future purchases of category and shopping-basket. To measure store-switching intentions, we used a 5-point Likert scale.[2]

To evaluate the response and loyalty of consumers towards the store, based on different compositions and sizes of the assortment, we performed an ANOVA analysis of variance. This method allows us to compare several means in different situations and, in this case, it will allow us to know the influence of the inclusion of high equity NB and in the different assortments. The results obtained are presented in Tables 1 (Spain) and 2 (U.S.).

---

[1]We selected the following four product categories: yoghurt (staples), fresh bread and rolls (niches), toilet tissue (variety enhancers) and laundry detergent (fill-ins).

[2]1—Definitely continue shopping in this store; 5—Definitely go to another store.

Table 2 ANOVA analysis (U.S.)

Assortment	F	Sig.
PL only	1311	.253
Small and 1/3 high equity NB	1504	.221
Small and 2/3 high equity NB	046	.830
Large and 1/3 high equity NB	085	.771
Large and 2/3 high equity NB	761	.384

Table 3 Summary of the significance values of the ANOVA analysis

Type of assortment	Sig. Spain	Sig. U.S.
PL only	.195	.253
Small and 1/3 high equity NB	**.017**	.221
Small and 2/3 high equity NB	.196	.830
Large and 1/3 high equity NB	**.030**	.771
Large and 2/3 high equity NB	.243	.384

Significant values are bolded

Results show significant differences between Spain and the U.S. regarding the influence of PL equity on store loyalty. In Spain, there are scenarios where the existence of high equity PL has influence on consumer loyalty to the store and others where it does not. However, we do not find these differences in the U.S., where its influence is not significant in any of the scenarios analysed. Specifically, the scenarios in the Spanish market where introducing a high-equity PL influences store loyalty are mixed assortments, both small and large, where high equity NB represents only one third of such assortments. Table 3 summarizes ANOVAs results (p-values) for all the scenarios analyzed in Spain and the U.S.

4 Conclusions and Managerial Implications

Based on our findings, introducing high equity PL has different consequences on store loyalty, showing important differences depending on both country and assortment configuration.

Regarding the Spanish market, the fact that the existence of high value PL does not affect the loyalty of stores with *assortments of a single brand (PL only)* could be due to customers of this type of stores, normally linked to the format discount, have a greater awareness of value and sensitivity to price, so that they are more faithful to the commercial format itself and to a specific purchasing behavior (search for low prices) than to a certain brand, even if it is of high equity. Thus, our recommendation for these retailers would be they only focus their customer loyalty actions on low and competitive pricing strategies.

In addition, the existence of high equity PL does not influence the store loyalty when it comes to *assortments in which most of the NB (two thirds) are of high equity.* This may be because these types of consumers are more likely to acquire NB, with the PL having relative importance. Normally, these retailers are characterized by having a greater commitment to quality and including brands of prestige. Hence the existence, or not, of high equity PL is not so influential on customer loyalty. Therefore, our recommendation is reinforce their commitment to brands of high reputation and all those elements that improve the store image, as all this can lead to strengthening customer loyalty. We also suggest offering a high equity PL, since consumers will expect, consistently with the quality of the brands of the assortment, a high equity store brand.

However, in scenarios with mixed assortments, whether small or large, where *only one third of the NB is high equity,* the existence of high equity PL does offer significant differences in terms of consumer loyalty. Thus, when consumers are faced with these assortments the fact of having a high equity PL will increase the store loyalty. This suggests that the PL does play a relevant role in this type of assortment, whose customers seek a balance between price and quality. Having a high equity PL facilitates the process of choice and store loyalty. Our recommendation to achieve store loyalty is develop a high equity PL, betting on quality, innovation and a good communication strategy of these brands. We think that the strategy of these retailers should focus on maintaining a balanced assortment, with a high equity PL, while paying attention to offer competitive prices, as relevant factors to achieve store loyalty. Retailers should capitalize their retail shelves, offering high equity brands, both PL and NB, that are well positioned among consumers and offer medium-high sales volume.

Regarding the U.S., no significant differences are obtained in any of the analyzed scenarios, neither PL only, nor mixed, whether small or large, which indicates that the PL equity in the U.S. could not be a determining factor for store loyalty. This difference with respect to the Spanish market could probably be due to the lower level of preference and market share of PL in the U.S., since in Spain PL have achieved a level of notoriety and significant market share, and this is appreciated by consumers. In addition, hard discount format has a long tradition in the U.S. and consumers are used to varying their purchases among several retailers.

This paper has some constraints, where we highlight we do not differentiate by product categories. It would be interesting to analyze if there are significant differences, in both countries, according to the type of product.

References

Ailawadi, K. L., Pauwels, K., & Steenkamp, J. B. (2008). Private label use and store loyalty. *Journal of Marketing, 72*(6), 19–30.

Chandon, P., Wansink, B., & Laurent, G. (2000). A benefit congruency framework of sales promotion effectiveness. *Journal of Marketing, 64*(4), 65–81.

Chernev, A. (2003). When more is less and less is more: The role of ideal point availability and assortment in consumer choice. *Journal of Consumer Research, 30*(2), 170–183.

Corstjens, M., & Lal, R. (2000). Building store loyalty through store brands. *Journal of Marketing Research, 37*(3), 281–292.

Dhar, S. K., Hoch, S. J., & Kumar, N. (2001). Effective category management depends on the role of the category. *Journal of Retailing, 77*(2), 165–184.

Dick, A., & Basu, K. (1994). Customer loyalty: Toward an integrated conceptual framework. *Journal of the Academy of Marketing Science, 22*, 99–114.

Dunn, R., & Wrigley, N. (1984). Store loyalty for grocery products: An empirical study. *Area, 16* (4), 307–314.

Farquhar, P. H. (1989). Managing brand equity. *Marketing Research, 1*, 24–33.

Gómez, M., & Okazaki, S. (2007). Estimating store brand shelf space: A new framework using neural networks and partial least squares. *International Journal of Market Research, 51*(2), 243–266.

Hansen, K., & Singh, V. (2008). Are store-brand buyers store loyal? An empirical investigation. *Management Science, 54*(10), 1828–1834.

Hoch, S., Bradlow, E. T., & Wansink, B. (1999). The variety of an assortment. *Marketing Science, 18*(4), 527–546.

Kahn, B. E., & Lehmann, D. R. (1991). Modeling choice among assortments. *Journal of Retailing, 67*(3), 274–299.

Keller, K. L. (2003). *Strategic brand management* (2nd ed.). New Jersey: Prentice Hall.

Knox, S., & Denison, T. (2000). Store loyalty: Its impact on retail revenue. An empirical study of purchasing behaviour in the UK. *Journal of Retailing and Consumer Services, 7*, 33–45.

Kotler, P. (1994). *Marketing management, analysis, planning, implementation and control* (8th ed.). Englewood Cliffs, NJ: Prentice Hall.

Porter, S. S., & Claycomb, C. (1997). The influence of brand recognition on retail store image. *Journal of Product and Brand Management, 6*(6), 373–385.

Rhee, H., & Bell, D. (2002). The inter-store mobility of supermarket shoppers. *Journal of Retailing, 78*, 225–237.

Rossiter, J. R. (2002). The C-OAR-SE procedure for scale development in marketing. *International Journal of Research in Marketing, 19*(4), 305–303.

Sirohi, N., McLaughlin, E., & Wittink, D. (1998). A model of consumer perceptions and store loyalty intentions for a supermarket retailer. *Journal of Retailing, 74*(2), 223–245.

Smith, A., Sparks, L., Hart, S., & Tzokas, N. (2003). Retail loyalty schemes: Results from a consumer diary study. *Journal of Retailing and Consumer Services, 10*, 109–119.

Steenkamp, J. E. M., & Gielens, K. (2003). Consumer and market drivers of the trial probability of new consumer packaged goods. *Journal of Consumer Research, 30*(3), 368–384.

Szymanowski, M., & Gijsbrechts, E. (2012). Consumption-based cross-brand learning: Are private labels really private? *Journal of Marketing Research, 49*(2), 231–246.

Verhoef, P., Langerak, F., & Donkers, B. (2007). Understanding brand and dealer retention in the new car market: The moderating role of brand tier. *Journal of Retailing, 83*(1), 97–113.

Youn, S., Sun, T., & Wells, W. D. (2001). Commercial liking and memory: Moderating effects of product categories. *Journal of Advertising Research, 41*(1), 7–13.

Part IV
Modelling and Theoretical Research

Can Stochastic Availability Predict Private Label Shares? Modelling Approach and Preliminary Results

Yutian Shen and Jack Cadeaux

Abstract Unless buying on-line, consumers only buy retail products from stores at which they shop. The objective of this paper is to answer the following research question: Can the realized availability of private label products, given their exclusive distribution, combined with consumer shopping patterns across multiple stores, when combined with revealed preferences from brand choices, be used to predict private label shares? By addressing this question, we hope to use a stochastic choice model approach to better understand the relationship between the exclusive distribution of private label brands and their market share by refining the measurement of distribution to account for their purchase occasion-specific availability.

Keywords Private labels · Exclusive distribution · Stochastic availability · Market share

1 Introduction

Highly aggregated measures of distribution do not generally capture the availability of products faced by different consumers on shopping trips. Jeuland (1979) and Bruno and Vilcassim (2008), examined effects of distribution on market share by considering consumer choice. Planned availability, even apart from stock-outs, means that some products may only be available in some stores. Arguably, the market share of brands depends on consumer preferences and whether the brands are available at the stores at which a shopper shops. This matter is quite general and problematic for national brands whose distribution status varies across brands and over time. For some brands and in some periods, national brand distribution can be quite intensive. In other cases, it can be much more selective. For fast moving consumer goods (FMCGs), it is rare, although possible, for national brands to

Y. Shen (✉) · J. Cadeaux
School of Marketing, University of New South Wales, Sydney, NSW, Australia
e-mail: yutian.shen@unsw.edu.au; j.cadeaux@unsw.edu.au

© Springer International Publishing AG, part of Springer Nature 2018
F. J. Martínez-López et al. (eds.), *Advances in National Brand and Private Label Marketing*, Springer Proceedings in Business and Economics,
https://doi.org/10.1007/978-3-319-92084-9_18

161

engage in exclusive distribution (Gielens et al. 2014). However, private labels present a special archetypical case, since their distribution is purely exclusive. That is, each retailer stocks only its private labels and not those of competitors. The converse is also true: one retailer only distributes each private label. This 1-1 correspondence between private labels and retailers is the defining feature of such brands.

Early studies made strong assumptions about consumer store loyalty, store size, store shopping patterns, brand independence in distribution, and purchase rates. This paper relaxes most of these assumptions and aims to answer the following research question: How can the realized availability of private label products, given their exclusive distribution combined with consumer shopping patterns across multiple stores, when combined with revealed preferences from brand choices, be used to predict private label shares? It uses a stochastic availability model that considers the essentially exclusive distribution of private labels. It tests the model with IRI (Information Resources Inc.) scanner panel data (Bronnenberg et al. 2008). It does this analysis for the laundry detergent, paper towels, and milk product categories with a benchmark comparison against naïve ACV-based predictions that managers are much more likely to be able to use in practice.

2 Stochastic Models of Store and Brand Choice

Stochastic models examine how consumers choose brands. By examining choices across purchase occasions, they reveal aggregate brand switching patterns and variations in choice probabilities. Most such models do not consider distribution and tend to assume that products are always available. Early on, analysts argued that a macro model of market share should include distribution and consider heterogeneity (Bass and Pilon 1980). As far as we know, to date, Jeuland (1979) and Bruno and Vilcassim (2008) are the only studies that present such models.

Jeuland (1979) considered brand availability within choice models instead of assuming that all brands are identically distributed across stores. He included unobserved heterogeneity in brand availability to account for this phenomenon. He begins with a random consumer choice model with preference strength related to consumers' choices across available brands. Choice probability depends on preference strength. Then, he integrates the individual consumer into the aggregate levels of market share, brand repeat buying, and brand-switching. This macro-model considers the heterogeneity of the population based on preference strength. The probability distribution of the quantity an individual consumer chooses is a function of the purchase rate of the product category, average quantity bought in each purchase occasion, and the probability of brand choice. Because of the assumption of independence, market share depends only on the expected value of brand choice. Jeuland (1979) thus incorporates distribution as unobserved availability. Jeuland's model also makes strict assumptions—namely, that a consumer always visits a certain store and has an "average" rate of purchase (i.e., are neither significantly heavier nor lighter buyers), that all outlets are equal in size, stock a brand independently of other brands, and have equal patronage.

Bruno and Vilcassim (2008) extend the traditional discrete-choice-based demand estimation method developed in Berry et al. (1995). They relax the availability assumption to correct the demand parameters. Their model uses information on *aggregate* availability to *simulate* the potential assortments that consumers may face when shopping. To measure aggregate availability, they use all-commodity volume (ACV) weighted retail distribution as the aggregate availability variable. Bruno and Vilcassim (2008) still use aggregate levels of retail distribution, rather than observing what is planned to be sold in each store on a purchase occasion. Yet it is easy to capture store-level distribution by observing it as implicit in panel data. This approach could substitute partially for ACV-weighted distribution scores.

Cadeaux (1997) questions Jeuland's (1979) assumptions about store choice and availability and describes store choice as preceding brand choice. Then, he combines the two into a revised availability model. That model assumes that distribution should capture product availability for a consumer at a *specific store-shopping occasion*. In this sense, store choice "precedes" brand choice. Although this assumption may be safe for many FMCG categories and for many FMCG national brands, it would seem to be ideally suited to private labels, although that assumption may not hold equally across categories. A very simple way to explore this question is to consider categories with widely varying private label shares.

3   Assumptions and Model Overview

The new model used here also makes a wide range of assumptions. It assumes that brand choice is substantially stochastic and that not all brands in the choice set are available in each shopping trip but that only a subset of all brands of the category choice set is available. It also assumes that a consumer's purchase rate, average quantity bought per purchase occasion, and the consumer choice probabilities are independently distributed. But is also assumes that a consumer does not always shop in one store and that consumers have different, albeit unobserved, preferences across different stores. The overall size of the clientele of these outlets is also assumed not to be significantly different from that of any other store. Thus, it does use a store weighting factor such as ACV or PCV. It assumes that the customers of these outlets are neither significantly heavier nor lighter buyers of the category; that is, each store attracts the same usage rate segment. Most importantly it assumes that consumers choose stores *before* they choose a brand or SKU and that these two steps are independent. A given product is not present in the distribution status matrix when there is no purchase of this product during the observed week in the aggregate scanned panel data. An assumption that unobserved individual preference strength follows a Gamma distribution, implies that the choice probability vector follows a Dirichlet distribution.

To describe how FMCG brands are purchased in the market, Dirichlet models are usually built when the market is stationary and unsegmented. In these markets, we commonly believe that there is little variation in brand sales and little obvious grouping for different brands in a category over a period. That assumption may or may not apply in a category that contains both national and private label brands. Specifically, we assume that purchase incidence and brand choice follow a mixture of distributions at four levels in the Dirichlet model. For purchase incidence, it is assumed that individual successive purchase behavior is random and independent across purchase occasions in a certain period (usually 1 week). This succession period chosen is equal and non-overlapping. The number of product-category purchases for an individual is assumed to follow a Poisson distribution. The purchasing rates for varying individuals take the form of the Gamma distribution. Therefore, the aggregate number of purchases of the product made by all individuals in a long period follows a Negative Binomial Distribution (NBD) (Goodhardt et al. 1984). The brand choices of an individual are assumed to be random over purchase occasions and the probabilities of choosing a given brand are fixed over time and independent over successive purchases. In addition, the number of purchases of a certain brand by one individual in a sequence of purchases follows a multinomial distribution (Wilks 1962). The choice probabilities for varying individuals follow a multivariate Beta or Dirichlet distribution. Here a Beta distribution is selected for choice probabilities because of its flexibility, tractability and successful applicability in various stochastic buyer behavior models. Therefore, the purchases of different brands by all individuals follow a mixture of a multinomial with a Dirichlet distribution (Goodhardt et al. 1984).

Briefly, the empirical analysis proceeds by observing a store repeat-switching matrix. This is used to estimate a store choice preference vector. Then, we observe the in-store distribution status. For example, we construct at the brand level, a (0, 1) distribution status matrix to indicates which stores stock which brand for the product category in each period where the status is 1 if there is a purchase record of this brand in each week over the period at the observed stores and 0 otherwise. We develop an aggregate distribution status matrix across weeks for each brand at every store based on weekly distribution status records. As a third step, an availability measure is developed by considering store preference (step 1) and brand distribution status (step 2); as the fourth step, by observing and calculating a brand repeat or switching matrix, brand choice preference is generated. Last, revised estimates for brand shares are obtained according to the availability measure (step 3) and the brand choice preference (step 4).

4   Preliminary Results

Table 1 shows the preliminary results of the model for private label brands only. The first column displays the actual market shares of the private label brands in each category. The second column shows the "naïve" predictions of an ACV model that

Table 1 Actual and predicted private label market shares

PL brand	Actual share (%)	ACV prediction (%)	Availability model (%)
Detergent PL a	0.55	1.10	0.11
Detergent PL b	0.59	0.49	0.18
Detergent PL c	0.04	0.06	0
Detergent PL d	0.04	0.08	0
Detergent PL e	1.91	1.41	1.30
Milk PL a	13.19	17.89	5.74
Milk PL b	12.04	7.93	5.57
Milk PL c	0	0.92	0
Milk PL d	0.55	1.23	0.05
Milk PL e	25.09	22.92	15.22
Paper towels PL a	4.4	5.48	2.49
Paper towels PL b	2.8	2.43	0.87
Paper towels PL c	0.4	0.28	0.02
Paper towels PL d	0.6	0.38	0.05
Paper towels PL e	7.4	7.02	4.57

Table 2 Some illustrative model fit statistics

Product context	ACV prediction (MSE)	Availability model (MSE)
Fifteen private labels of three categories in this paper	0.000314	0.001411
Four national brands of laundry detergent in another related study	0.101771	0.024143
Six national brands of paper towels in another related study	0.092510	0.029566

simply projects store ACV shares against the most recent historical aggregate share of PL sales in the category [i.e., Predicted share of store i PL = (ACV for store i) * (PL share of category sales)]. Finally, the third column shows the predictions of the new stochastic availability model. Given five retailers in the market and the fact each retailer in this market offers one PL brand in each category, Table 1 displays the results for five PL brands in each category. The categories were chosen because (a) they are among the categories for which scanner panel data were available, (b) that are categories that consist of well-defined sets of substitutes, and (c) they represent a wide range of PL brand penetration. The first category, laundry detergent, has a very low PL share of total category sales (3.13%), the second, milk, has a very high PL share (50.87%), while the third, paper towels, has a moderate overall PL share (15.60%). The ACV shares for the five stores are as follows: store 1 (35.16%), store 2 (15.58%), store 3 (1.80%), store 4 (2.41%) and store 5 (45.05%).

To demonstrate fit, Table 2 presents the average mean squared errors (MSEs) for three sets of products: the 15 private label products in three categories from this study and two other sets of national brand products from another larger study in this project. Clearly, the higher MSEs show that the quite complex availability model used here does not fit as well as a naïve ACV model for the private label products. However, for the national brands in a related study, it does fit much better than a naïve ACV model. It thus seems that *any* sort of distribution-based model predicts market share much better for private labels than it does for national brands, not doubt due to their one-to-one exclusivity. However, a preliminary yet clear conclusion would be that there is little to be gained by using a more sophisticated stochastic choice availability model to predict *private label* shares. A much more naïve model does quite well, if not much better. Nevertheless, there is much to be gained by using a more sophisticated stochastic availability model for *national brands*, the complete evidence for which is contained in another related study.

Several observations arise from these preliminary results. First, it is important to note that the PL shares and the predictions arise in categories that are dominated by national brands, except for milk for which PL brands slightly dominate. The results show that the new stochastic availability model always tends to under-predict overall PL share and shares for each PL entry. It is possible to speculate on some reasons for this. One might be that a sophisticated availability model simply makes more sense for national brands than for private labels in the sense that while store choice may "precede" brand choice for national brands, private label brands, as exclusive brands, are not only exclusive in distribution but create in a sub-segment in the category or a market partition (Grover and Srinivasan 1987). That is, in a general sense, shoppers, unless highly brand loyal, may plan a basic category purchase for goods such as detergent, milk, and paper towels, then make a brand choice that is restricted to the choice set on offer at the store. Private label buyers may be a *different segment* in the sense that they *jointly* plan a brand and category purchase. In which case, a naïve ACV model is a reasonably sufficient predictor for their market share. Nevertheless, it is also clear, that in the big picture, distribution no matter how modelled, means more for private labels than for national brands whose market share results depend also on other marketing mix factors.

This work is part of a much larger application of this stochastic availability model for national brands and national brand SKUs, which compares its performance against a range of models of increasing complexity. We hope that that larger study will shed further light on some aspects of the problem discussed here.

References

Bass, F. M., & Pilon, T. L. (1980). A stochastic brand choice framework for econometric modeling of time series market share behavior. *Journal of Marketing Research, 17*(4), 486–497.

Berry, S., Levinsohn, J., & Pakes, A. (1995). Automobile prices in market equilibrium. *Econometrica: Journal of the Econometric Society, 63*(4), 841–890.

Bronnenberg, B. J., Kruger, M. W., & Mela, C. F. (2008). Database paper – The IRI marketing data set. *Marketing Science, 27*(4), 745–748.

Bruno, H. A., & Vilcassim, N. J. (2008). Research note-structural demand estimation with varying product availability. *Marketing Science, 27*(6), 1126–1131.

Cadeaux, J. M. (1997). Distribution status, brand availability, and market share. In *Paper Presented at the 9th International Conference on Research in the Distributive Trades*. Belgium: Katholieke Universiteit Leuven, Leuven.

Gielens, K., Gijsbrechts, E., & Dekimpe, M. G. (2014). Gains and losses of exclusivity in grocery retailing. *International Journal of Research in Marketing, 31*(3), 239–252.

Goodhardt, G. J., Ehrenberg, A. S., & Chatfield, C. (1984). The dirichlet: A comprehensive model of buying behaviour. *Journal of the Royal Statistical Society. Series A (General), 147*(5), 621–655.

Grover, R., & Srinivasan, V. (1987). A simultaneous approach to market segmentation and market structuring. *Journal of Marketing Research, 24*(2), 139–153.

Jeuland, A. P. (1979). The interaction effect of preference and availability on brand switching and market share. *Management Science, 25*(10), 953–965.

Wilks, S. S. (1962). *Mathematical statistics*. New York: Wiley.

A Bibliometric Analysis of the Private Label Literature

Marcello Sansone, Annarita Colamatteo, and Maria Anna Pagnanelli

Abstract This work analyses a dataset of 567 papers (from 1990 to 2017) about private label and store brand, providing a framework of the scientific literature in terms of trends in publications over time, the most productive and most cited authors, and the most relevant scientific journals. Moreover, an analysis of the co-occurrence of the keywords, synthesized in a co-word map, provides a representation of the content of the research about the private label and defines the cognitive structure of the field, involving information about the core topic, the active research fronts and emerging topics.

The results show an increasing relevance of the private label literature over time, the main core of research that concerns the determinants and model for private label purchase, and numerous aspects that can be explored in research about the private label.

Keywords Private label · Store brand · Bibliometric analysis · Co-occurrence · Co-word analysis

1 Introduction

Despite the uncertainty of the macroeconomic scenario, in recent years the private label has shown great vitality, establishing itself as a key factor for the retail industry. The private label arises at the centre of the relationship with the customer and assumes a great role within the economic system in terms of investment, employment and support for companies and small and medium-sized enterprises. The performance data at the European level highlight the strategic relevance of the private label in consumption dynamics and the increasing role in the market over

M. Sansone (✉) · A. Colamatteo · M. A. Pagnanelli
University of Cassino and Southern Lazio, Cassino, Italy
e-mail: m.sansone@unicas.it; a.colamatteo@unicas.it; mariaanna.pagnanelli@unicas.it

© Springer International Publishing AG, part of Springer Nature 2018   169
F. J. Martínez-López et al. (eds.), *Advances in National Brand and Private Label Marketing*, Springer Proceedings in Business and Economics,
https://doi.org/10.1007/978-3-319-92084-9_19

time [in 1990, the private label market share was 21% (Nielsen); in 2016, it was 44% (PLMA)].

The literature on the subject of the private label has addressed several topics: the definition and its evolution over time (Cristini 1992; Fornari 2007; Pastore et al. 2007; Castaldo et al. 2013); the determinants of market share (Lamey et al. 2007; Rubio and Yague 2009; Sethuraman and Gielens 2014); the role of the private label in the management policies of retailers and in the retail marketing mix levers (Ailawadi and Keller 2004; Fornari 2009; Lugli 2003); and the consumer behaviour, purchase preferences and the factors that influence consumer choices (Ailawadi et al. 2001; Dalli and Romani 2003; Sprott and Shimp 2004; De Wulf et al. 2005; Dolekoglu et al. 2008).

Considering the importance of this topic, we implement a bibliometric analysis of contributions to the literature on the private label that aims at identifying the most studied issues and the emerging topics under consideration, useful for both academics and managers (Galvagno 2011).

The relevance of the bibliometric analysis of scientific studies is underlined by literature. Firstly, the studies within this discipline start from the scientific contribution of Alan Pritchard, who in 1969 proposed the introduction of the term 'bibliometric' to indicate "*the application of mathematics and statistical methods to books and other forms of written communication*". The definition of 'bibliometric' over time (British Standard Institution 1976; Fairthorne 1969; Burton 1988; Tague-Sutcliffe 1992) has not changed substantially from that provided by Pritchard; in fact, researchers define the objectives, the instruments and the topic under study to delineate the current role of bibliometrics in the quantitative analysis of large-scale scientific products. A bibliometric analysis can also instigate citation analysis and a content analysis methodology. This methodology can be summarized using maps representing the topic being researched; such activity is considered a proven research methodology, and the application of bibliometrics is useful to outline the research branches, the recurring themes and emerging aspects. A map of science is a two- and three-dimensional representation of a research branch (Noyons 2004), whose elements are the topics or themes of the same mapped research branches.

For the construction of such maps, bibliometrics uses the principle of co-occurrence of bibliographic elements. Where more than two elements appear together in the same document, then the probability is greater that they have a structural correlation with the concepts characteristic of that research branch; their position on the map is represented by neighbouring points (De Bellis 2005).

To identify what are the most studied issues and the most important topics in relation to the private label, we carry out a bibliometric analysis; such an analysis can be used by scholars and managers to understand the growing strategic role of the private label within the retail industry.

2 Methodology

This paper aims to detect what are the most studied issues and emerging topics in research on the private label through a bibliometric analysis of literature.

In general, analysis of the intellectual structure and evolution of a science (or a research branch) is believed to be useful for both academics and managers: for the scholars, the utility resides in the ability to place their own research in a field well delineated and to identify new ways to progress and new opportunities; for the managers, it may provide guidance on the development of the conceptual foundation on which practical knowledge essential to their profession is developed (Galvagno 2011).

Therefore, on these premises, it is useful to outline the current state of research on the private label through a descriptive bibliometric analysis of 567 papers, aimed at detecting temporal trends in scientific publications, the most relevant authors, the most cited authors, the most important journals and the most used keywords. The selection process for the contributions to the literature was performed on the Web of Science database using the keyword "private label/s" or "store brand/s" as the main topic of the article and sorting results according to the increasing number of citations over time.

The same dataset was analysed through VosViewer, a leading software for the construction of bibliographic maps and networks, processing research maps according to the methodology of co-word analysis.

Such maps represent better than others the content of research contributions and the cognitive structure of a scientific field (Courtial et al. 1984), since they provide information about the core topic, namely the active research fronts within a scientific theme and emerging topics. It is also helpful to understand the network of correlations between primary, secondary and emerging topics that goes beyond the simple content analysis of research contributions.

The implication behind this methodology is that being able to map the co-occurrences and the frequency with which they recur within the most relevant papers on the subject is useful in classifying how many and which research branches emerge and what are the most studied aspects of the keyword's topic.

3 Results and Discussion

To define products sold by retailers with their name or the brand owned by the retail companies, the terms 'private label' and 'store brand' are the most frequently used in international literature. Therefore, to perform a descriptive bibliometric analysis and a co-word analysis, a double level of selection of papers has been made ex ante.

The first selection of the papers was performed on the database Web of Science, using the keywords "private label" or "private labels" as the principal topic and sorting results according to the increasing number of citations over time: 370 papers are identified.

Hereinafter are the results of the descriptive bibliometric analysis performed, summarized according to trends in scientific publications over time, most productive and most cited authors, and the most important scientific journal.

The first results of the analysis refer to the temporal distribution of the 370 publications analysed. From 1990 to 2017, the number of publications per year on the topic of the private label registers a trend which is definitely growing, reaching the maximum number in the year 2015 (#49) and maintaining over the last 5 years an average number per year higher than previously. This trend is confirmed by the relative number of publications, in relation to the total number of publications in the dataset, which highlights the exponential increase in research contributions on the private label over time.

The second point of the results is related to the most relevant authors of research on the private label. To that effect, two indexes were considered: the number of published contributions on the subject and the number of citations of each author. In particular, referring mainly to the latter indicator and considering the relevance of citations, Hoch, Ailawadi and Narasimhan emerge, along with a larger number of authors with fewer citations around the same average. We also noted a correlation between the number of papers published and the number of citations obtained.

Following the same criterion, the most relevant journals and book series on the topic of the private label are considered. In terms of the number of publications on this topic among the total publications in the journals, in first place, there is a specializing Springer series, *Advances in National Brand and Private Label Marketing*, followed by the *Journal of Marketing* and the *Journal of Retailing*. In terms of citations, the *Journal of Marketing* and the *Journal of Retailing* considerably outdistance other journals. The rest achieve a decreasing number of citations, with minor differences between values.

Due to the frequency of use of the term 'store brand' as synonymous with 'private label', the analysis presented thus far was replicated for 197 selected papers from the Web of Science using the keywords "store brand" or "store brands" as the principal topic of the paper and sorting the results according to the increasing number of citations over time.

The first results of the analysis are related to the temporal distribution of the 197 analysed publications. From 1992 to 2017, the number of publications per year on the topic of store brand recorded a significant growing trend, reaching the maximum number in the year 2015 (#25) and maintaining for the past 3 years an average number per year higher than previously.

This trend is confirmed by the relative number of publications (in relation to the total number of publications in the dataset), which highlights the exponential increase of research contributions on store brand from 2010 to the present.

The second point of the results is related to the most relevant authors of researches on store brand. To that effect, two indexes were considered: the number of published contributions on the subject and the number of citations of each author.

Table 1 Indicators of private label literature

Indicator	Keyword: Private label	Keyword: Store brand
Publication per years	Significant increase since 2010	Significant increase since 2008
Relative publication volume	Exponential increase since 2010	Exponential increase since 2013
Productive authors (first three)	Nenycz-Thiel; Amrouche; Beneke	Rubio; Diallo; Gonzalez-Benito
Most cited authors (first three)	Hoch; Ailawadi; Narasimhan	Richardson; Ailawadi; Verhoef
Relevant journals (first three)	*Advances in National Brand and Private Label Marketing*; *Journal of Retailing*; *Journal of Marketing*	*Journal of Retailing*; *Marketing Science*; *International Journal of Retail and Distribution Management*
Most cited journals (first three)	*Journal of Marketing*; *Journal of Retailing*; *Marketing Science*	*Journal of Retailing*; *Journal of Marketing*; *Marketing Science*

According to the latter criterion, the most relevant authors are Richardson, Ailawadi, Verhoef, Dhar and Raju. In this case, there is a correlation between the number of papers published and the number of citations obtained.

Following the same approach, the most relevant journals and book series in terms of store brand are considered. This reveals different results from the previous analysis: in terms of number of publications on this topic in total publications in the journals, at the top of the ranking are the *Journal of Retailing*, *Marketing Science* and the *International Journal of Retail and Distribution Management*. In terms of citations, the *Journal of Marketing*, the *Journal of Retailing* and *Marketing Science* are at the top with a very similar average number of citations.

All the results described are summarized in Table 1.

The same papers (unified in a single database, eliminating repetitions and considering the first 500 papers) are analysed through VOSviewer, a leading software for the construction of bibliographic maps and networks, to develop a map of the research according to the methodology of co-word analysis, aimed at highlighting graphically the main topic studied by prevailing literature related to the terms 'private label' and 'store brand'.

Since the latter aspect is considered very important to identify the main topic analysed by literature and the emerging aspects for future research, a textual analysis of the keyword was conducted.

Figure 1 reveals a main core of research linked to the terms 'private label/s' and 'store brand/s', which highlights the frequent comparison with national brands and the core of research about perceptions of private label products and certain factors that determine performance and competition, such as quality, price or loyalty.

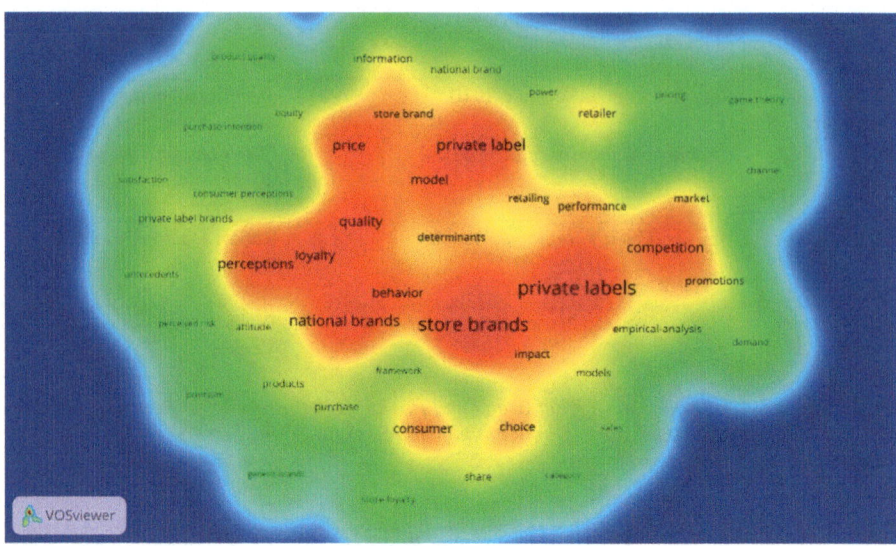

Fig. 1 Co-word map of private label literature

Table 2 Summary of research topics about private label and store brand

Main research topics
National brand
Perceptions
Price
Quality
Competition
Loyalty
Research sub-topics
Consumer behaviour, choice, performance, model, retailer/retailing, impact, brands, determinants, promotions, information, market.
Emerging aspects
Premium products, generic brand, category choice, perceived risk, antecedents, satisfaction, channel, demand, sales purchase, purchase intention, equity, product quality, power, game theory

Moving away from the centre, we can see aspects mainly related to consumer behaviour, the choices that the consumer makes, and the role that other factors play in the private label, such as promotions or information. Finally, in the (green) cold zone are a higher number of topics with fewer co-occurrences, which could represent emerging aspects for future research. Table 2 synthesizes the main topics, the sub-topics and the emerging aspects of research into the private label and store brand.

4 Conclusions, Limitations and Further Research

The present work highlights the growing relevance of the private label topic in scientific research. Analysis of the literature through the two main keywords "private label/s" and "store brand/s" has shown a growth in the number of published papers per year and a relative publication volume exponential from 2010 to 2017.

Analysis of the indicators related to the authors reveals a small group in terms of high productivity and high number of publications. These authors stand out among the others and are evidently recognized by the reference field as experts on the topic. Overall, the number of authors who have studied the topic is not high but is growing over time.

Analysis of the journals reveals little specialization in private label research: only two journals are specific: *Advances in National Brand and Private Label Marketing* and *National Brands and Private Labels in Retailing*; the others concern marketing, retailing, management or food products.

The results of this bibliometric analysis imply that the role assumed by the private label in the exchange system has led scholars to take an interest and to explore the reasons for the evolution of the private label that justify the current market shares. The map of co-words in the main papers in terms of citations on the Web of Science has in fact revealed a main core of research which, in addition to constant comparison with national brands, concerns the determinants and purchase models of the private label, and the role of quality, price and loyalty. In the area of emerging topics, numerous factors are added (e.g. purchase intentions, perceived risk, satisfaction, search for information) that can be explored in future research on the private label.

This research has some limitations, mainly linked to the method of obtaining the information to build the dataset. We used only the Web of Science: although it is one of the main references for scientific research, it is not exhaustive, and it is therefore very probable that some works on the subject are not contained in this analysis. Furthermore, the research considered only those papers in English.

Further research could therefore include other databases and build a more specific initial set of papers—for example, by including additional keywords or translating them into other languages. Furthermore, the results presented can be investigated in depth through other bibliometric indicators.

References

Ailawadi, K. L., & Keller, K. L. (2004). Understanding retail branding: Conceptual insights and research priorities. *Journal of Retailing, 80*(4), 331–342.

Burton, H. D. (1988). Use of a virtual information system for bibliometric analysis. *Information Processing and Management, 24*(1), 39–44.

Castaldo, S., Grosso, M., & Premazzi, K. (2013). *Retail and channel marketing*. Cheltenham: Edward Elgar.

Courtial, J. P., Callon, M., & Sigogneau, M. (1984). Is indexing trustworthy? Classification of articles through co-word analysis. *Information Scientist, 9*(2), 47–56.

Cristini, G. (1992). *Le strategie di marca del distributore. Milano: Egea.*

De Bellis, N. (2005). *La citazione bibliografica nell'epoca della sua riproducibilità tecnica.*

Fairthorne, R. A. (1969). Content analysis, specification, and control. *Annual Review of Information Science and Technology, 4*, 73–109.

Fornari, E. (2007). *Economia della marca commerciale: Le dimensioni del branding distributivo.* Milano: EGEA.

Galvagno, M. (2011). Anti-consumption research. Analisi bibliometrica della letteratura internazionale. *Mercati e Competitività*, (2), 55–75

Lugli, G. (2003). *Branding distributivo: Dalla marca di prodotto alla marca di categoria.* Milano: Egea.

Noyons, C. M. (2004). Science maps within a science policy context. In H. F. Moed, W. Glänzel, & U. Schmoch (Eds.), *Handbook of quantitative science and technology research* (pp. 237–255). Netherlands: Springer.

Pastore, A., Fornari, E., & Cecconi, V. (2007). Sviluppo e riposizionamento delle marche commerciali. *Finanza, Marketing E Produzione, 2*, 61–86.

Pritchard, A. (1969). Statistical bibliography or bibliometrics. *Journal of Documentation, 25*(4), 348–349.

Tague-Sutcliffe, J. (1992). An introduction to informetrics. *Information Processing and Management, 28*(1), 1–3.

Printed by Printforce, the Netherlands